Economic Development in the Middle East and North Africa

Economic Development in the Middle East and North Africa

Challenges and Prospects

Edited by

Mohamed Sami Ben Ali

palgrave
macmillan

ECONOMIC DEVELOPMENT IN THE MIDDLE EAST AND NORTH AFRICA

First published 2016 by
PALGRAVE MACMILLAN

Palgrave Macmillan in the UK is an imprint of Macmillan Publishers Limited, registered in England, company number 785998, of Houndmills, Basingstoke, Hampshire, RG21 6XS.

Palgrave Macmillan in the US is a division of Nature America, Inc., One New York Plaza, Suite 4500, New York, NY 10004-1562.

Palgrave Macmillan is the global academic imprint of the above companies and has companies and representatives throughout the world.

Hardback ISBN: 978–1–137–48646–2
E-PUB ISBN: 978–1–137–48068–2
E-PDF ISBN: 978–1–137–48066–8
DOI: 10.1057/9781137480668

Distribution in the UK, Europe and the rest of the world is by Palgrave Macmillan®, a division of Macmillan Publishers Limited, registered in England, company number 785998, of Houndmills, Basingstoke, Hampshire RG21 6XS.

Library of Congress Cataloging-in-Publication Data is available from the Library of Congress.

A catalogue record for the book is available from the British Library.

Contents

Figures and Tables

Figures

TABLES

Acknowledgments

The editor would like to thank Qatar University and the College of Business and Economics for all the support.

Disclaimer

The findings, interpretations, and conclusions expressed in this book reflect the opinions of the authors and not those of their respective institutions or countries.

Editor's Introduction: The Problem under Analysis

The Middle East and North Africa (MENA) region covers over 15 million square kilometers ranging from the African Atlantic coast to central Asia, as well as from the Mediterranean Sea to the Sahara Desert. MENA is comprised of over 336 million individuals representing approximately 6 percent of the Earth's population. The MENA region's location and many different resources make it strategic in a number of ways. MENA divides Asia and the African region and includes countries such as Algeria, Bahrain, Egypt, Iran, Iraq, Jordan, Kuwait, Lebanon, Morocco, Qatar, Saudi Arabia, Syria, the United Arab Emirates, Yemen, and so on. With 60 percent of the oil reserves and around 45 percent of the natural gas reserves of the world, the MENA region's wealth is expected to allow a great standard of living coupled with sustained growth that will last for a long time.

Economic Development in MENA Countries as a field of study offers promising research opportunities. This volume will attempt to elucidate the economic development and help with understanding its underlying constraints in MENA countries.

The MENA economies are characterized by public sector dominance in economic activity that ensures a large part of domestic production and that relies mainly on domestic financing resources, which in most cases fail to meet the economies' needs. These countries radically changed their economic policies and turned to more liberalized economic policies, in order to foster their development. As a result, MENA countries now play a crucial role in regional and global economic growth. The economic development issue therefore raises many issues related to research. This volume stems from our desire to bring answers to these questions. In looking ahead to the future of these countries, this volume is a useful collection of different chapters on MENA countries' specific characteristics and their interactions with the global economy.

The volume is a compilation of chapters. Each chapter deals with subjects such as economic growth, workers' remittances, intra-regional and international trade, inflation, corruption, foreign direct investment, and exchange regime policies, which give this volume rather diverse theoretical and empirical evidence on a variety of issues facing policymakers, investors, and other stakeholders in the region.

One of the unique aspects of the chapters in the volume is that each chapter offers a well-conceived testing of economic and finance theories as well as an application of the most recent trends in theory and empirics. All of the chapters in the volume will be dedicated to different subjects that address economic development but are articulated around a common region, which is a unique experience in this field.

Economic development is a main subject of interest for policymakers and researchers. Institutions and their quality are considered as one of the major pillars of economic development for all countries. We discuss in the first chapter of this volume the effect of institutions on economic development while focusing on the MENA countries.

The second chapter of this volume is dealing with the sources of economic growth. The absence of a dynamic private sector, rigid labor markets, low levels of competitiveness, low trade diversification, low intraregional trade, and job skills mismatches were among the primary factors leading to weak economic performance in the MENA region. MENA countries need to reach high long-term economic growth rates to improve the living standards of populations, especially in resource-poor MENA countries. This chapter contributes to the empirical and theoretical literature through refining and lengthening the debate on economic growth. Understanding this issue could assist policymakers in designing appropriate economic growth policies.

Natural resources are a common feature between most of the MENA countries. Theory stipulates that natural resources are not always synonyms of steady economic growth. In the third chapter, we analyze the natural resource curse in the MENA countries by considering its role in shaping government policies and spending on health and education.

International remittance inflows have significantly grown in developing countries in the past several decades. The scale and growth of remittances has helped them stick out on an aggregate and per capita basis, which has made their importance recognized. This importance of transfers stems from the fact that workers' remittances, compared with other capital flows, are more stable and have a habit of increasing throughout phases of economic downturn. Governments and international financial institutions in developing countries have grown more interested in remittances. Past literature has focused on how these flows impact economic development. Chapter 4 is shedding light on the effect that remittances have on economic development.

The harmful effect that high inflation has on social welfare and economic performance is increasingly agreed upon; even though price stability has been witnessed for quite some time in both developed and developing nations, inflation has reemerged with severe socioeconomic implications of which MENA as well as oil-exporting countries are predominantly concerned about. The region has witnessed a sharp rise in average inflation to double-digit levels for specific countries, with significant surges recorded for others. Chapter 5 sheds light on the new inflation trends in MENA countries by focusing on many facets of inflation issues in the region and mainly on the inflation-central bank independence.

A growing body of literature asserts the negative effects of corruption—or what Transparency International describes as an "abuse of entrusted power for private gain"—on macroeconomic performance. This literature argues that its presence is a major obstacle to good policymaking and economic development. Fighting corruption and knowing its sources and effects on an economy is an issue that has gained in importance in economic circles in recent decades. Recently, a number of increasingly important studies have focused on the effects of corruption. Many dimensions have been considered in the literature, which focuses on the various, intimately interconnected potential ways in which corruption may affect economic activity and therefore economic development. Pervasive corruption and lack of accountability and transparency have been, at different levels, common features for many MENA countries. In line with this strand of thought, the issue of corruption needs to be addressed in MENA countries; particularly as economic development is needed to unleash the region's economic potential. We consider in chapter 6 the role of corruption and economic growth.

Researchers disagree sharply about the role of the financial sector in economic performance. Differences in economic performances due to disparities in the financial sector will shape the future of policy implications, especially for reforming the financial sectors in MENA countries. Chapter 7 will address the impact of the financial development on economic growth.

Historically, growth phases have resulted from strong international trade development. In the case of MENA countries, the last two decades have been marked by their numerous efforts to pursue economic liberalization, aiming to integrate into the global economy to ensure faster economic growth. As a result, exports from the MENA region as a whole have increased considerably over the last two decades. At first glance, these countries display higher export levels compared to other regions. However, a closer look reveals that the weight of resource-rich countries is mostly due to hydrocarbons, and many resource-poor countries register persistent current account deficits. At the same time, MENA economies' international trade diversification varies from country to country, but show low levels of diversification. Trade diversification and intra-regional trade are prominent issues that need to be addressed as a top priority in the region; they are among the drivers of economic development to unleash the region's economic potential. They will be addressed in chapter 8.

FDI as a share of GDP has increased over the last two decades both for resource-poor and rich countries. In absolute terms, these inflows have been much more important to resource-rich, labor importing countries (e.g., Saudi Arabia accounted for more than 44% in 2010). In relative terms, however, their scale was more important to resource-poor countries, which points to the increasing attractiveness of resource-poor countries, such as Lebanon and Egypt, as hosting countries. In resource-poor countries, FDI outside the energy sector, has mostly been in non-tradable sectors, such as telecommunications, tourism and construction. In chapter 9, we seek to address these trends in FDI flows in MENA countries, explain the main driving factors, and focus on the impact they have on economic development in the region.

Overall, this volume will be an excellent handbook for global graduate students and academicians doing research on various economic and financial issues related to MENA countries. It will provide readers a comprehensive understanding of the general framework of where MENA countries stand, challenging problems, and prospects for the upcoming years. This volume serves as a useful reference for both Masters and PhD level students to find suitable research or thesis topics, as well as to write reviews on the literature.

1

The Role of Institutions in Economic Development

Mohamed Sami Ben Ali and
Sorin M. S. Krammer

Despite the global liberalization of trade, financial and technological flows, there still are tremendous disparities in terms of income per capita and growth rates across countries (Hall and Jones, 1999). Among the plethora of explanations proposed in the economic literature on this phenomenon, institutions have become a common factor for long-term economic performance (Acemoglu et al., 2001) as well as international activities such as trade (Dollar and Kraay, 2003) and foreign direct investments (Ali et al., 2010) and the legitimacy or failure of states (Subramanian et al., 2004). Given these pivotal implications of institutions for the social and economic welfare of countries, this chapter proposes to review the current institutional background of countries in the Middle East and North Africa (MENA) region and provide some insights into the historical and more recent evolution of formal institutions in this part of the world.

Quality of Institutions and Economic Development

Definition and Classification of Institutions

Economists and political scientists provide many definitions for the concept of institutions. North's (1990) pioneering analysis was that institutions are "the rules of the game in a society or, more formally, are the humanly devised constraints that shape human interaction." Other researchers have contradicted the definition provided by North by noting that public communications are organized by the coordination of traditional and deep-rooted codes of the society, and these constitute institutions (Hodgson, 2006). Institutions are also defined as a structure of societal features, like organizations, codes, faiths, and criteria. These features direct, empower, and restrain the activities of persons (Greif, 2000; Dixit, 2004). The perceptions about institutions and organizations are combined so that organizations are seen as instances of institutions. Institutions are also considered as policies to be chosen by persons (Dixit, 2004). According to Schotter (1981), institutions are seen as uniformity in societal conduct that is acceptable to every constituent of the community. This conduct is controlled either by the self or by a foreign power.

Overall, there are many facets of institutions that are considered in the literature as the results of different typologies that are discipline-specific (i.e., sociological, political science, managerial, etc.); consequently, certain studies center on the role of informal elements (i.e., more tacit, embedded aspects of institutions—such as societal trust or cultural values), while others emphasize the impact of formal aspects (i.e., codified elements that govern societal interactions—such as laws, regulations, or policies). Within the realm of economics, the emphasis is clearly on the latter, as these formal institutions are a key moderating factor in all interactions between different economic agents, such as firms, individuals, or governments (North, 1990). Thus, the present chapter follows this tradition and subscribes to the Northian view of institutions.

Importance of Institutions

Institutions make up some of the most significant determinants of any economic outcome, for numerous reasons. First, institutions safeguard investors' academic privileges, provide a fitting atmosphere for inspiration and creation, and boost competition for opportunities. Institutions are then essential to society. Although each individual is treated without prejudice or preference, institutions increase the competition for possibilities. The value of institutions also impacts countries as well as persons. In case the decree of rule is enforced and visibly defined, shielded rights of assets exist in a nation, and consequently result in relatively better economic growth, even in nondemocratic governments (Olson, 1993).

Second, a substantial amount of research demonstrates the major influence of institutions on economic growth. After all, economic growth is affected by numerous elements such as assets or location, but a lack of well-built institutions affects economic growth negatively, even when these elements are favorable. Institutions influence more than just growth in an economy. Direct overseas endeavors are stimulated by a well-organized judicial structure, less bribery, and national dependability (Asiedu, 2006). The degree of corruption decreased when there was an increase in overall overseas distribution allotted to minerals and fuels and, as a result, it was seen to have a clear impact on foreign direct investment, which resulted in growth among African countries.

Finally, decreasing the level of corruption went a long way in leading to a positive impact on economic growth. Although democracy might not constantly add to growth, it is more advantageous to economic prosperity because it involves capitalist conduct and helps persons scrutinize prospective expenditures liberally (North, 1990). Since democratic systems protect public privileges and rights of assets, they are more favorable to economic growth, but they do not always lead to development. Democratic systems could employ bad strategies to expand politically, but dictatorships may not be subjugated by such demands. Long-term stability is not seen in dictatorships although, when they are stable, they contribute to the growth of the economy. Sought-after institutions offer safety of assets, rights, implementation of agreements, motivation for free enterprise, sustained steadiness of economic science, supervision of venturesome fiscal mediators, and public assurances and security dividends. This results in improved influence and liability (Rodrik, 2008). Rodrik (2000) claims that managing conflict prospects in nations with participatory institutions produces less growth instability than in nondemocratic civilizations.

Measuring Institutions

Systematic reviews of existing literature suggest that there is less agreement on how to empirically measure institutions (Woodruff, 2006). Dietsche (2007) partly attributes this challenge to the fact that different theorists and empirical researchers have defined institutions and the functions they provide on the basis of various ontological frames of reference. According to her, those who are intellectually grounded in economic theory tend to view institutions as incentive structures and constraints to the pursuit of individuals' self-interest. In contrast, those more closely associated with sociology and anthropology ascribe to institutions cognitive roles through which individuals' behavior are coordinated. Nevertheless, efforts to measure institutions can take on one or more of the following forms: measures of formal institutions, measures of a mixture of formal and informal institutions, expansive measures of property rights, and slim measures of specific institutions; yet, some are founded on impressionistic surveys performed by legal experts, business people, or academics, and others are constructed on analyses of laws and constitutions (Woodruff, 2006). Some specific examples of proxies—identified by Dietsche (2007)—to measure the quality of institutions include:

(1) Governance index: an average of six measures of institutions, such as
 a) Voice and accountability;
 b) Political stability and absence of violence;
 c) Government effectiveness;
 d) Regulatory burden;
 e) Rule of law; and
 f) Freedom from corruption.
(2) Corruption perception index, by Transparency International
(3) Checks and balance, as measured by Keefer and Stasavage (2002)
(4) Doing Business Indicators, by the World Bank
(5) Fragmentation of the political field, by Database on Political Institutions (DPI)
(6) Polity measures regarding level of democracy and autocracy in a country and democratic measures concerning the extent to which electoral competition prevails, by Polity IV database
(7) Civil liberties and political rights, by Freedom House
(8) Index of social division (e.g., ethnicity)

While these measures (i.e., proxies) of institutional quality have been particularly useful and have aided empirical research, a number of concerns have frequently been raised in the literature. First, Arndt and Oman (2006) show that the problem with proxies that measure institutional quality is that they often do not fully capture the attributes that are associated with them. For example, Glaeser et al. (2004) have argued that most current measures of institutions found in the literature measure outcomes rather than institutions. Another critique is that the proxies indicators used to measure institutional quality were often not originally designed for that purpose and, in some instances, indices have been created retroactively, such as the Polity IV data that goes back to 1800 (Dietsche, 2007; Woodruff, 2006). Finally, it has also been suggested that in almost all cross-country or cross-regional studies, measured institutions are interconnected with other measured or unmeasured institutions, which limits what can be said about this approach (Woodruff, 2006).

Taking most of these critiques seriously, Voigt (2013) has proposed that a measure of institutions should be exact, objective, and account for *de jure* and *de facto* elements. In addition, he suggested that when estimating the economic effect of institutions, there is the need to incorporate a number of covariate proxies for informal institutions.

Impact of Institutions on Economic Development

Although many studies propose that institutions are indeed vital to economic growth, they are not, however, the only cause of growth; for instance, Knack and Keefer (1995) show that the explanatory influence of the regressions is greater when indicators of political violence are involved. However, due to data restrictions, the empirical investigation of cross-country growth was constrained to a constricted investigation of the institutions' role. Many other studies were done, such as the one by Acemoglu et al. (2000), in which they discovered the presence of a solid correlation between colonial institutions and economic performance. By studying European colonization practices, they show how the only effect on per capita GDP was witnessed through the use of institutions, and so it goes to show that the process of improving institutions will beget an improvement in the per capita income. It has been proven time and time again that institutions seem to have a rather strong influence on economic performance, one that could be powerful when related to other factors.

Through continued empirical studies, it has been highlighted that even considering economic growth determinants such as geography and integration, as well as institutions, yields results showing that the latter trumps all else (Rodrik et al., 2004). Integration does not possess a direct effect on income, and geography displays only a weak and rather inaccurate one. On the other hand, integration is positively and significantly affected by institutional quality; Robinson et al. (2006) reason that institutions regulate the comparative statics of the equilibrium as well as the income level and its growth rate. The secret lies in the strength of institutions, such that a response would be positive in the company of solid institutions. Institutions then clarify, more than any other aspect, the disparities in growth among countries.

Besides their direct influence, it is important to consider the indirect impact institutions have on growth and how this impact is twofold and involves either intermingling with additional variables or through operating as a network to govern the impact of those variables on growth. The variables to be considered are trade, policy, democracy, and human capital. When it comes to trade, varied studies done by Dollar and Kraay (2003), Acemoglu et al (2005)., and Baliamoune-Lutz and Ndikumana (2007), in different parts of the world, display that the core factor shaping the impact of trade on growth is the presence of institutions. When it comes to policy, Easterly and Levine (2002) as well as Fatás and Mihov (2005) found that the influence policy has on growth is largely dependent upon the nation's institutional quality. In studying democracy, Acemoglu and Robinson (2008), Commander and Nikoloski (2010), and Rigobon and Rodrik (2005) found that there was very little association between democracy and growth, but by studying the relationships between different institutions, the results suggested that democracy as well as the rule of law are valuable to economic performance. Asiedu (2003), Banerjee et al. (2005), Lee and Kim (2009), and Miletkov and Wintoki (2012) primarily examine institutional quality, low-income countries, and financial development's role in improving property rights. Woodruff (2006) suggested that scholars like Acemoglu et al. (2001; 2002) and Engerman and Sokoloff (2000) developed a historical perspective of the links between institutions and economic development. At its core, this perspective addresses the problem of reverse logic and associated criticisms that were leveled against the previous arguments linking institutions to economic development.

Although the notion is that institutions are essential, some have confronted it. Bardhan (2005) argues that the measures of institutions are being confused, while North (1981) contends that institutions must be "designed." Glaeser et al. (2004) debate the measurements used as a way to point out how the lack of relationship between economic growth and the proposed constitutional measures of institutions. Their claim is that the reason the quality of institutions could possess significance when it comes to the growth regression is because there is improvement in the quality of institutions as income increases. Other scholars bring up some other valid critiques, but despite that, none of it hampers the empirical research performed on institutions.

Quality of Institutions: Where Do MENA Countries Stand?

Overview of the Region

History and civilizing legacy are shared among the MENA countries. The region has historically always tried to maintain its inimitable geopolitical importance, having always been a booming hub of business.

The MENA province has always been very affluent, when compared to other provinces of the globe. In the tenth century, the region had the highest GDP per capita among five nation pools. The region's uniqueness remains, despite the disappearance of its dominant role. This zone has the greatest heritage bond with practically every part of the globe because it is centrally situated between three continents: Asia, Europe, and Africa.

The MENA region has the world's largest oil reserves, and its fiscal reserves are significant. The province shows dazzling potential in the sphere of renewable energy resources—especially solar energy (Müller-Steinhagen and Trieb, 2007). After gaining independence during the twentieth century, the nations have focused on industries of their own choices, health structure, and edification. During the 1970s, Most of the nations in the MENA region had an agenda to recover from the effects of colonialism on citizens' class of living, by exploiting the monetary reserves from native supplies. As the oil boom petered out in this period, so too did its economic accomplishments, despite having invested in infrastructure ventures, edification, and civic wellbeing. Economic reforms had to do with privatization and trade liberalization as the gear to progress business capabilities. Many such endeavors were found to be successful to some extent, letting these economies adjust internationally.

22 self-governing countries are included in the MENA zone, possessing a surface area of 14.8 million sq. km. This region covers 61% of the globe's known oil resources and 21 percent of the natural gas resources. Among the Organization of the Petroleum Countries (OPEC) member nations, eight are in this zone. According to World Bank (2008), the region is sparsely inhabited—relatively speaking—with nearly 38 occupants per km^2. This is due to the lowered availability of water reserves. The oil-producing nations are Saudi Arabia, UAE, Qatar, Kuwait, Oman, Libya, Bahrain, and Algeria. The employment opportunities created by the oil sector is nearly 5 percent. In these countries, there is scarcity in non-consumer and consumer supplies, which makes household fund attraction scarce. FDI, tourism, transmittals, and export play a vital part in the process of economic development of the second bunch of countries—Egypt, Lebanon, Jordan, Morocco, Syria, and Tunisia—in terms of creating more jobs. The rest of the states in the MENA region are facing grave issues in the arena of economic and community development due to the inadequacy in funds.

The minority of this country pool are successful in discovering proper approaches to adjusting the ever-varying global setting. The UAE, Oman, Tunisia, and Bahrain provide a positive approach in this regard. In the Gulf Cooperation Council (GCC), Oman, Bahrain, and the UAE are affluent in reserves while Tunisia is affluent in having a skilled and profuse work force. These four countries constitute one-fourth of the GDP of the region even though they are comparatively less populated.

Institutions in MENA Countries

In this section, we are going to focus on several formal institutional proxies that are widely used in the literature, and examine them from the perspective of MENA countries. Specifically, we will be looking at:

- The degree of economic freedom (using data from the Heritage Foundation)
- The quality of governance (using the Worldwide Governance Indicators from the World Bank)
- The "friendliness" of the business environment (using the Doing Business Indicator from the World Bank)
- The perceptions of firms in these markets regarding the institutional environment in which they are active (using the Enterprise Surveys from the World Bank)

Heritage Foundation's Economic Freedom Index (EFI)

For several decades, the EFI has been a useful tool for policymakers to assess and improve their institutional environment in order to spur economic dynamism and, subsequently, prosperity. Scholarly work performed while using the EFI has revealed a strong connection between economic growth and several institutional features: low tax rates, limited government, a stable currency, openness to global trade and financial flows, strong private property rights, and lower regulatory burden. The EFI evaluates countries using 10 specific categories, such as property rights, freedom from corruption, and more, which are then averaged to create an overall score for each state.

Overall, the average level of economic freedom in the MENA region has remained comparable to that of previous years, with economic and political policies that hamper growth and development in the region, as suggested by the limited involvement of private enterprises and relatively high unemployment rates (Kim and Miller, 2015). Most of the MENA countries are in the "moderately free" or "mostly unfree" groupings of this index. Israel (70.5), Bahrain (73.4), United Arab Emirates (72.4), and Qatar (70.8) are the regional leaders in terms economic freedom, while Iran (41.8) and Algeria (48.9) have the lowest scores in the region. In comparison with previous years, Israel has improved its position with 2.1 points, achieving the highest EFI score ever via improvements in management of public spending, property rights, regulatory prescriptions, as well as trade, labor, and fiscal policies. In contrast, both Algeria and Yemen have experienced significant decreases (1.9 and 1.8), further contributing to the international perception of them being "mostly unfree" countries. Some countries (Syria, Libya, and Iraq) remain uncovered by this Index as a result of ongoing violence and unrest in these nations, which suggests that the true regional average (61.6) is likely to be lower than the one reported, which is still above the world average of 60.4. The areas of most pressing concerns remain property rights (39.4), corruption (38.4), and financial (45.3) and investment freedom (44.4), while trade (74.1), monetary (73.4), and fiscal freedom (88.8) score above average. A sustained decline in the business freedom (64.0) in 11 out of 18 countries suggests the potential for more social and political unrest in the region, despite heavy subsidies for energy and food (Kim and Miller, 2015).

World Bank's Worldwide Governance Indicators (WGI)

In its simplest form, governance can be viewed as the way authority is exercised in a nation through political, economic, and institutional mechanisms. Previous work in this area associates good governance to growth and development, particularly in the medium and long run (Kaufmann and Kraay, 2003), as countries affected by misgovernance are closely associated with lower investment and economic development rates as a result of weaker private sectors (Kaufmann, 2011). To measure governance in the MENA region, we will employ the widely popular Worldwide Governance Indicators (WGI). The WGI comprises of six composite indicators covering 200 countries since 1996, and captures six broad dimensions of governance using several hundred variables from survey respondents, nongovernmental organizations, public sector organizations, and commercial business information providers worldwide (Kaufmann et al., 2010). These are:

- *Voice and accountability*
- *Political stability and absence of violence*
- *Government effectiveness*
- *Regulatory quality*
- *Rule of law*
- *Control of corruption*

On average, the WGI data suggests that governance in the Middle East and North Africa is low, and practically unchanged in the last decade or so (Figure 1.1). Only a couple of countries (Qatar and the UAE) have, on average, improved their governance scores, while for most others, their governance metrics have stayed unchanged or even deteriorated slightly over the past decade. These numbers are consistent with the general perception of mishandling and misrule perpetuated by several of the region's governments prior to the "Arab Spring," and the subsequent unrest stemming from political volatility and power voids.

Taken individually, most MENA countries have negative scores on all six dimensions considered by the WGI, and are ranked in the thirty-sixth percentile or lower worldwide—in stark contrast to the scores displayed by advanced, high-income OECD countries (Table A1.2). Among them, four countries (Israel, Oman, Qatar, and the UAE) stand out as regional leaders in terms of governance. All these countries have, on average, positive scores across most of the WGI components. Still, Israel scores negatively on political stability, while the other three performers lack in terms of voice and accountability. On the other side of the spectrum, we find many countries with high negative scores across all these dimensions, as both a result of and

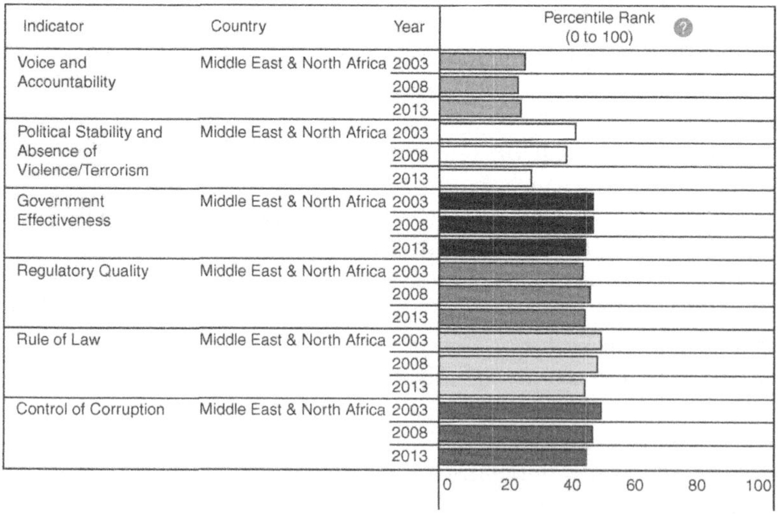

Figure 1.1 Quality of Governance in MENA countries.

Source: Kaufmann D., A. Kraay, and M. Mastruzzi (2010), The Worldwide Governance Indicators: Methodology and Analytical Issues. Available at: www.govindicators.org.

cause for continuous unrest in the region (Syria, Iraq, and Yemen) or lack of democracy (Iran). As expected, given the political and social contexts of the region, all MENA countries (except Israel) score very low (actually negative scores) on voice and accountability criteria, confirming a relative lack of freedom and participation of the citizenry in elections or expressions of opinion. Formal institutional environment (rule of law and regulatory quality) is especially strong in higher-income countries like Bahrain, Qatar, Israel, and the UAE, with few other exceptions (Jordan and West Bank/Gaza). Higher incomes are also associated with more political stability and superior governmental efficiency, while in terms of control of corruption laws and regulations, a few countries are doing extremely well (Qatar, the UAE, and Israel) while most of the region remains on the negative side, with a couple of extreme cases, such as Libya (–1.52), Syria (–1.24), or Yemen (–1.20).

The explanations for these severe governance failures focus on three key aspects. First, the lack of governments' accountability as a result of diminished democratic institutions and weak political freedom is ubiquitous. The historical deficit of democratic tradition in the region has kept many autocrats from being held accountable for the lack of major improvements in terms of economic growth, human development, or other social indicators. Moreover, the lack of free speech and free press in many instances has further amplified this failure for accountability. Second, from a purely economic perspective, many MENA countries suffer from adoption of subpar economic policies dating back to the 1950s, which have resulted in a misguided allocation of authority over natural resources. As a result, a common characteristic of the region is the presence of an overinflated public sector, in which state-owned enterprises often under perform as a result of mismanagement and the inefficient allocation of resources (Pfeifer, 1999). Finally, the presence of rampant corruption exacerbates these aforementioned risks, reducing the efficiency and transparency of governance, with significant negative consequences for growth in the region. Although the primary explanation for the prevalence and severity of corruption resides in the failure of these states, in many instances, bribes and kickbacks are deeply rooted in the cultural and social background of these countries. Hence, corruption in MENA nations takes on a very different meaning from corruption in Western societies, and ranges from being tolerated to often being considered a normal "form of democracy" (Rosen, 2006), which has been used for centuries, as a way to forge relationships in these societies.

World Bank's Doing Business Indicator (DBI)

Given the high rate of unemployment[1] (especially among young people, the highly educated, and women) and the lack of a strong private sector in many of the MENA countries, one avenue through which these countries can improve on these aspects is by facilitating the development of private business and attracting significant volumes of foreign investments. In this regard, the Doing Business Indicator from the World Bank highlights how difficult or easy it is for an entrepreneur in these countries to open and run a business, given the local institutional requirements—as measured by differences across regulatory frameworks between countries. In capturing these differences, the DBI tracks changes in regulations (mostly in terms of number of procedures, duration/time, and monetary costs associated with these steps) across ten areas, specifically:

- Starting a business (including minimum capital required to open a new business)
- Dealing with construction permits
- Getting electricity
- Registering property
- Obtaining credit (including the legal rights index strength, and credit information depth)
- Protecting investments (including the degree of disclosure needed, liability involved)
- Paying taxes (number of taxes and the bureaucratic burden of complying with and paying them)
- Trading across borders (approvals, signatures for import-export operations)
- Enforcing contracts
- Resolving insolvency issues (including the expected recovery rate of debts).

Overall, the DBI indicator provides a bird's eye view of the ease of doing business across 189 economies in the world, and is commonly used in policy analysis aimed to identify areas for regulatory improvements and targeted future reforms. Countries are assigned scores in all 10 aforementioned areas, and are subsequently ranked based on their aggregate performance across these indicators. The standing of each topic is a simple average of the percentile ranking on its component indicators. This is a useful tool for international comparisons, although it obviously faces some methodological tradeoffs (i.e., inability to measure all factors that matter for the survival and performance of the firm; sampling of firms usually being biased toward big cities/major business hubs; the underlying conditions of the existing regulatory frameworks, which are endogenous to the business environment, etc.) that prevent it from telling the whole story regarding the comparative competitiveness of one business environment versus another.

So, how do MENA countries do in terms of ease of doing business vis-à-vis other regions? Overall, MENA countries score 107 in terms of ranking, which places them in the lowest quartile of the circulation in terms of friendliness of the business environment, thus confirming some of our previous conjectures regarding the characteristics of governments in the region and the lack of a strong private sector (Figure 1.2). Most MENA countries are in the lower half of the DBI ranking, and only few economies in the region manage to be competitive in this respect (i.e., UAE, Bahrain, Oman, Saudi Arabia, Qatar, and Tunisia). The areas with the largest regulatory deficits are in terms of obtaining credit (ranked 133 for the region), enforcing contracts (ranked 118), resolving insolvency (ranked 105), protecting investments (ranked 113), but also the effort needed to start a business (ranked 112). Historically, MENA countries have actually become worse over the last decade or so, as the "distance to the frontier" (i.e., the best practice/score in the world) in all these areas has increased, with some cases—such as starting a business—registering

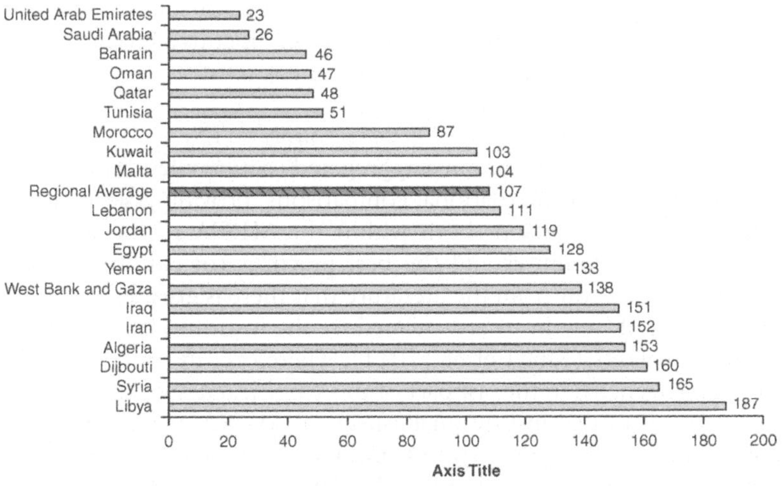

Figure 1.2 Ranking of MENA countries in terms of Ease of Doing Business (2014).
Source: Doing Business database. http://www.doingbusiness.org/.

an increase in this distance of around 30 percentage points from 2005 to 2013 (Doing Business, 2014). Some of these setbacks are driven by several countries in the region who constantly score low on many of these indicators, resulting in very low rankings, like Libya, Djibouti, or Iraq (see Table A1.3). At the opposite end of the spectrum, Saudi Arabia as well as the United Arab Emirates are the regional leaders in the majority of the categories as they continue to improve on their global rankings.

In conclusion, the weakness of the private sector in most MENA countries can be traced back to some several regulatory drawbacks as well as the limited access to credit, which subsequently constricts the number of private employment opportunities and perpetuates the usage of informal authority and corrupt practices (e.g., "wasta," or having connections) to get a public sector job or a job in a state-owned enterprise. This further spills over into the capacity of these countries to raise taxes (given that the informal sector is relatively large) and the ability to attract competitive foreign investments in the region to address the existing unemployment and achieve a better match in terms of skills and education available in these countries. However, these regulatory provisions are very dynamic, and the most recent Doing Business report summarizes some of the major reforms undertaken by these countries in terms of spurring the creation of new businesses and facilitating access to credit and development resources for new firms in these economies. More of these efforts, adapted to the particularities of these markets, are needed to spur reform and promote MENA as a friendlier and more competitive business environment for both domestic and foreign enterprises.

World Bank's Enterprise Surveys (ES)

Although these aforementioned aggregated (country-level) indicators are widely used for international comparisons, providing some useful international comparisons both within the MENA region and also between these countries and the best practices (of countries at the forefront), we know from the literature that there is great heterogeneity in terms of how firms are affected by the institutional constraints in these markets (Kinda et al., 2011). Therefore, in order to tackle this heterogeneity, in the last part of this empirical descriptive exercise of capturing formal institutional aspects in MENA, we are going to concentrate on the perceived institutional constraints experienced by firms in these countries, using firm-level numbers from the Enterprise Surveys produced by the World Bank. In this way, we are going to complement the existing macroeconomic evidence on the status quo of formal institutions in the MENA region with some microeconomic evidence derived from these surveys. According to these sources, small and medium size enterprises (SMEs) constitute about 80 to 90 percent of the formal private sector in MENA, being responsible for 20–40 percent of the private employment and with real growth opportunities in the future, if complemented by regulatory actions regarding access to finance and streamlined legislation for operation.

Interestingly enough, when examining the aggregate responses of firms with respect to the biggest obstacles faced by firms in these economies, besides "Access to finance" which has already been discussed in previous paragraphs, other factors—pertaining to infrastructure ("Access to electricity") and institutional/political background ("Political instability")—appear even more important (see Table 1.4). More than a quarter of the firms in the MENA region (27.5%) perceive the ongoing political unrest and frequent regime changes as a major challenge to their activities, and the latest wave of violence in the region is clearly represented in these responses (Yemen 49%; West Bank and Gaza 31%; Lebanon 58%). This is almost three times higher than the world average for this indicator (10.5%). Although the majority of MENA countries appear to benefit from good (and in some cases, excellent) infrastructure, several outliers such as Djibouti (48.8%), Iraq (19.7%), and Yemen (23.7%) indicate that excessive instability and violence affects firms also via reduced and cumbersome access to important factors of production, such as electricity. Besides these general prescriptions applicable to all MENA nations, there are also strong idiosyncratic effects at the country-level that are emphasized by these surveys. For example, many enterprises in Egypt perceive informal competition to be a major obstacle to their activities (25.5%), as opposed to excessive taxation (23.2%) in Jordan or corruption in Yemen (26.6%) and Syria (14.2%).

The joint-importance of these factors is also documented by previous studies in the literature. Their results support the hypothesis that in the region, economic growth has been significantly hampered by these country-specific characteristics, as likened to other regions in the world. Thus, an improvement to the labor skill shortages faced by firms in MENA countries could increase real GDP per capita by over 0.4 percent annually (Bhattacharya and Wolde, 2010). These average elasticities of growth rates suggest that addressing all these institutional deficiencies in the region pays off significantly over the long run. Conversely, such solutions require major changes in the institutional underpinnings of these nations, such as labor market policies to improve skill level and job matching especially for private firms (via subsidies, training, and incentive schemes), measures to improve access to finance (via specialized agencies for SMEs, public promotion measures of private credit, etc.), and investment in infrastructure (i.e., generation, transmission, and distribution of electricity, perhaps through greater public-private and foreign partnerships). Addressing some of these extremely pressing concerns will positively influence both labor productivity and technical efficiency of firms in the region, with a clear objective of improving export-capacity and diversification possibilities for many resource-driven MENA countries (Kinda et al., 2011) as a sustainable avenue for economic growth in the future.

NOTE

1. According to the latest numbers provided by the UN, the Middle East and North Africa show 18.8 and 24.4 percent youth unemployment (ages 15–24) respectively, compared to 13.1 percent in OECD and Europe, or 9.1 in East Asia.

REFERENCES

Acemoglu, D., Johnson, S., and Robinson, J. A. (2000). The Colonial Origins of Comparative Development: An Empirical investigation. *National Bureau of Economic Research Working Paper Series*, No. 7771.

Acemoglu, D., Johnson, S., and Robinson, J. A. (2001). The colonial origins of comparative development: An empirical investigation. *American Economic Review*, 91 (5): 1369–1401.

Acemoglu, D., Johnson, S., and Robinson, J. A. (2002). Reversal of fortune: geography and institutions in the making of the modern world income distribution. *Quarterly Journal of Economics*, 117: 1231–1294.

Acemoglu, D., Johnson, S., and Robinson, J. A. (2005). The rise of Europe: Atlantic trade, institutional change, and economic growth. *American Economic Review*, 95 (3): 546–579.

Acemoglu, D., and Robinson, J. A. (2008). Persistence of power, elites, and institutions. *American Economic Review*, 98 (1): 267–293.

Ali, F. A., Fiess, N., and MacDonald, R. (2010). Do institutions matter for foreign direct investment? *Open Economic Review*, 21 (2): 201–219.

Arndt, C., and Oman, C. (2006). *Uses and Abuses of Governance Indicators.* Paris: Development Centre, OECD.

Asiedu, E. (2003). Debt relief and institutional reform: A focus on heavily indebted poor countries. *The Quarterly Review of Economics and Finance*, 43 (4): 614–626.

Asiedu, E. (2006). Foreign direct investment in Africa: The role of natural resources, market size, government policy, institutions and political instability. *The World Economy*, 29 (1): 63–77.

Baliamoune-Lutz, M., and Ndikumana, L. (2007). The Growth Effects of Openness to Trade and the Role of Institutions: New Evidence from African Countries. *Working Paper*, No. 2007–05.

Banerjee, A., Iyer, L., and Somanathan, R. (2005). History, social divisions, and public goods in rural India. *Journal of the European Economic Association*, 3 (2–3): 639–647.

Bardhan, P. (2005). Institutions matter, but which ones? *Economics of Transition*, 13 (3): 499–532.

Bhattacharya, R., and Wolde, H. (2010). *Constraints on Growth in the MENA Region*. International Monetary Fund: Washington, D.C.

Commander, S. J., and Nikoloski, Z. (2010). Institutions and Economic Performance: What Can Be Explained? *IZA Discussion Papers*, No. 5247.

Dietsche, E. (2007). Why the Quality of Institutions Is Not a Cure for the "Resource Curse." *The Journal of Energy and Development*, 32 (2): 262–282.

Dixit, A. (2004). *Lawlessness and Economics: Alternative Modes of Governance*. Princeton, NJ: Princeton University Press.

Doing Business. (2014). *Understanding regulations for small and medium-size enterprises*. The World Bank: Washington, D.C.

Dollar, D., and Kraay, A. (2003). Institutions, trade, and growth. *Journal of monetary economics*, 50 (1): 133–162.

Easterly, W., and Levine, R. (2002). Tropics, Germs, and Crops: How Endowments Influence Economic Development. *NBER Working Papers*, No. 9106. National Bureau of Economic Research.

Engerman, S. L., and Sokoloff, K. L. (2000). Institutions, factors endowments, and paths of development in the new world. *The Journal of Economic Perspectives*, 14 (3): 217–232.

Fatás, A., and Mihov, I. (2005). Policy volatility, institutions and economic growth. *The Review of Economics and Statistics*, 95 (2): 362–376.

Glaeser, E., La Porta, R., Lopez-de-Silanes, F., and Shleifer, A. (2004). Do institutions cause growth? *Journal of Economic Growth*, 9 (3): 271–303.

Greif, A. (2000). The fundamental problem of exchange: A research agenda in historical institutional analysis. *European Review of Economic History*, 4 (3): 251–284.

Hall R.E. and Jones, C. (1999). Why do some countries produce so much more output per worker than others? *Quarterly Journal of Economics*, 114 (1): 83–116.

Hodgson, G. M. (2006). What Are Institutions? *Journal of Economic Issues*, 40 (1): 1–25.

Kaufmann, D., and Kraay, A. (2003). Governance and Growth: Causality Which Way? Evidence for the World, in brief. *Manuscript. World Bank publication.*

Kaufmann, D., Kraay, A., and Mastruzzi, M. (2010). The Worldwide Governance Indicators: Methodology and Analytical Issues. *World Bank Policy Research Working Paper*, No. 5430.

Kaufmann, D. (2011). Governance and the Arab World Transition: Reflections, Empirics and Implications for the International Community. *Brookings Report.*

Keefer, P. and Stasavage, D. (2002). Checks and balances, private information, and the credibility of monetary commitments. *International Organization*, 56 (4): 751–774.

Kim A. B., and Miller, T. (2015). *Index of Economic Freedom.* Washington, DC: The Heritage Foundation and Dow Jones & Company Inc.

Kinda, T., Plane, P., and Véganzonès-Varoudakis, M. A. (2011). Firm productivity and investment climate in developing countries: how does Middle East and North Africa manufacturing perform? *The Developing Economies*, 49 (4): 429–462.

Knack, S., and Keefer, P. (1995). Institutions and economic performance: Cross-country tests using alternative institutional indicators. *Economics & Politics*, 7 (3): 207–227.

Lee, K., and Kim, B. Y. (2009). Both institutions and policies matter but differently for different income groups of countries: Determinants of long-run economic growth revisited. *World Development*, 37 (3): 533–549.

Miletkov, M., and Wintoki, M.B. (2012). Financial development and the evolution of property rights and legal institutions. *Emerging Markets Review*, 13 (4): 650–673.

Müller-Steinhagen, H., and Trieb, F. (2007). Renewable Energies in the MENA Region: Potential for Sustainable Energy Provision and Export to Europe. *Oberpfaffenhofen: German Aerospace Center, DLR, Institute of Technical Thermodynamics.*

North, D. C. (1981). *Structure and Change in Economic History. Douglass C. North,* New York.

North, D. C. (1990). *Institutions, Institutional Change and Economic Performance.* Cambridge: Cambridge University Press.

Olson, M. (1982). *The Rise and Decline of Nations: Economic Growth, Stagflation, and Social Rigidities.* New Haven, CT and London: Yale University Press.

Olson, M. (1993). Dictatorship, democracy, and development. *American Political Science Review*, 87 (03): 567–576.

Pfeifer, K. (1999). Parameters of economic reform in North Africa. *Review of African Political Economy*, 26 (82): 441–454.

Rigobon, R., and Rodrik, D. (2005). Rule of law, democracy, openness, and income. *Economics of Transition*, 13 (3): 533–564.

Robinson, J. A., Torvik, R., and Verdier, T. (2006). Political foundations of the resource curse. *Journal of Development Economics*, 79 (2): 447–468.

Rodrik, D. (2000). Institutions for high-quality growth: what they are and how to acquire them. *Studies in Comparative International Development*, 35 (3): 3–31.

Rodrik, D. (2008). The real exchange rate and economic growth. *Brookings papers on economic activity*, 2008 (Vol 2): 365–412.

Rodrik, D., Subramanian, A., and Trebbi, F. (2004). Institutions rule: The primacy of institutions over geography and integration in economic development. *Journal of Economic Growth*, 9 (2): 131–165.

Rosen, L. (2006). Expecting the Unexpected: Cultural Components of Arab Governance. *The Annals of the American Academy of Political and Social Science*, 603 (1): 163–178.

Schotter, A. (1981). *The Economic Theory of Social Institutions.* New York: Cambridge University Press.

Subramanian, A., Trebbi, F. and Rodrik, D. (2004). Institutions rule: The primacy of institutions over geography and integration in economic development. *Journal of Economic Growth*, 9 (2): 131–165.

Voigt, S. (2013). How (Not) to measure institutions. *Journal of Institutional Economics*, 9 (1): 1–26.

Woodruff, D. M. (2006). Understanding rules and institutions: possibilities and limits of game theory. *Qualitative Methods Newsletter*, 4 (1): 13–17.

World Bank. (2008). World Development Indicators. The World Bank, Washington DC

Appendix

Table A1.1 Economic Freedom scores in MENA countries (2015)

Country	World Rank	2015 Score	Change in Score from 2014	Property Rights	Freedom from Corruption	Fiscal Freedom
Algeria	157	48.9	−1.9	30.0	36.0	80.0
Bahrain	18	73.4	−1.7	60.0	48.0	99.9
Egypt	124	55.2	2.3	20.0	32.0	85.8
Iran	171	41.8	1.5	10.0	25.0	81.2
Iraq	N/A	N/A	N/A	N/A	16.0	N/A
Israel	33	70.5	2.1	75.0	61.0	61.9
Jordan	38	69.3	0.1	60.0	45.0	93.7
Kuwait	74	62.5	0.2	45.0	43.0	97.7
Lebanon	94	59.3	−0.1	20.0	28.0	91.3
Libya	N/A	N/A	N/A	10.0	15.0	95.0
Morocco	89	60.1	1.8	40.0	37.0	70.9
Oman	56	66.7	−0.7	55.0	47.0	98.5
Qatar	32	70.8	−0.4	70.0	68.0	99.7
Saudi Arabia	77	62.1	−0.1	40.0	46.0	99.7
Syria	N/A	N/A	N/A	10.0	17.0	N/A
Tunisia	107	57.7	0.4	40.0	41.0	74.3
United Arab Emirates	25	72.4	1.0	55.0	69.0	99.5
Yemen	133	53.7	−1.8	30.0	18.0	91.5

Source: Kim and Miller (2015). ***Index of Economic Freedom***. http://www.heritage.org/index

Gov't Spending	Business Freedom	Labor Freedom	Monetary Freedom	Trade Freedom	Investment Freedom	Financial Freedom
38.7	66.6	50.5	71.2	60.8	25.0	30.0
73.1	72.5	83.1	74.2	78.6	65.0	80.0
68.0	65.4	53.6	67.4	70.0	50.0	40.0
93.0	57.0	51.3	48.7	41.4	0.0	10.0
43.8	57.7	74.4	73.6	N/A	N/A	N/A
47.8	72.4	67.1	81.6	88.6	80.0	70.0
70.7	59.1	74.4	80.6	79.6	70.0	60.0
61.1	58.6	64.2	74.0	76.2	55.0	50.0
70.6	54.7	60.7	72.0	75.8	60.0	60.0
37.5	46.8	66.7	71.4	80.0	5.0	20.0
61.0	68.8	33.4	81.9	78.2	70.0	60.0
44.2	68.4	76.1	76.2	76.8	65.0	60.0
71.9	70.5	71.2	79.7	81.8	45.0	50.0
61.9	65.8	72.7	68.4	76.4	40.0	50.0
N/A	57.3	49.1	N/A	N/A	0.0	20.0
70.8	81.2	69.1	74.8	61.2	35.0	30.0
85.8	74.7	83.8	83.8	82.4	40.0	50.0
59.9	54.0	57.1	68.5	77.6	50.0	30.0

Table A1.2 The quality of governance in MENA countries in comparison with OECD countries (2013)

Country \ Indicator	Voice and Accountability	Rule of Law	Regulatory Quality	Political Stability	Government Effectiveness	Control of Corruption
OECD countries	1.29	1.37	1.36	0.94	1.43	1.39
Algeria	−0.89	−0.68	−1.19	−1.17	−0.60	−0.48
Bahrain	−1.32	0.35	0.60	−1.34	0.58	0.45
Djibouti	−1.44	−0.76	−0.55	−0.12	−1.18	−0.44
Egypt, Arab Rep.	−1.04	−0.60	−0.70	−1.62	−0.89	−0.60
Iran, Islamic Rep.	−1.60	−0.98	−1.50	−1.27	−0.70	−0.68
Iraq	−1.10	−1.47	−1.26	−1.99	−1.08	−1.25
Israel	0.63	0.95	1.16	−1.09	1.22	0.84
Jordan	−0.82	0.39	0.11	−0.62	−0.11	0.09
Kuwait	−0.65	0.39	−0.09	0.14	−0.07	−0.15
Lebanon	−0.44	−0.78	−0.09	−1.69	−0.39	−0.92
Libya	−1.00	−1.36	−1.83	−1.81	−1.50	−1.52
Morocco	−0.72	−0.25	−0.17	−0.50	−0.07	−0.36
Oman	−1.00	0.56	0.47	0.48	0.21	0.08
Qatar	−0.86	1.04	0.74	1.22	1.07	1.24
Saudi Arabia	−1.82	0.26	0.08	−0.41	0.06	−0.01
Syrian Arab Republic	−1.77	−1.48	−1.61	−2.68	−1.34	−1.24
Tunisia	−0.11	−0.20	−0.35	−0.91	0.00	−0.15
United Arab Emirates	−1.03	0.64	0.78	0.92	1.17	1.29
West Bank and Gaza	−0.87	−0.44	0.15	−1.90	−0.78	−0.71
Yemen, Rep.	−1.35	−1.16	−0.74	−2.35	−1.20	−1.20

Source: The Worldwide Governance Indicators. Available at: www.govindicators.org
Note: All six WGI indexes range from −2.5 to 2.5.

Table A1.3 Summary of regulatory quality in the MENA region (2014): Ease of doing business

Indicator	Worse regional performance	Best regional performance	Regional average	Best global performance
Starting a Business (rank)	Libya (171)	UAE (37)	112	New Zeeland (1)
Procedures (number)	Algeria (14)	3 Economies* (5)	8	New Zeeland (1)
Time (days)	West Bank and Gaza (45.0)	3 Economies* (8.0)	19.9	New Zeeland (1.0)
Cost (% of income per capita)	Djibouti (184.7)	Bahrain (0.9)	28.9	Slovenia (0.0)
Paid-in Min. Capital (% of income per capita)	Bahrain (266.6)	9 Economies* (0.0)	45.4	112 Economies* (0.0)
Dealing with Construction Permits (rank)	Libya (189)	Bahrain (4)	108	Hong Kong SAR, China (1)
Procedures (number)	Kuwait (24)	Iraq (10)	16	Hong Kong SAR, China (6)
Time (days)	Iran, Islamic Rep. (320.0)	United Arab Emirates (44.0)	145.7	Singapore (26.0)
Cost (% of income per capita)	Djibouti (1,949.2)	Qatar (1.1)	283.3	Qatar (1.1)
Getting Electricity (rank)	Iran, Islamic Rep. (169)	United Arab Emirates (4)	77	Iceland (1)
Procedures (number)	3 Economies* (7)	United Arab Emirates (3)	5	10 Economies* (3)
Time (days)	Djibouti (180)	United Arab Emirates (35)	86	Germany (17)
Cost (% of income per capita)	Djibouti (7,487.0)	Qatar (4.0)	1,038.0	Japan (0.0)
Registering Property (rank)	Libya (189)	United Arab Emirates (2)	93	Georgia (1)
Procedures (number)	Algeria (10)	United Arab Emirates (2)	6	4 Economies* (1)
Time (days)	Morocco (60.0)	Saudi Arabia (8.0)	33.0	New Zealand (1.0)
Cost (% of income per capita)	Syrian Arab Republic (27.8)	Saudi Arabia (0.0)	5.9	5 Economies (0.0)
Getting Credit (rank)	Libya (186)	Saudi Arabia (55)	133	Malaysia (1)
Strength of legal rights indes (0–10)	Djibouti (2)	Saudi Arabia (5)	3	10 Economies* (10)
Depth of credit information index (0–6)	Djibouti (1)	Saudi Arabia (6)	4	31 Economies *(6)
Public registry coverage (% of adults)	Djibouti (0.3)	Oman (21.0)	11.9	Portugal (100.0)
Pribate bureau coverage (% of adults)	Egypt, Arab Rep. (19.6)	Saudi Arabia (44.3)	28.4	22 Economies (100.0)
Protecting Investors (rank)	Libya (187)	Saudi Arabia (22)	113	New Zealand (1)
Extent of disclosure index (0–10)	Malta (3)	Saudi Arabia (8)	6	10 Economies* (10)

Continued

Table A1.3 Continued

Indicator	Worse regional performance	Best regional performance	Regional average	Best global performance
Extent of director liability index (0–10)	Lebanon (1)	Saudi Arabia (8)	5	Cambodia (10)
Ease of shareholder suits index (0–10)	Djibouti (0)	Malta (8)	3	3 Economies* (10)
Strength of investor protection index (0–10)	Djibouti (2.3)	Saudi Arabia (6.7)	4.5	New Zealand (9.7)
Paying Taxes (rank)	Algeria (174)	United Arab Emirates (1)	64	United Arab Emirates (1)
Payments (number per year)	Yemen, Rep. (44)	Saudi Arabia (3)	18	Hong Kong SAR, China (3)
Time (hours per year)	Algeria (451)	United Arab Emirates (12)	220	United Arab Emirates (12)
Trading Across Borders (rank)	Iraq (179)	United Arab Emirates (4)	89	Singapore (1)
Documents to export (number)	Iraq (10)	United Arab Emirates (3)	6	Ireland (2)
Time to export (days)	Iraq (80)	United Arab Emirates (7)	20	5 Economies (6)
Cost to export (US$ per container)	Iraq (3,550)	Morocco (595)	1.127	Malaysia (450)
Documents to import (number)	Iraq (10)	United Arab Emirates (5)	8	Ireland (2)
Time to import (days)	Iraq (82)	United Arab Emirates (7)	24	Singapore (4)
Cost to import (US$ per container)	Iraq (3,650)	United Arab Emirates (615)	1.36	Singapore (440)
Enforcing Contracts (rank)	Syrian Arab Republic (179)	Iran, Islamic Rep. (51)	118	Luxembourg (1)
Time (days)	Djibouti (1,225)	Iran, Islamic Rep. (505)	658	Singapore (150)
Cost (% of claim)	Malta (35.9)	Oman (13.5)	24.6	Bhutan (0.1)
Procedures (number)	Syrian Arab Republic (55)	Yemen, Rep. (36)	44	Singapore (21)
Resolving Insolvency (rank)	3 Economies *	Bahrain (27)	105	Japan (1)
Time (years)	Djibouti (5.0)	Tunisia (1.3)	3.2	Ireland (0.4)
Cost (% of estate)	Egypt Arab Rep. (22)	Oman (4)	14	Norway (1)
Recovery rate (cents on the dollar)	Iraq (0.0)	Bahrain (67.4)	29.4	Japan (92.8)

Source: Doing Business database. http://www.doingbusiness.org/
Note: * Two or more economies share the top ranking in this indicator.

Table A1.4 The biggest obstacles to firm activities in MENA countries

Economy	Year of the survey	Access to finance	Access to land	Business licensing and permits	Corruption	Courts	Crime, theft and disorder	Customs and trade regulations	Electricity	Inadequately educated workforce	Labor regulations	Political instability	Practices of the informal sector	Tax administration	Tax rates	Transportation
All Countries		16.6	3.4	2.6	6.7	1	4.5	3.5	10.1	7.4	2.9	10.5	12.2	3.4	11.9	3.2
Middle East & North Africa		9.8	3.8	2.4	6.4	0.9	2.1	3.4	19.8	3.5	2.8	27.5	6.3	1.3	9.2	1.2
Djibouti	2013	1.9	0.8	1.8	12.6	0.7	0	3.8	48.8	6.6	1.7	1	4	1.3	12.4	2.6
Algeria	2007															
Egypt, Arab Rep.	2007	7.1	3.1	2.2	14.8	1.1	0	2.5	6.7	8.7	4.6	0	25.5	3	19.8	1.1
Egypt, Arab Rep.	2008	7.4	7.5	2.3	8.1	0.5	0.2	3	4.7	18.1	3.4	0	25.5	2	14.4	3.1
Iraq	2011	4.7	10.5	6.4	2.9	0	1.4	4.3	19.7	7	5	15.1	16.7	1.3	4.6	0.5
Jordan	2006	9.2	3.7	25.4	6.1	0.5	0.5	3.5	1.2	9.2	6	7.7	6	11.3	8.6	1.1
Jordan	2013	31.2	4.8	1.9	4.6	1.4	0.6	3.2	1.8	4.8	6	10.6	3.3	1.1	23.2	1.6
Lebanon	2009	10.6	1.3	0.5	4.8	4.5	1.1	2.1	11.6	4.2	1.3	45.2	4	0.3	5.6	2.9
Lebanon	2013	6.6	1.9	0.6	6.7	1.8	1.4	2.1	11.1	0.7	1	58	2	1.6	4.4	0.1
Morocco	2007															
Syrian Arab Republic	2009	6.6	3.2	3.2	14.2	9	0.2	9.4	11.8	12.8	7.8	0	11.2	5	4.8	0.6
West Bank and Gaza	2006	10.7	1.8	4	4	0	1.3	1.3	11.2	0.5	0.5	45.1	6.7	1.8	0.5	10.7
West Bank and Gaza	2013	9.4	3.2	3.6	3.9	0.5	1.3	6	13.4	1	2.1	31.1	10.6	2	10	2.1
Yemen, Rep.	2010	5	6.6	0.9	26.6	1.5	1.3	0.8	32.1	5.4	0.2	7.7	2.1	2.6	6.8	0.5
Yemen, Rep.	2013	4.8	1.5	0	7.9	0.8	7.8	0.7	23.7	0.8	1.3	49	1.1	0.3	0.2	0.2

Notes: This indicator refers to the percentage of firms that have identified obstacle "x" as a major constraint for their activity; this indicator is computed using data from manufacturing firms only.
Source: World Bank Enterprise surveys. http://www.enterprisesurveys.org

2

Sources of Economic Growth in MENA Countries

Technological Progress, Physical or Human Capital Accumulations?

Senay Acikgoz, Mohamed Sami Ben Ali, and Merter Mert

Economic growth is an increase in the productive capacity of an economy. The productive capacity can be increased by an increase in factors of production, such as capital, labor, or the level of technology. Economic growth can also be defined briefly as an increase in the level of output that an economy can produce. From a supply-side view, the main *sources of economic growth* are expected to be from capital (both physical and human), accumulation and technological progress. The literature on economic growth examines whether the sources of economic growth stem mostly from technological progress, physical capital accumulation, or human capital accumulation. Besides, it is a fundamental debate about a simple question: *Why does rapid growth occur in some countries when some others cannot achieve such a performance?* Important literature analyzing the high and sustained economic growth of countries already exists. The main concern is to disentangle the contributions of capital accumulation and technological progress from this growth process. In light of this main concern, sources of growth should also be investigated for the countries in the Middle East and North Africa (MENA). Our study explores the sources of economic growth for the MENA countries and contributes to the debate over whether they stem from technological progress, physical capital accumulation, or human capital accumulation, and deliberates on the identifying assumption used in growth accounting theories. Specifically, the study asks the following question: *What are the theoretical and empirical results of assuming the nature of technological progress as Harrod-neutral in growth accounting for the MENA countries?*

Sources of Economic Growth: A Literature Overview

The basic literature on sources of economic growth is an attempt to calculate the contributions of the various factors and the level of technology to the growth rate of the output. The main problem is to disentangle the contributions of capital accumulation and technological progress.

A pioneering work on economic growth is the study by Solow (1957). The author uses a production function by connecting output to inputs that are capital and labor-based in physical units. Solow phrases any kind of shift in the production function as "technical change." He also defines the multiplicative factor, which measures the cumulated effect of shifts over time and differentiates the production function totally with respect to time. After rearranging this special form, Solow makes an application to the US economy for the period 1909–1949. This study leads many further studies in the literature. Later on, Nishimizu and Hulten (1978), investigate the sources of economic growth in Japan between 1955 and 1971 by assuming that the level of technology of each sector is characterized by a Hicks-neutral technological progress. According to their results, produced factors of production capital and intermediate goods are the principal sources of sectorial economic growth, rather than productivity. Collins and Bosworth (1996) examine eight East Asian, five South Asian, twenty-one sub-Saharan African, nine Middle Eastern and North African, 22 Latin American, and 23 industrial countries for the period 1960–1994. Their results mainly *point to capital accumulation* rather than productivity growth for East Asian countries. Klenow and Rodríguez-Clare (1997) use a production function that is rearranged and based on Mankiw, Romer, and Weil (1992). They document that *productivity contribution is the main source* of growth for Hong Kong, the Republic of Korea, and Taiwan. They also generalize this result for their sample 98 countries, stating that 90 percent of the country differences in *output per worker growth are attributable to differences in total factor productivity growth.* In a similar setting, Kim and Lau (1994) examine sources of economic growth for China, Hong Kong, Indonesia, Japan, Malaysia, the Philippines, Singapore,

South Korea, Taiwan, Thailand, France, West Germany, the United Kingdom, and the United States. They use the meta-production function model. Their results find that the main source of growth is capital accumulation rather than technological progress for China, Hong Kong, Indonesia, Japan, Malaysia, the Philippines, Singapore, South Korea, Taiwan, and Thailand. However, the main source of growth is technological progress rather than capital accumulation for France, West Germany, the United Kingdom, and the United States. Wang and Yao (2003), using a simple growth accounting exercise, analyze sources of growth for the Chinese economy from 1952 to 1999. The 1952–1977 and 1978–1999 periods are called the prereform and reform periods, respectively. The authors use a production function that connects the real GDP to total factor productivity, real capital stock, total employment, and the average schooling years of population age 14–65 (i.e., human capital stock). They find that while the growth of total factor productivity has a positive and significant role during the reform period, its contribution is negative in the prereform period. Wang and Yao (2001) show that total factor productivity growth is the driving force for China in the long run.

Iwata et al. (2003) investigate sources of economic growth for East Asian countries (Hong Kong SAR, Indonesia, Korea, Malaysia, Philippines, Singapore, Taiwan Province of China, Thailand, and China) for the period 1960–1995 by employing nonparametric derivative estimation techniques. According to their results, *the growth of total factor productivity had been main factor* for economic growth in these countries.

De Brun (2005) analyzes Uruguay's growth pattern over the period 1957–1999. He also employs a growth accounting exercise based on a production function with GDP, depending on physical capital, labor, human capital, and an index of productivity or technological change that evolves over time. The growth accounting exercise shows that *factor accumulation is the main contributor* to economic growth in Uruguay.

Park and Ryu (2006) show that physical capital accumulation accounts for most of the economic growth seen in East Asian economies, if a homothetic function is used. However, technical progress accounts for most of the economic growth if the Cobb-Douglas production function with constant returns to scale is used.

Fuentes et al. (2006) examine the sources of economic growth for Chile during the 1960–2005 period, based on a production with adjusted total factor productivity, capital adjusted for utilization, hours worked, and labor quality. These authors find different results for different periods. While the main contributor to the 1961–1973 period of modest growth is capital, it is labor during the slow-growth period of 1974–1989. *During the high-growth period of 1990–2005, the main contributor is total factor productivity* in the Chilean economy.

Bosworth et al. (2007) analyze sources of economic growth based on a growth accounting framework for the Indian economy for the period 1960–2004. The production function accounts for total factor productivity and a measure of returns to scale. According to their results, while the main source was factor inputs before 1973, in subsequent decades, *the contribution of total factor productivity has grown in importance*. De la Escosura and Roses (2009) investigate the sources of economic growth for Spain for the period of 1850–2000 using a translog index of total factor productivity. According to their results, up to 1950, factor accumulation is the main source of long-term growth. However, *the main source becomes total factor productivity during periods of growth acceleration*. More recently, Madsen (2010) uses data for 16 industrialized countries for the period 1870–2006 based on the empirical implications of the Abel–Blanchard model. Madsen (2010) finds evidence that conventional growth accounting studies attribute too much weight to factor accumulation and emphasizes *TFP-induced factor accumulation*.

van der Eng (2010), analyzes Indonesian economic growth during the 1880–2008 period. Findings of this study show that total factor productivity growth is negative during key growth periods 1900–1929 and 1975–1997, while it was substantial particularly during some subperiods. Lee and Hong (2012) make an analysis for 12 developing Asian countries. According to their results, *fast growth stems from capital accumulation* rather than education and total factor productivity for these 12 economies over the analyzed period. Molinari et al. (2013) examine Australia, Japan, South Korea, and the US economies from 1980 to 2006. They take into account disembodied and factor-embodied technical change. They show that *while capital accumulation is the main sources of GDP growth in Australia, Japan, and the United States, it is total factor productivity in South Korea*.

Ferreira et al. (2013), using the data covering the 1960–2007 period for 18 Latin American countries among 83 developed and developing countries, find evidence that, until the late 1970s, total factor productivity was not the main source. However, the main sources of low level of output per worker were physical and human capital accumulation. On the other hand, total factor productivity decreased after the late 1970s, and the sample economies began to stagnate.

Acikgoz and Mert (2014) study sources of economic growth for Hong Kong, the Republic of Korea, Singapore, and Taiwan, between the 1950s and 2007, using a production function under the assumption of Harrod-neutral technological progress. Their results emphasize that the main sources of economic growth is the technological progress in the short term, rather than technology.

Studies on the sources of economic growth for the countries in the MENA region are not copious. In their study, Abu-Bader and Abu-Qarn (2007) investigate whether technological progress or capital accumulation is the leading contributor to economic growth. They use growth accounting analysis for 10 MENA countries for the period 1960–1998 by using both time series analysis and panel data methods. They find that the contribution of productivity gains to growth is negligible; that is, factor accumulation is the driving force of the economy for the MENA economies. However, as it is stated by Dani Rodrik, who criticizes Collins and Bosworth (1996) in the same study, using the production function without assuming labor-augmenting technical change (i.e., Harrod-neutral technical change) may underestimate total factor productivity growth in arriving at results (Collins and Bosworth 1996).

FROM WHERE DOES ECONOMIC GROWTH STEM IN MENA?

In this chapter, we explore sources of economic growth in the MENA countries and contribute to the debate over whether sources of economic growth stem from technological progress, capital accumulation, or human capital accumulation. We also deliberate on the identifying assumption generally used in growth accounting studies; the long-term relationships among the variables should be investigated since Harrod-neutral technological progress identification is compatible with long-term analyses.

Our analysis covers the period from 1970 to 2011 for 15 MENA countries: Bahrain, Egypt, Iran, Iraq, Israel, Jordan, Kuwait, Malta, Morocco, Qatar, Saudi Arabia, Syria, Tunisia, and Turkey. Data has been obtained from the Penn World Table Version 8.0 (Feenstra et al., 2013). The real gross domestic product (GDP), capital stock, and the index of human capital are taken per worker. The original human capital index is per person. For this reason, this index is multiplied by population and then divided by the number of persons engaged (workers) in the country. All data except the number of workers are in at constant 2005 national prices.

Our analysis starts with a graphical discussion of movements in the main variables over time for all MENA countries. Then we present some empirical results. Graphs are based on the logarithmic values of the variables. In the Figures 2.1–2.15, the first two graph plots the real GDP per worker and capital stock per worker. The last graph shows the index of human capital per worker.

Since most economic time series are expected to be nonstationary, we also looked at the first differences among the logged values or growth rates of these series. In general, the mean and median values of the growth rates of output per worker, physical capital stock per worker, and human capital per worker of most of the MENA countries (Egypt, Iran, Jordan, Malta, Morocco, Sudan, Syria, Tunisia, and Turkey) are positive for the period of study. Average growth rate of output per worker in Egypt and Malta are 3.8 and 3.5 percent, respectively. Egypt and Turkey have the highest averages of physical capital stock per worker growth rate among 15 MENA countries. Egypt and Turkey also score the highest on the index of human capital per worker growth rate for the duration of the analysis.

Sources of Economic Growth: Preliminary Results

Bahrain

Bahrain is an island state in the MENA region and its main export is oil. The state attained its independence in 1971. Although Bahrain has been diversifying its economy by communication and transport facilities, oil and gas are its main sources of income. Figure 2.1 plots the real GDP per worker, physical capital stock per worker, and the index of human capital per worker of Bahrain from 1970 to 2011, respectively. In the analyzed period, the average growth rate of the number of workers per year is 6.4 percent, which is greater than the growth rates of the real GDP (4.3%) and physical capital stock (5.8%). As noted in Devlin (2010), the MENA region, compared to other developing regions, has a vibrant and growing population. Bahrain's average population growth rate per year has been recorded at 4.5 percent during the aforementioned period. These higher growth rates in employment and population lead to such time plots (as in Figure 2.1). While physical capital stock per worker was relatively stable until 1980, the real GDP per worker series had decreasing rates. Between 1985 and 2000, both the real GDP per worker and physical capital stock per worker did not change; however, the log of physical capital stock per worker was greater than the log of the real GDP per worker. As can be seen from Figure 2.1, these three series reached a peak value and they started to decrease after 2005. This is because there was a decrease in the number of person engaged between 2002 and 2005.

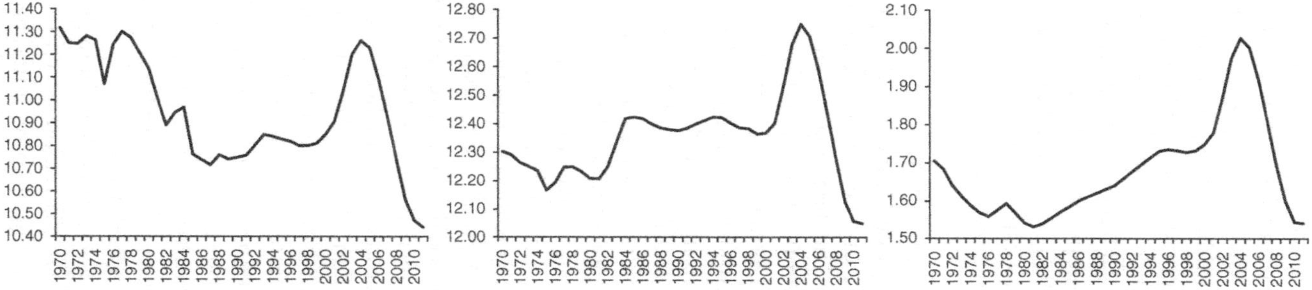

Figure 2.1 Bahrain: Real GDP, real physical capital stock, and human capital per worker.

"Increasing human capacity is the key to economic success in a global economy where countries compete increasingly in terms of skilled labor and ideas" (World Bank, 1991). "The MENA region has made significant strides in the education sector, having started in the 1960s and 1970s from very low levels of human capital accumulation" (World Bank, 2008). Bahrain's index of human capital per person has increased by an average of 1.6 percent per year from 1970 to 2011. The log of human capital per worker series in Figure 2.1 started to increase with the year 1981; it declined after 2005, since the growth rate of the index of human capital per person stayed under the growth rate of the number of workers.

Egypt

The process of economic development in Egypt can be divided into three phases, depending on the economic policies adopted by the Egyptian governments. The first phase, referred to as the socialist revolution, covers the 1960s. The second phase is referred to as the Open Door Policy years, covering the 1970s. Finally, the Economic Reform and Structural Adjustment Project (ERSAP) phase, covering the 1990s. As can be seen in Figure 2.2, the economy had enjoyed a relatively high growth rate after the mid-1970s. The fairly high GDP growth rates (6.3% on average) during this period brought about high growth rates in physical capital stock (7.8% on average). The Egyptian economy had been affected by two wars between 1967 and 1973, and the open door policy was initiated in 1974. The open door policy led to high growth rates in the real GDP and physical capital stock up to the mid-1980s. Since the number of persons engaged during these years was stable, the real GDP per worker and physical capital stock per worker exhibited an increasing trend (Figure 2.2).

The Egyptian government launched the ERSAP with the International Monetary Fund and the World Bank. The aim of this plan was to move the economy from one dominated in the public sector to one dominated in the private sector, by assuming the largest responsibility for generating investment and leading growth (Abu-Bader and Abu-Quarn, 2005). As can be seen from Figure 2.2, although there are fluctuations in the growth rates of these series because of policy changes over time, the main variables of this plan also have an increasing trend in the 1990s and 2000s.

Egypt does not have good record on human capital, which is the general situation in the MENA region—even the level of the human capital index per worker is raised constantly. The highest growth rate was recorded in the period from 1980 to 1990 (2.2% on average).

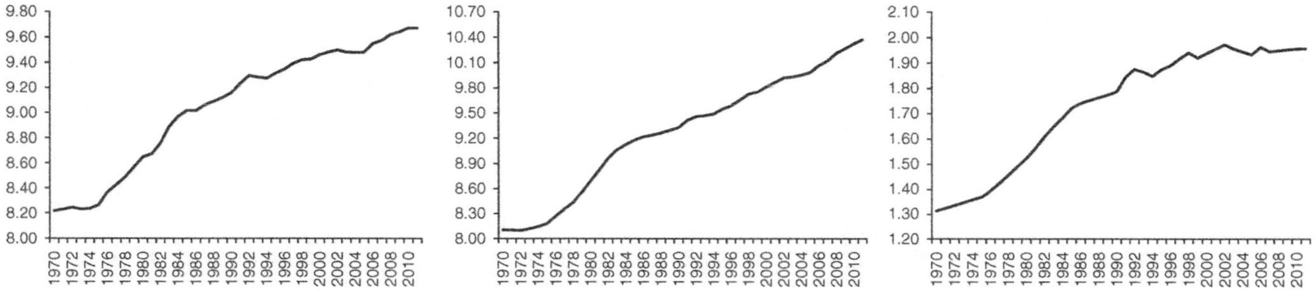

Figure 2.2 Egypt: Real GDP, real physical capital stock, and human capital per worker.

Yearly growth rate in the human capital index per worker is 1.6% on average. Education has been a priority investment for governments and households. "In the 1960s and 1970s, the majority of investment in education in Egypt was devoted to capital expenditure through rapid expansion of school construction, although this has shifted toward a greater emphasis on teacher salaries, training and curriculum development. Education has also been a priority expenditure item at the household level" (Devlin, 2010).

Iran

Iran is one of the larger states in the MENA region. There has been a remarkable deterioration in the economic growth performance of Iran since the 1980s because of the Iran-Iraq war. In the Iranian economy, the years between 1970 and 1975 were an impressive period, in terms of higher growth rates in labor productivity and the capital-labor ratio—since import substitution industrializing strategies were being applied (first graph in Figure 2.3). After the Islamic revolution, "a considerable portion of large-scale modern industry and the entire banking and insurance system were nationalized by the government" (Hakimian, 2009). This changed the ownership from the private sector to public sector. These developments caused fluctuations in the real GDP per worker (i.e., labor productivity). Physical capital accumulation also lost its increasing pattern after the revolution. As it is noted in Alizadeh (2000), "the economy not only endured the effects of the disruption of the revolution itself but also the protracted and costly war with Iraq, a continuing economic embargo but the United States."

"The First Five Year Economic, Social and Cultural Plan (1989–1994) aimed to regenerate the economy by carrying out the reconstruction of the war-damaged regions, promoting private investment, and initiating a reform and liberalization programme"(Pesaran, 2000). During the period of the plan, the real GDP, capital stock, and human capital per worker grew by the rates of 3.7 percent, 0.6 percent, and 2.8 percent, respectively. In the ten years following the plan period, the growth rate of physical capital stock was 3.2 percent on average, while the number of workers and the real GDP grew by 5.4 percent and 6.3 percent, respectively. The growth rate of the number of workers started to decrease with the year 2006 and it was recorded as –2.9 percent in 2008. The index of human capital grew by less than 1 percent per year after 2005. The economy reached positive and higher growth rates in labor productivity and capital-labor ratio with the year 2009.

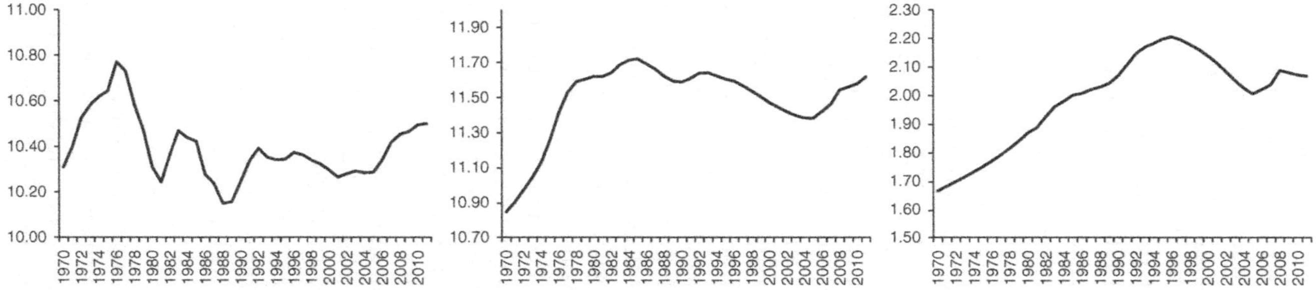

Figure 2.3 Iran: Real GDP, real physical capital stock, and human capital per worker.

Iraq

There are three important periods affecting the economic development of Iraq: the war with Iran covering the 1980–1988 period, Iraq's invasion of Kuwait covering 1990 and 1991, and the 2003 invasion of Iraq until 2011. Before the war against Iran in September 1980, Iraq was showing a 2500 percent increase in oil revenues, when compared to its earnings in 1970. Thus, the real GDP per worker showed positive growth rates between 1970 and 1980 because the government was able to increase "spending simultaneously on infrastructure, goods producing sectors, social services, imports and the military" (Alnasrawi, 2001). The war with Iran brought about increases in the labor force, the armed forces, and military expenses. During the war years, both labor productivity and the capital-labor ratio stayed relatively stable, since yearly growth rates of the real GDP and capital stock were about –0.1 percent and 5.3 percent on average. During the same period, employment increased annually by 2.1 percent.

After Iraq's invasion of Kuwait, the United Nations Security Council, under the leadership of the United States, initiated applications for very severe sanctions that continued until early 2000s. The sanction process had caused severe decreases in the real GDP per worker that reached its lowest value in 1990 and 1991. Capital stock per worker also steadily decreased during the sanction period. The 2003 invasion of Iraq also had negative effects on the process of economic development and other reconstruction policies that had already been put into action. These policies can be summarized as policies aiming to stimulate more entrepreneurship, more economic openness, and a decrease in the informal economy. However, the success of economic policies still depends on the security situation in Iraq.

"Economic development plans in Iraq were founded on the idea of investing in physical plant and infrastructure and did not give development of human capital a high priority" (Looney, 1992). The 1971–1975 and 1976–1980 National Development Plans included policies that would help to overcome the lack of skilled workers. Thus, the human capital per worker series of Iraq steadily increased until the 1990s. After that, its growth rate did not change (Figure 2.4).

Israel

Israel is one of the high-income countries in the MENA region. This relatively high level of income was attained by rapid growth. Labor productivity had also increased steadily in the 1970s and 1980s. However, as can be seen from Figure 2.5, the real GDP per worker has been fluctuating around its trend over the period. One of the

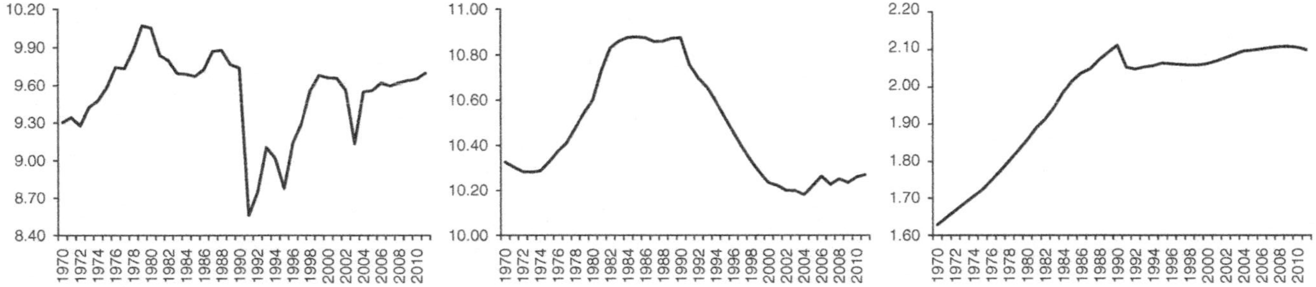

Figure 2.4 Iraq: Real GDP, real physical capital stock, and human capital per worker.

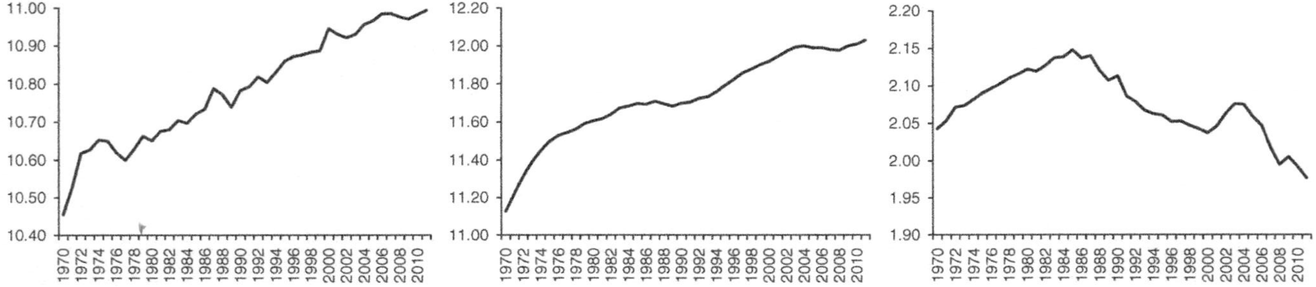

Figure 2.5 Israel: Real GDP, real physical capital stock, and human capital per worker.

reasons for these fluctuations was the fact that the Israeli government had been attempting to liberalize the economy, especially in the late 1970s. These attempts could not break "the protectionism, union domination, and high defense outlays by the central government and this inevitably led to an unsustainable public debt burden, monetization, and hyperinflation" (Rivlin, 2011). These economic issues made the policymakers change the structure and performance of the Israeli economy and the 1985 Economic Stabilization Program (ESP) was imposed. "Turning point of the ESP were to eliminate government intervention to the economy and to construct an economy increasingly based on market forces" (Ben-Bassat, 2002). Capital stock per worker between 1970 and 1975 increased at an increasing rate; however, it increased at a declining rate after 1975 to 1985. In other words, the Israeli economy was able to accumulate capital per worker during the 1970–1985 years—while labor productivity had been fluctuating.

The 1990s can be characterized by a sharp increase in investments due to economic growth, decreases in military expenses following the Oslo agreement in 1991, and the reduction in inflation rates. In the year 2000, which was "a period of rapid growth, particularly in the High Technology being one of the stronger sectors of Israel's economy" (Nathanson, 2011), the annual growth rate was 8.85 percent. During the economic downturn arising from the international crisis in the hi-tech industry in 2001 and 2002, declines in the real GDP in 2001 and 2002 were –0.22 and –0.58 percent. After this period, the economy stabilized to an annual growth rate of close to 5 percent, including in 2008. However, our calculations also showed that since growth rate of employment was greater than the economic growth rate, growth rates of labor productivity and capital-labor ratio became negative in 2008.

These results require reviewing the structure of employment and human capital in Israel for the analyzed period. One can define Israel as a state receiving migration from the world. As noted in Raijman (2012), "the origin of labor migration to Israel can be traced to the end of the Six-Day War in 1967. In the aftermath of this war, the non-citizen Palestinian workers from the West Bank and the Gaza Strip had begun joining the Israeli economy with low-paying jobs in construction, agriculture and services." During the 1990s, with the disintegration of the Soviet Union, Israel had an inflow of migrants who enriched the economy with human capital. According to PWT8.0 data, Israel has a higher index of human capital values among the MENA countries. However, index values have grown with decreasing rates over the analyzed period. In the economic downturn of 2001 and 2002, human capital per person grew by 0.18 percent, which is less than the 0.50 percent yearly average growth rate between 1970 and 2011. The index of human capital per worker has gradually been decreasing after 1985 while the number of workers has been increasing, with small downs, during the analyzed period.

Jordan

Jordan is an upper middle income country with a population of 6.3 million and annual per capita real GDP of JD 5199. Jordan enjoyed higher growth rates of around 6 percent per annum during the 1970s. Upon erecting the extractive mineral industry as the pillar its economic expansion in the 1970s and 1980s and establishing modern infrastructure, Jordan was able to increase its capital stock by 10.4 percent per annum (Piro, 1998 and Wilson, 2005). The school system established in these years resulted in best-educated population of the entire Arab world (Wilson, 2005). As can be seen from Figure 2.6, although there is a small decline in the index of human capital per worker between 1995 and 2005, it shows an increasing trend at a declining rate over the 42 years.

Jordan can be described as "small open economy and it is vulnerable to external shocks and dependent on workers remittances and foreign aid" (Jaradat, 2010). The roots of having an open economy have come from collaboration with the International Monetary Fund and World Bank in the late 1980s. Successfully implemented economic adjustment programs resulted in an increase in labor productivity after the mid-1990s. The second and third graphs in Figure 2.6 show that there is a level shift in physical capital stock and human capital per worker. "The Jordanian economy was negatively affected by the sharp increase in international oil prices combined with a drop of external grants" (Jaradat, 2010). The effects of these factors have been a slowed-down increase in labor productivity.

Kuwait

As a member of the Gulf Cooperation Council (GCC), the State of Kuwait increased its oil revenues because of major spikes in the price of oil during 1973–1974 and 1979, and the economic growth of Kuwait fluctuated around its ten-year average growth rate, which was –2.2 percent during the 1970s. Since the growth rate of employment was high because of the large immigration of expatriate workers in Kuwait, economic growth rates were generally smaller in those years, leading to a downward trend in the real GDP per worker.

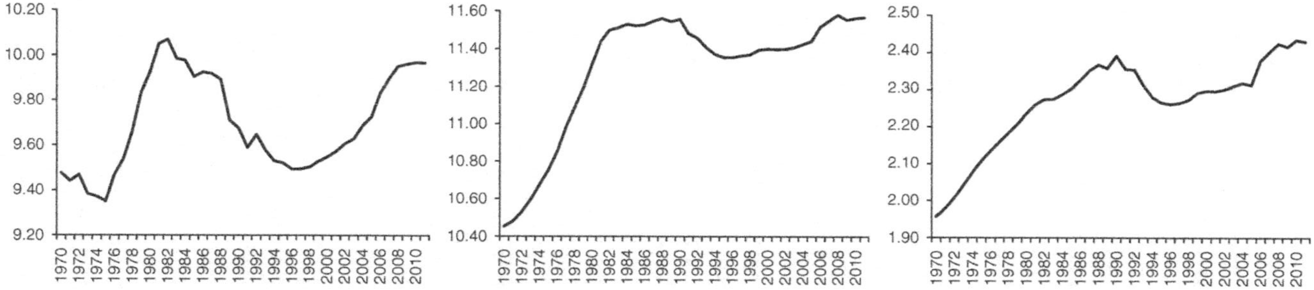

Figure 2.6 Jordan: Real GDP, real physical capital stock, and human capital per worker.

The economy of Kuwait depends heavily on oil exports. Recent data from the Organization of the Petroleum Exporting Countries (OPEC) indicates that the oil and gas sector of Kuwait accounts for about 60 percent of its GDP and about 95 percent of export revenues. For this reason, the Kuwaiti government has been encouraging economic diversification since the 1980s. This process had broken off during major events such as Iraq's invasion and the recent global financial crisis. Since both the real GDP and the number of workers declined in 1990 and 1991, a sharp decrease in the real GDP per worker occurred. Capital accumulation per worker was also affected by changes in the economic environment because of fluctuations in oil revenues and the corresponding budget surpluses and deficits. As it is noted in Ramadhan et al. (2013), "after the liberation of Iraq in 2003, the private sector has benefited from government spending on developmental projects and the opportunity of increased business activities due to the rebuilding of Iraq." The effects of these activities can be seen in the upward trend of the capital-labor ratio given in Figure 2.7.

Early immigrants to Kuwait were primarily Arab. Since the mid-1970s, the Kuwaiti government had "pursued a policy to increase the inflow of Asian migrants. Because of this policy, the Asian population increased to more than one third and the Arab population declined to two thirds of the expatriate population. The impressive growth in the education and training system is reflected in increasing numbers of qualified Kuwaitis entering the labor force" (Allak, 1989 and Al-Enezi, 2002). This showed itself in the human capital per worker exhibiting high values before the mid-1990s. "Despite improvements in some social indicators, Kuwait is largely lagging behind in education and health quality, infrastructure development, and business climate and regulations" (IMF, 2013).

Malta

"Malta is a small and open economy which is highly dependent on external trade and investment, and tourism" (Azzopardi, 2009). Malta enjoyed high labor productivity growth rates in the 1970s, and this continued into the early 2000s. After gaining independence from Britain in 1964, the main economic objectives of the government were "to increase the productive capacity of Malta and reduce emigration by creating jobs in the industrial and service sectors" (Werker, 2012). During the 1990s, Malta decided to follow "a series of economic policies in order to create a market economy, even if perhaps at the expense of higher government deficits and stock of government debt" (Camilleri and Falzon, 2013). Although Malta had higher

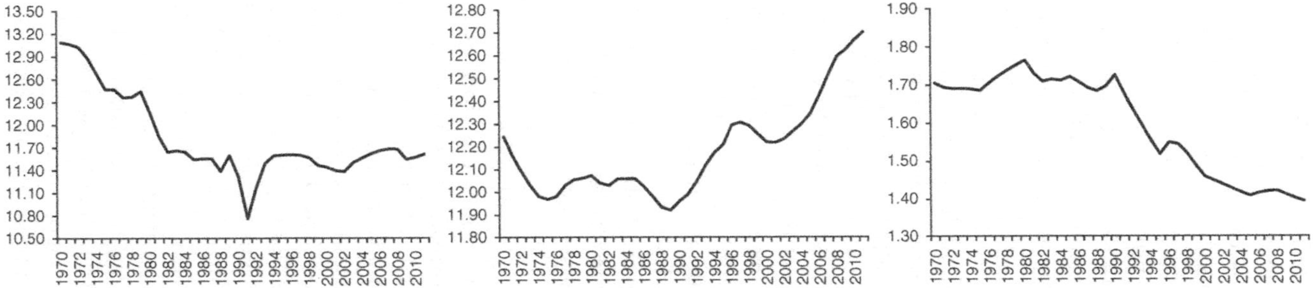

Figure 2.7 Kuwait: Real GDP, real physical capital stock, and human capital per worker.

labor productivity growth in the 1990s, its average decreased from 8.3 percent to 3.7 percent by the end of the decade.

The 1980s and 1990s can be described as good years in terms of the capital-labor ratio. It can be said that those highly productive years with some fluctuations helped the Maltese economy accumulate physical capital. Efforts, started with gaining independence, toward becoming a member of the European Union, high government spending, and investment by public enterprises contributed to economic growth and capital accumulation of the Maltese economy. "Tourism industry were also heavily promoted by the governments" (Katircioglu, 2009) even the tourism sector has been highly vulnerable over the analyzed period. Malta joined the European Union (EU) in 2004 and the currency became the euro in 2007. In the early 2000s, "Malta was affected by exogenous shocks in the electronics and tourism industries, leading to a lower rate of employment growth, made worse for Malta by the rising competitiveness of emerging economies where wages are lower than European averages" (Ebejer, 2006). Although the real GDP per worker and capital stock per worker have been steadily increasing over time, their averages per annum were 0.1 percent between 2000 and 2011.

The human capital index per labor exhibits fluctuations around an increasing trend during the 1980s and 1990s. A decline in the index after 2004 can be explained by "early school leaving and decreases in enrolling in upper secondary vocational training" (Ebejer, 2006).

Morocco

"The Moroccan economy is often described as an economy with high potential and low performance" (Cherkaoui and Ben Ali, 2007). Chronologically evaluated, Morocco's real gross domestic product grew by about 5 percent a year during the 1970s and between 2000 and 2011. The country has higher capital accumulation growth rates during these two periods. The 1980s and 1990s are the years that have lower growth rates, leading to decreases in the capacity of job creation in the economy over the analyzed period. Thus, employment grew at an average rate of 2.5, 2.4, 1.5, and 1.1 percent per decade from 1970 to 2011, respectively. As can be seen from Figure 2.8, these movements in employment and the real GDP led to fluctuations in the real GDP per worker and it also affected the growth pattern of the capital-labor ratio. According to the World Bank (2006), "rigidities of the labor market, importance of the tax burden, the exchange rate regime, the level of protectionism, the weakness in information, coordination of the private and public sectors and the training of

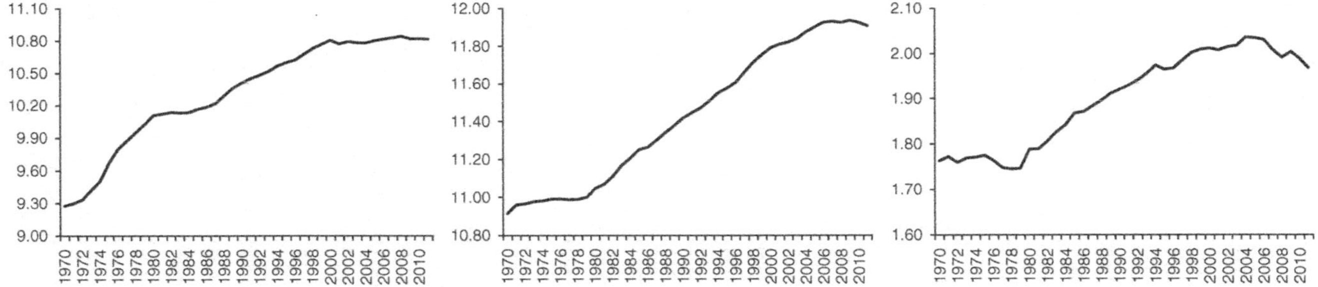

Figure 2.8 Malta: Real GDP, real physical capital stock, and human capital per worker.

employees" are the main reasons for fluctuations in labor productivity, the capital-labor ratio, and human capital per worker in Morocco.

The human capital index per worker almost did not change during the 1970s. It grew by 1.1 percent a year from 2000 and 2011 because of declines in fertility, increasing schooling and urbanization, and a shift from the agricultural sector toward the industry and services sector. As it is noted in the first paragraph, although the Moroccan economy has higher potential among the MENA countries, its potential did not create higher growth rates in human capital (Figure 2.9).

It can be said that Morocco was able to resist the direct effects of the financial crisis in 2008 and 2009, since it grew by 5.2 percent a year from 2000 to 2011. The structural reforms, strong and healthy financial system, and efficient exchange rate regime influenced this pattern during the crisis period.

Qatar

Qatar is a small country with a population of about 2.2 million at the end of 2014. Qatar is different from other MENA countries in terms of its economic growth rates. The economy grew by about 6.5 and 13.5 percent during the 1990s and in the first decade of the new millennium because of the recent development of its natural resources. Thus, with more than 70 percent of the total government revenue, more than 60 percent of its GDP, and 85 percent of its export earnings come from the oil sector, Qatar also has the world's wealthiest citizens. As a migration-friendly country, expatriate labor accounts for the labor and domestic labor markets (about 15%). Urbanization is high and almost all of the population lives in urban areas.

After gaining its independence from Britain in 1971, the economy has converted from a tribal society to a modern state. Declines in the oil prices during the 1980s negatively affected this process and made the economy diminished. This also determined the capital accumulation capacity of the economy. As can be seen from Figure 2.10, the economy started to be recovered with the mid-1990s. 1995 is accepted as a turning point in Qatar's economic history. After the coup in 1995, a huge economic and social transformation has been started by structural reforms.

As a developing country with huge migration, both population and employment growth rates are high in Qatar. High employment rates with high growth rates, especially in the new millennium, gave rise to negative growth in labor productivity and the capital-labor ratio.

As it is noted in Berrebi et al. (2009), "prior to the discovery of oil and the subsequent economic boom, few opportunities for formal

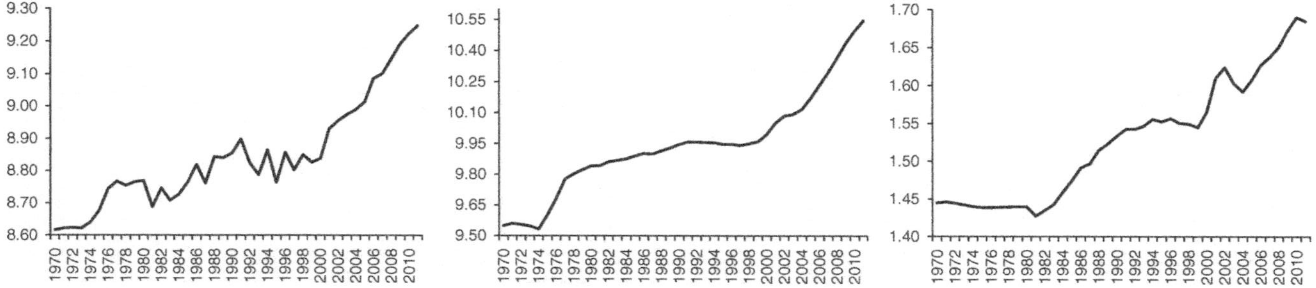

Figure 2.9 Morocco: Real GDP, real physical capital stock, and human capital per worker.

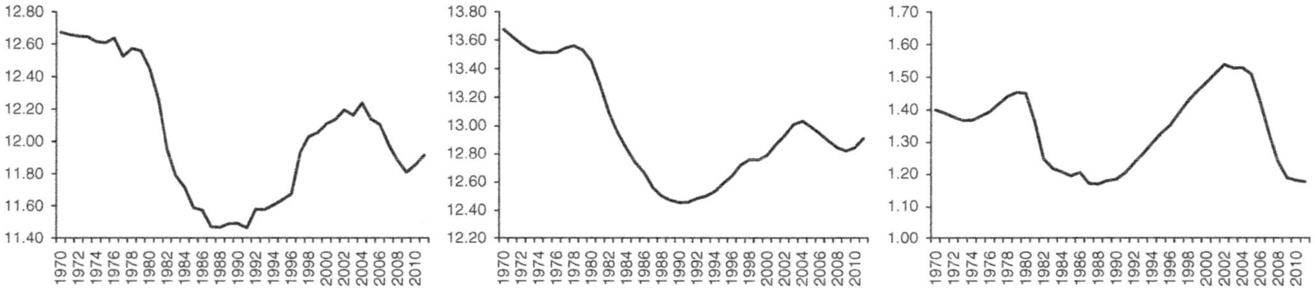

Figure 2.10 Qatar: Real GDP, real physical capital stock, and human capital per worker.

education existed in Qatar." During the 1970s and after the coup of 1995, leaders of Qatar made large investments in education in Qatar. These investments helped human capital accumulation for the country. Although the index of human capital exhibits an increasing trend over the 1970–2011 period, high growth rates in employment after 2000 have led to a decrease in human capital per worker for this period.

Saudi Arabia

As can be seen from Figure 2.11, the real GDP per worker series shows a level shift in the mid-1980s, since the economic situation of Saudi Arabia changed significantly. Saudi Arabia had its fastest growing period in the early 1970s with 10.9 percent per annum. The country enjoyed "a substantial surplus in its overall trade, its imports increased rapidly and sufficient government revenues were available for development, defense and aid to other countries" (Alkhathlan, 2013). Depending on the oil revenues had made the Saudi Arabian economy volatile. This volatility might show itself as a cyclical pattern in the capital accumulation process of the economy. Like other MENA countries, Saudi Arabia also has been diversifying its economic structure. Thus, the non-oil output was around 77 percent of the GDP in the mid-1980s, and its share became about 54 percent in 2011. According to one view, "these increases in the non-oil sector are merely the result of the fluctuation in the world's oil demand that reflects swings in world oil prices" (Al-Hassan et al., 2010). Changes in oil prices might have also resulted in a decrease in growth rate of output per labor (Figure 2.11).

The highest value of capital stock per worker was observed around the 1980s, and it shows troughs in 1974, 1990, and 2004–2005. "Saudi Arabia's major improvements were achieved in the provision of public services, particularly in health, education and social services" (Alsahlawi and Gardener, 2004). In Saudi Arabia, human capital per worker stayed relatively low and stable during the period 1970–1992. After 1992, it sharply increased and returned to a value of two at the end of the analyzed period.

Sudan

Sudan gained its independence from joint British and Egyptian rule in 1956. Its independent history has seen several armed conflicts that affected the country's economic development and its natural resources. Because of civil wars between 1955 and 1972 and 1983–2005, the real GDP per worker growth fluctuated around 2 percent over the analyzed period. Internal conflicts resulted in two countries

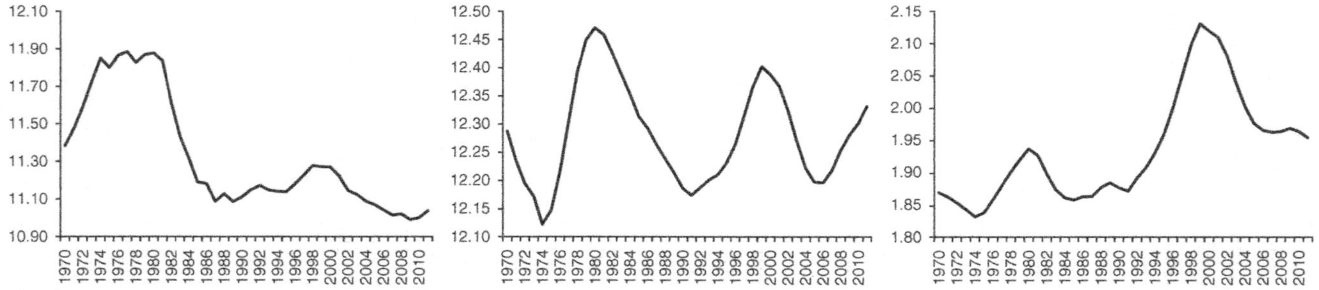

Figure 2.11 Saudi Arabia: Real GDP, real physical capital stock, and human capital per worker.

being formed in the middle of 2011: Sudan and South Sudan. The increasing contribution of the oil sector had been used to improve the country's economic performance. However, since oil resources are located in South Sudan, Sudan lost most of its oil reserves, and this also means the loss of oil revenues. In 2011, the labor productivity growth was 0.9 percent, deviating from its long-term average of about 2 4 percent.

In Sudan, as in other MENA countries, the labor market is under the public sector. "The structure of the labor market is constrained by weak and inefficient regulations and institutional settings, rigidity and lack of dynamism, deficiency in employment, monitoring, planning and skill upgrading; the high incidence of duality (rural–urban; traditional-modern and formal-informal sectors) and prevalence of high rates of unemployment, especially among youth population and child labor" (Nour, 2013). While human capital stock per worker of Sudan had dramatic increases until the mid-1990s, it stayed at around 1.8 until 2011 (Figure 2.12).

Syria

Syria has borders with five MENA countries: Lebanon, Iraq, Israel, Jordan, and Turkey. In the Syrian economy, which shows a growth of about 5 percent a year from 1970 until 2011, the rate of capital accumulation is about 5 percent on average. When the economy is reviewed in ten-year periods, Syria experienced rapid growth, averaging 9.5 percent per year in the 1970s, with high growth rates in capital accumulation. Employment also increased in those years and these developments gave rise to increases in the labor productivity and the capital-labor ratio. 1973 and 1977 oil shocks also affected the Syrian economy, and it shrank by 9 and 4 percent in these two years. The 1980s are years of low economic growth, despite employment in Syria having increased. This brought about fluctuations in the labor productivity. The slowdown in the 1980s was mainly due to "poor agricultural crops and related drop in trade, transport and other non-government services, combined with stagnation in petroleum and mining, and a fall in value added in manufacturing and utilities" (World Bank, 1986). The MENA region generally had problems in the process of economic development during the 1990s, and Syria shared this problem, in terms of having lower capital stock per worker. It continued its process of growth because "the country benefited from increased oil production and agricultural performance, as well as an aid windfall during the Gulf war in the 1990s" (Dasgupta et al., 2001). "Syria's economic transition away from an

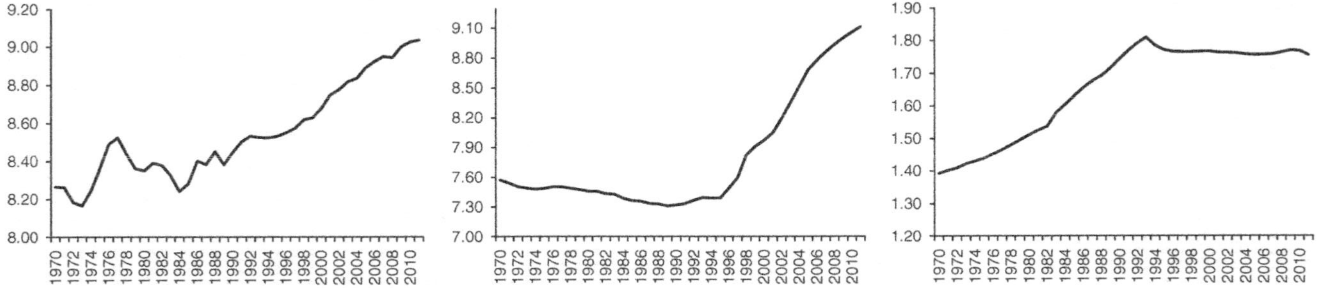

Figure 2.12 Sudan: Real GDP, real physical capital stock, and human capital per worker.

oil-exporting, centrally-planned economy toward an economically diverse, market-based system began at the turn of the 21st century, with economic reforms that gradually integrated the economy with the global trading system" (Lim and Saborowski, 2005). Thus, Syria closed the first decade of the twenty-first century with 4.5 percent economic growth rates.

According the last two graphs in Figure 2.13, as physical capital stock per worker increased, human capital per worker increased, implying that there is a positive correlation between capital stock and human capital per worker. The 2000s have witnessed increases in capital stock and human capital per workers.

Tunisia

The economy of Tunisia has the real GDP per worker series growing gradually over the period 1970–2011. Tunisia completed the 1970s with high economic growth and capital accumulation rates (with 7 percent per year). During the last 30 years of the analyzed period, although Tunisia has achieved consistently good macroeconomic performances, its employment grew at a decreasing rate with the declines its population, leading to fluctuations in its labor productivity especially until the mid-1990s. Data set used in this study shows that most of MENA countries have positive employment growth over time. However, "almost all of them entered the new millennium with large unemployment rates" (Ben Jelili and Goaied, 2009). For example, unemployment rates changed between 12.5 and 18.3 in the 2006–2011 period. Unemployment rate among higher education graduates was 17 percent in 2006 and it became 29.2 percent in 2011. Although the index of human capital of Penn World Table for Tunisia has an increasing trend over time, decreases in the number of workers led to increasing an increasing trend in the index of human capital per worker (Figure 2.14).

Turkey

Turkey is one of the MENA countries that has shown a consistent growth pattern in the variables of interest. The growth rate of labor productivity was positive for the period 1970–1977 and 1980–1988, however it was negative for 1977–1980, which includes the year of crisis. During 1988–2001, rises and falls occur relatively more frequently. Note that Turkey's financial liberalization process began after 1989, and financial liberalization might be the reason for those movements. After 2001 until 2007, growth rate of the real GDP per worker was positive and it grew negatively during 2007–2009, which

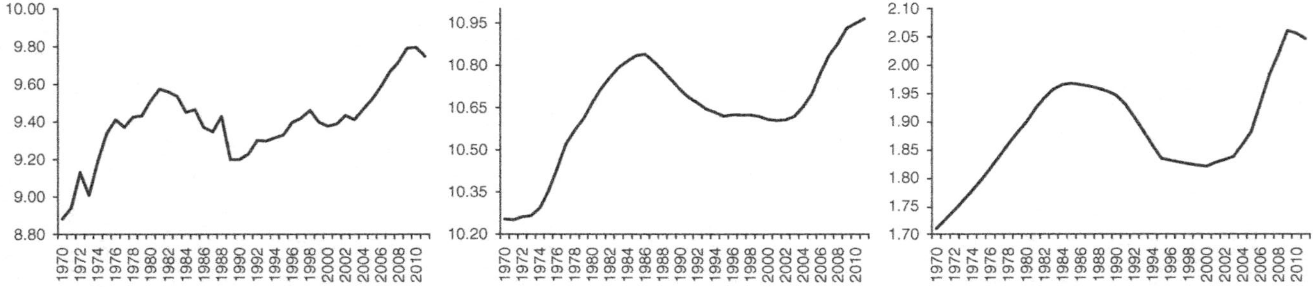

Figure 2.13 Syria: Real GDP, real physical capital stock, and human capital per worker.

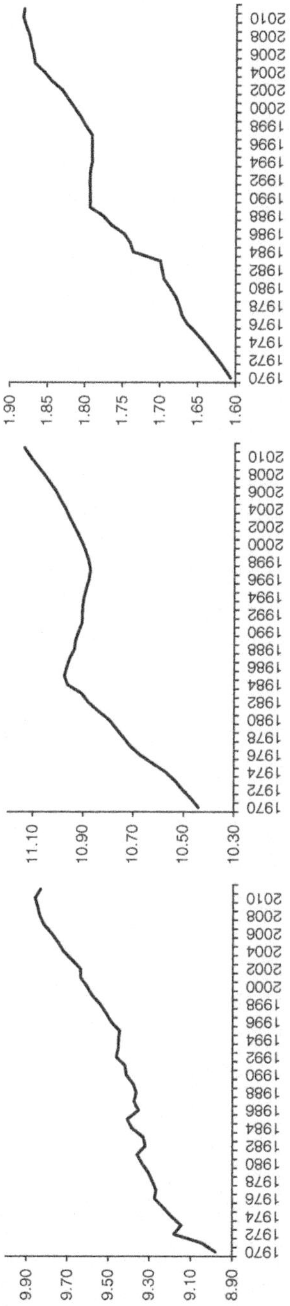

Figure 2.14 Tunisia: Real GDP, real physical capital stock, and human capital per worker.

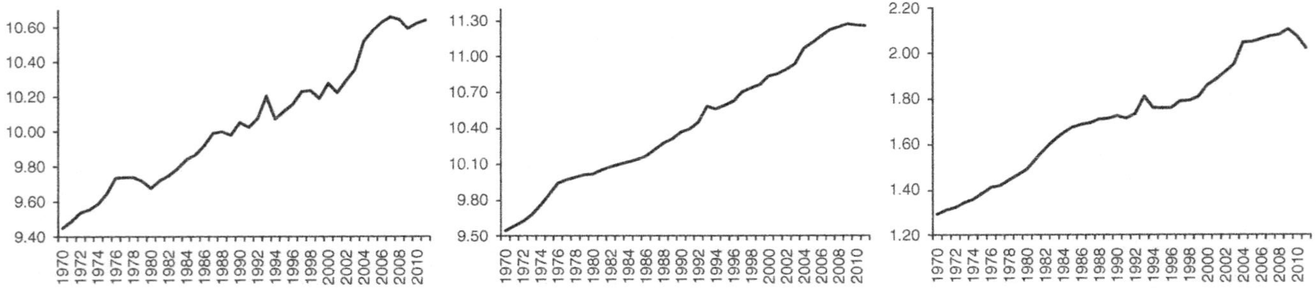

Figure 2.15 Turkey: Real GDP, real physical capital stock, and human capital per worker.

is the crisis period; labor productivity growth was recorded as positive during 2009–2011. Growth rate of the capital-labor ratio was positive for the period 1970–2001, except for 1993 and 2009–2011. Its growth rates are relatively high during 1970–1976, 1992–1993, and 2003–2004. Growth rate of the index of human capital per worker was greater than during 1980–1983, relative to 1970–1980. After 1983, except for 1993, its growth rate was low. Although there is an increasing trend during 1999–2004, the growth rate of the index of human capital per worker became less during 2004–2009. For the period 2009–2011, its growth rate was negative. The Turkish economy has also been affected by global economic problems because of its open economy structure. Average growth rates of the real GDP per worker, real physical capital stock per worker, and human capital per worker are recorded as 2.9, 4.2, and 1.8 percent, respectively (Figure 2.15).

As can be seen from the figures in this section, the real GDP per worker series for half of the MENA countries increases steadily over time. This suggests, at least initially, that the real GDP per worker is not linear.

Sources of Economic Growth: Some Empirical Results

In this chapter, we explored different sources of economic growth for Egypt, Iran, Israel, Morocco, Qatar, Saudi Arabia, Sudan, and Turkey. Different empirical studies have been done so far on the sources of economic growth in developed and in developing countries. However, studies dealing with the Middle East and North Africa on sources of economic growth are not copious. Economic growth may stem from different sources—as explained in this chapter—both in a general framework and in MENA countries as well. However, the question here is, *from where does economic growth stem in MENA countries?*

While considering a Harrod-neutral technological progress in their paper, Acikgoz et al. (2015) argue that the main source of economic growth stems from physical capital accumulation. As presented in Table 2.1, the authors show that for Egypt, Morocco, Sudan, and Turkey, the main source is physical capital accumulation, which has a contribution of between 57 percent and 64 percent. For these countries, the contribution of human capital stock is also important, and that contribution is between 21 percent and 39 percent. Among these countries, for Egypt and Turkey, the contribution of technological progress is very small at 2.9 percent and 2.26 percent, respectively. However, it is greater in Morocco and Sudan, at 13.27 percent and

Table 2.1 Growth accounting results

Country	Best global performance	Contribution of capital stock per labor (2)	Contribution of human capital stock per labor (3)	Contribution of technological progress (4) = (1) – (2) – (3)
Egypt	0,0355	**57,5860**	39,5131	2,9008
Iran	0,0046	**175,4500**	83,3137	-158,7637
Israel	0,0131	32,1674	-0,3003	**68,1329**
Morocco	0,0154	**58,2939**	27,6266	14,0795
Qatar	-0,0184	**91,8789**	23,5584	-15,4373
Saudi Arabia	-0,0084	-7,4409	-23,4345	**130,8755**
Sudan	0,0187	**59,7692**	21,2485	18,9823
Turkey	0,0290	**64,1659**	33,5705	2,2636

Source: Acikgoz, et al. (2015).

18.98 percent, respectively. Interestingly, Iran and Qatar show a negative contribution of technological progress. For Iran, the contribution of physical capital stock is 175.45 percent and the contribution of human capital stock is 83.31 percent, which are very high compared to the others. However, the contribution of technological progress is negative, at –158.76 percent. Apart from the others, for Israel and Saudi Arabia, the technological progress is their main source of economic growth, which shows a contribution of 68.13 percent and 130.87 percent, respectively.

Thus, our results justify the argument that the main source of economic growth is physical capital accumulation for the MENA countries—except for Israel and Saudi Arabia, where the main source is technological progress.

Figures given in the Appendix show contributions of K/L growth, H/L growth, and technological progress to Y/L growth for each of the sample countries for a two-year period, based on Harrod-neutral technological progress. These figures give information about possible determinants of cyclical movements in Y/L growth. For Egypt, until 1990–1992, the contribution of technological progress was pro-cyclical with Y/L growth. However, after 1990–1992, the contributions of K/L growth and H/L growth were more compatible with Y/L growth. It is similar to Iran until and after 2002–2004, Saudi Arabia until and after 1992–1994, and Turkey until and after 1996–1998.

Israel's cyclical movements of Y/L growth is mainly determined by the contribution of technological progress for all of the periods. For

Sudan, cyclical movements of Y/L growth are mainly determined by the contribution of technological progress for the period 1970–1994 and 2000–2011. However, it is the contribution of K/L growth for 1994–2000 for Sudan. Morocco's cyclical movements of Y/L growth are determined by the contribution of technological progress, except for 1980–1984 and 2000–2006. For Qatar, contributions of K/L growth and H/L growth seem to have been the main determinant of cyclical movements of Y/L growth, except for 1970–1974, 1976–1978, and 1998–2002.

CONCLUSION AND POLICY IMPLICATIONS

This study examines the sources of economic growth for the MENA countries and asks the following question: *What are the theoretical and empirical results of assuming the nature of technological progress as Harrod-neutral in growth accounting for the MENA countries?*

Our study finds evidence that economic growth stems from capital accumulation rather than total factor productivity for all the MENA countries except Israel and Saudi Arabia. Thus, assuming the nature of technological progress as Harrod-neutral in growth accounting for the MENA countries does not have a critical impact on the results.

Note that for the fast growing economies among our sample (Egypt and Turkey), the main source is capital accumulation, and the contribution of technological progress is unimportant. A similar interpretation can be made for Sudan and Morocco. Thus, for those countries, it is important to raise savings and capital accumulation. However, it should be emphasized that this comment is only valid among MENA countries. For Iran, although the contribution of capital stock is very high, the growth rate of output per labor is low. Likewise, Qatar grows negatively although it shows a high contribution of capital stock. These results point to policies that focus on technological progress rather than capital accumulation for Iran and Qatar. Conversely, Saudi Arabia grows negatively although it shows a high contribution of technological progress. This result indicates the importance of policies on capital accumulation rather than technological progress for Saudi Arabia.

REFERENCES

Abu-Bader, S., and Abu-Qarn, A. (2007). Sources of growth revisited: Evidence from selected MENA countries. *World Development*, 35 (5): 752–771.

Abu-Bader, S., and Abu-Qarn, A. (2005). Financial Development and Economic Growth: Time Series Evidence from Egypt. *MPRA Paper*, No. 1113. http://mpra.ub.uni-muenchen.de/1113/.

Acikgoz, S., and Mert, M. (2014). Sources of growth revisited: The importance of the nature of technological progress. *Journal of Applied Economics*, 7 (1): 31–62.

Acikgoz, S., Mert, M., and Ben Ali, M. S. (2015). Where does economic growth in MENA countries come from? Forthcoming

Al-Enezi, A. K. (2002). Kuwait's employment policy: Its formulation, implications, and challenges. *International Journal of Public Administration*, 25 (7): 885–900.

Al-Hassan, A., Khamis, M., and Oulidi, N. (2010). The GCC Banking Sector: Topography and Analysis. *IMF Working Paper*, 10–87. Washington, DC: International Monetary Fund.

Alizadeh, P. (2000). *The Economy of Iran: The Dilemma of an Islamic State*. London: I. B. Tauris and Co.

Alkhathlan, K. A. (2013). Contribution of oil in economic growth of Saudi Arabia. *Applied Economics Letters*, 20 (4): 343–348.

Allak, M. H. (1989). The composition and growth of the labor force in Kuwait. *Dissertations available from ProQuest*. Paper AAI9004755. http://repository.upenn.edu/dissertations/AAI9004755.

Alnasrawi, A. (2001). Iraq: economic sanctions and consequences, 1990–2000. *Third World Quarterly*, 22 (2): 205–218.

Alsahlawi, K. A. A., and Gardener, E. P. M. (2004). Human resources and economic development: The case of Saudi Arabia. *Journal of Third World Studies*, 20 (1): 175–189.

Azzopardi, R. M. (2009). Malta's open economy: Weathering the recessional storm? *South European Society and Politics*, 14 (1): 103–120.

Ben Bassat, A (2002). "The Obstacle Course to a Market Economy in Israel," in *The Israeli Economy, 1985–1998: From Government Intervention to Market Economics*, edited by A. Ben Bassat. MIT Press.: United States of America.

Ben Jelili R., and Goaied, M. (2009). Entry, Exit, and Productivity in Tunisian Manufacturing Industries. *MPRA Paper*, No. 52222. http://mpra.ub.uni-muenchen.de/52222/1/MPRA_paper_52222.pdf.

Berrebi, C., Martorell, F., and Tanner, J. C. (2009). Qatar's labor markets at a crucial crossroad. *Middle East Journal*, 63 (3): 421–442.

Bosworth, B., Collins, S. M., and Virmani, A. (2007).Sources of Growth in the Indian Economy. *NBER Working Paper Series*, No. 12901.

Camilleri, S. J., and Falzon, J. (2013). The challenges of productivity growth in the small Island States of Europe: A critical look of Malta and Cyprus. *Island Studies Journal*, 1 (8): 131–164.

Cherkaoui, M., and Ben Ali, D. (2007). The political economy of growth in Morocco. *The Quarterly Review of Economics and Finance*, 46 (5): 741–761.

Collins, S. M., and Bosworth, B. P. (1996). Economic growth in East Asia: Accumulation versus assimilation, brookings papers on economic activity. *The Brookings Institution*, 27 (2): 135–204.

Dasgupta, D., Keller, J., and Srinivasan, T. G. (2002). *Reform and Elusive Growth in the Middle-East: What has Happened in the 1990s?* Washington, DC: World Bank.

de Brun, J. (2005). "Growth in Uruguay: Factor Accumulation or Productivity in Gains?," in *Sources of Growth in Latin America: What is Missing?*, edited by E. F. Arias, R. Manuelli, and J. S. Blyde. Washington, DC: Inter-American Development Bank.

de la Escosura, Prados, L., and Roses, J. R. (2009). Human Capital and Economic Growth in Spain, 1850–2000. *Working Papers in Economic History wp09–06*. Universidad Carlos III, Instituto Figuerola de Historia y Ciencias Sociales.

Devlin, J. C. (2010). *Challenges of Economic Development in the Middle East and North Africa Region*. Singapore: World Scientific Studies in International Economics.

Ebejer, I. (2006). Malta's growth predicament: from frontrunner to laggard…and back? *Economic analysis from the European Commission's Directorate-General for Economic and Financial Affairs*, 3 (14): 1–8.

Feenstra, R. C., Inklaar, R., and Timmer, M. P. (2013). The Next Generation of the Penn World Table. *NBER Working Papers*, No. w19255. National Bureau of Economic Research.

Ferreira, P. C., Pessôa S. D. A., and Veloso, F. A. (2013). On the evolution of total factor productivity in Latin America. *Economic Inquiry*, 51 (1): 16–30.

Fuentes, R., Larraín, M., and Schmidt-Hebbel, K. (2006). Sources of growth and behavior of TFP in Chile. *Latin American Journal of Economics*, 43 (127): 113–142.

Hakimian, H. (2009). "Iran's Free Trade Zones: Challenges and Opportunities". Conference on Iranian Economy at a Crossroads: Domestic and Global Challenges, 18–19 September, University of Southern California (USC), Los Angeles, California (available at http://eprints.soas.ac.uk/8297/1/FreeZonesinIran_HH_USCSept2009.pdf).

International Monetary Fund (IMF). (2013). Kuwait Selected Issues. *IMF Country Report*, No. 13/337. Washington, DC: International Monetary Fund.

Iwata, S., Khan, M. S., and Murao, H. (2003). Sources of economic growth in East Asia: A nonparametric assessment. *IMF Staff Papers*, 50 (2): 157–177.

Jaradat, H. (2010). Jordan's Economy Crisis, Challenges and Measures. *3rd Annual Meeting of Middle East and North African Senior Budget Officials* (MENA-SBO) Dubai, UAE October 31–November 1, 2010.

Katircioglu, S. T. (2009). Testing the tourism-led growth hypothesis: The case of Malta. *Acta Oeconomica*, 59 (3): 331–343.

Kim, J., and Lau, L. J. (1994). The sources of economic growth of the East Asian newly industrialized countries. *Journal of the Japanese and International Economies*, 8 (3): 235–271.

Klenow, P. J., and Rodríguez-Clare, A. (1997). The neoclassical revival ingrowth economics: Has it gone too far? *NBER Macroeconomics Annual*, 12: 73–102.

Lee, J. W., and Hong, K. (2012). Economic growth in Asia: Determinants and prospects. *Japan and the World Economy*, 24 (2): 101–113.

Lim, J. J., and Saborowski, C. (2011). Export Diversification in a Transitioning Economy: The Case of Syria. *World Bank Policy Research Working Paper*, No. 5811.

Looney, R. E. (1992). Economic Development in Iraq: Factors Underlying the Relative Deterioration of Human Capital Formation. *Journal of Economic Issues*, 26 (2): 615–622.

Madsen, J. B. (2010). The anatomy of growth in the OECD since 1870. *Journal of Monetary Economics*, 57 (6): 753–767.

Mankiw, N. G., Romer, D., and Weil, D. N. (1992). A contribution to the empirics of economic growth. *Quarterly Journal of Economics*, 107: 407–437.

Molinari, B., Rodríguez, J., and Torres, J. L. (2013). Growth and technological progress in selected Pacific countries. *Japan and the World Economy*, 28: 60–71.

Nathanson, R. (2011). Growth, Economic Policies and Employment Linkages: Israel, International Labor Office Employment. *Sector Employment Working Paper*, No. 83.

Nishimizu, M, and Hulten, C. R. (1978). The sources of Japanese economic growth: 1955–71. *Review of Economics and Statistics*, 60 (3): 351–361.

Nour, S. M. (2013). *Technological Change and Skill Development in Sudan*. Berlin: Springer-Werlag.

Park, J., and Ryu, H. (2006). Accumulation, technical progress, and increasing returns in the economic growth of East Asia. *Journal of Productivity Analysis*, 25 (3): 243–255.

Pesaran, M. H. (2000). "Economic Trends and Macroeconomic Policies in Post-Revolutionary Iran," in *The Economy of Iran: The Dilemma of an Islamic State*, edited by P. Alizadeh. London: I. B. Tauris and Co.

Piro, T. J. (1998). *The Political Economy of Market Reform in Jordan*. Boston, ML: Rowman and Littlefield.

Raijman, R. (2012). Foreigners and outsiders: Exclusionist attitudes towards labour migrants in Israel. *International Migration*, 51 (1): 136–151.

Ramadhan, M., Hussain, A., and Al-Hajji, R. (2013). Limitations of Kuwait's economy: An absorptive capacity perspective. *Modern Economy*, 4: 412–417.

Rivlin, P. (2011). *The Israeli Economy from the Foundation of the State through the 21st Century*. Cambridge, UK and New York: Cambridge University Press.

Solow, R. M. (1957). Technical change and the aggregate production function. *Review of Economics and Statistics,* 39 (3): 312–320.

van der Eng, P. (2010). The sources of long-term economic growth in Indonesia, 1880–2008. *Explorations in Economic History,* 47 (3): 294–309.

Wang, Y., and Yao, Y. (2003). Sources of China's economic growth 1952–1999: incorporating human capital accumulation. *China Economic Review,* 14 (1): 32–52.

Werker, E. (2012). Rapid Response Note: Learning from Double-Digit Growth Experiences, International Growth Center. *Working Paper,* March 2012. http://www.theigc.org/wp-content/uploads/2014/10/Werker-2012-Working-Paper.pdf (Accessed March 15, 2015).

Wison, R. (2005). *Politics and the Economy in Jordan.* New York: Taylor and Francis, E-Library.

World Bank. (1986). Syria Recent Economic Developments and Prospects, Report No. 5563-SYR, Country Program Department II Europe, Middle East and North Africa Region.

World Bank. (1991). *The Challenge of Development. World Development Report.* Washington, DC: International Bank for Reconstruction and Development.

World Bank. (2006). *Fostering Higher growth and Employment in the Kingdom of Morocco: A World Bank Country Study.* Washington, DC: The World Bank.

World Bank. (2008). *The Road Not Traveled: Education Reform in the Middle East and North Africa.* Washington, DC: International Bank for Reconstruction and Development.

Appendix

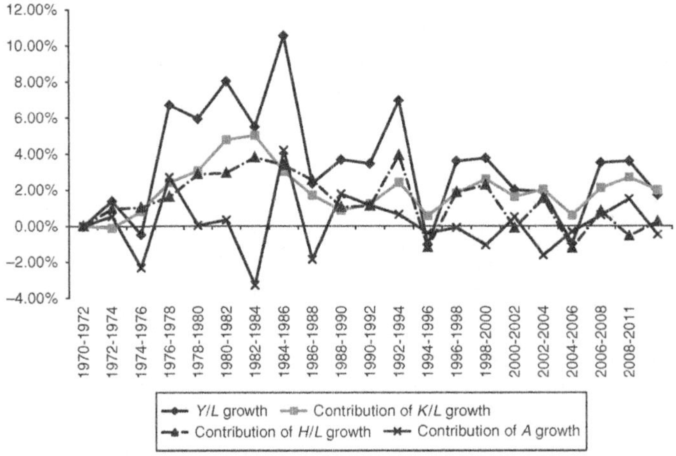

Figure A2.1 Growth rate of output per labor and contributions (for two-year periods, Egypt).

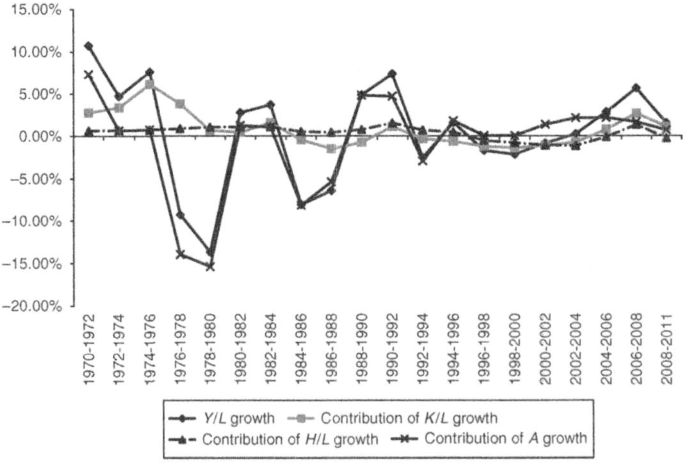

Figure A2.2 Growth rate of output per labor and contributions (for two-year periods, Iran).

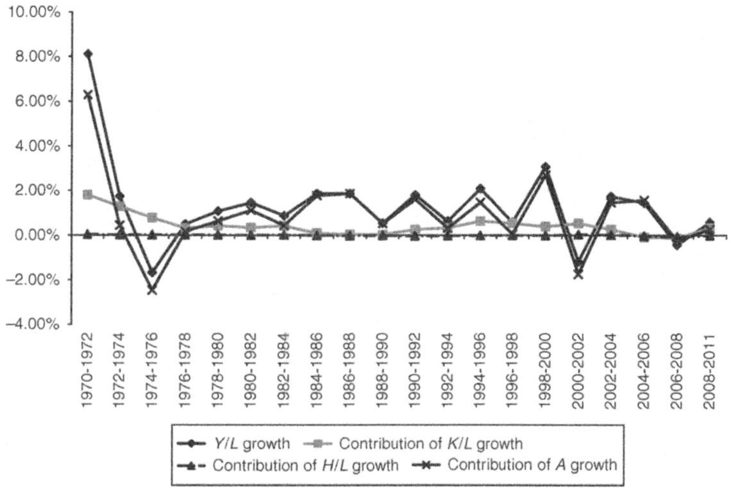

Figure A2.3 Growth rate of output per labor and contributions (for two-year periods, Israel).

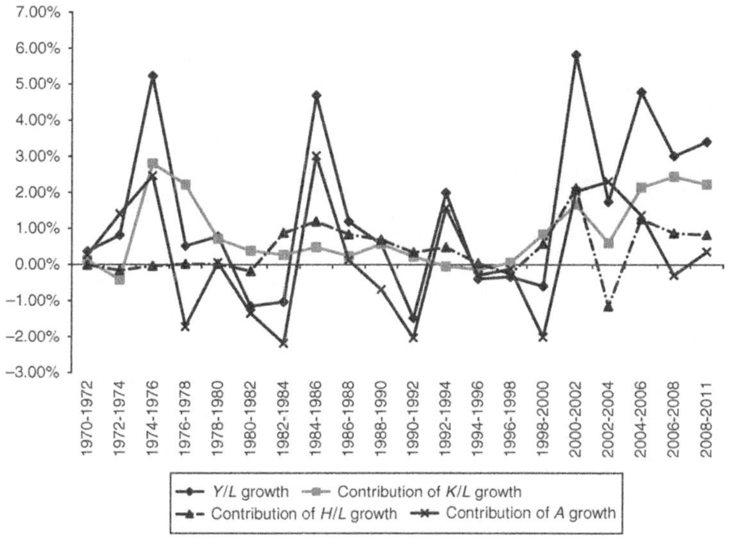

Figure A2.4 Growth rate of output per labor and contributions (for two-year periods, Morocco).

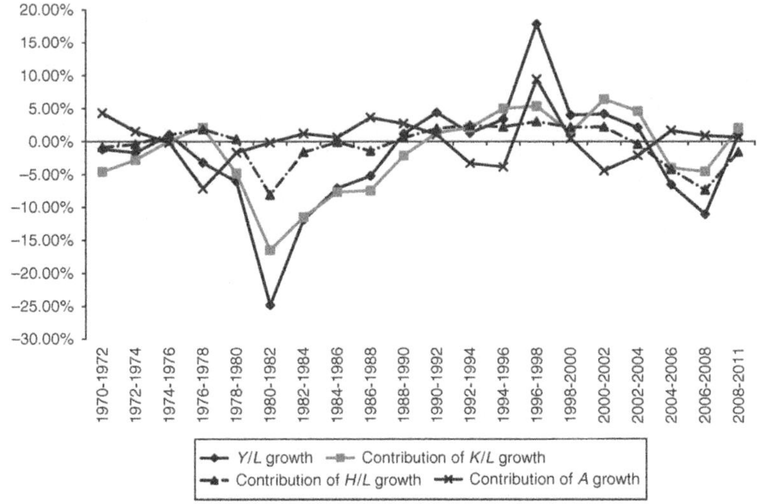

Figure A2.5 Growth rate of output per labor and contributions (for two-year periods, Qatar).

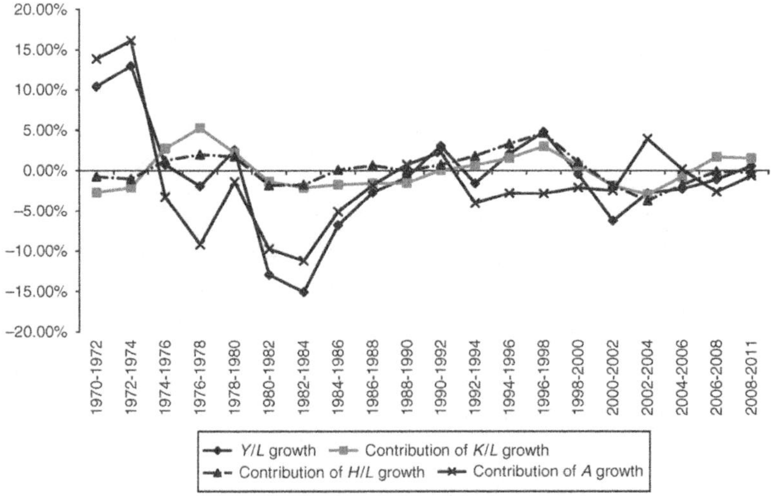

Figure A2.6 Growth rate of output per labor and contributions (for two-year periods, Saudi Arabia).

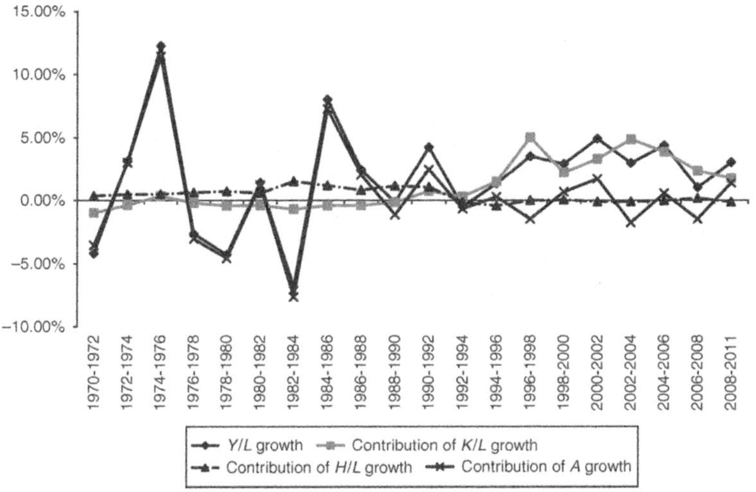

Figure A2.7 Growth rate of output per labor and contributions (for two-year periods, Sudan).

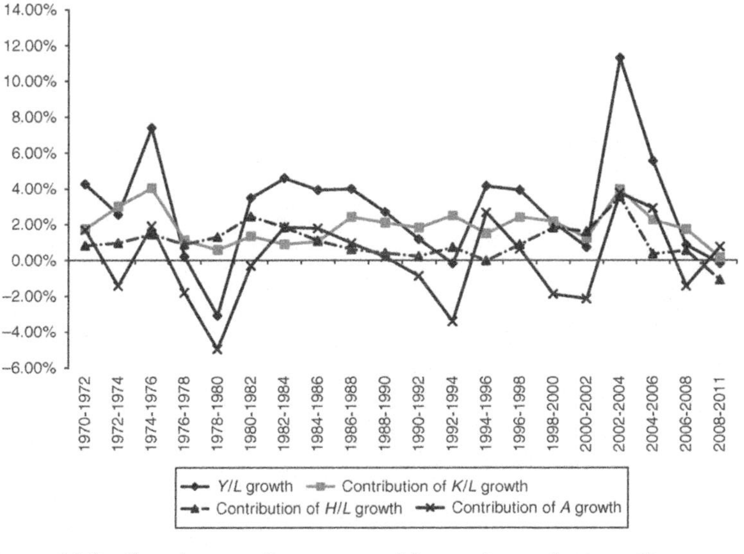

Figure A2.8 Growth rate of output per labor and contributions (for two-year periods, Turkey).

3

The Middle East and North Africa

Cursed by Natural Resources?

Mohamed Sami Ben Ali, Lara Cockx, and Nathalie Francken

The relationship between natural resource wealth and economic growth has been extensively studied. As opposed to basic intuition, the results of several empirical studies suggest that vast natural capital endowments don't necessarily generate prosperity, giving rise to the idea that natural resource wealth represents a curse rather than a blessing for economic development.

Pioneering empirical research from Sachs and Warner (1995) provides empirical support for this hypothesized resource curse effect, as the authors demonstrate a significant inverse association between the share of natural resource exports in GDP of 1970 and economic growth between 1970 and 1990 that holds even when several additional covariates are included. The groundbreaking work of Sachs and Warner was replicated and confirmed by Davis (2013), and has inspired numerous other studies. Sachs and Warner (1997; 2001) confirm their findings in an analysis on growth in developing countries between 1965 and 1990. Neumayer (2004) concludes that the resource curse holds for growth in "genuine income" as well. Kronenberg (2004) demonstrates the existence of a resource curse effect for transition economies. Papyrakis and Gerlagh (2004) distinguish between the direct and indirect effects of natural resource abundance on per capita income growth and find that the indirect adverse effects outweigh the direct positive effects. Collier and Goderis (2007) demonstrate that while natural resource booms have a favorable short-term impact on output, the effects for high-rent, nonagricultural commodities are negative in the long run.

A general picture of course masks some variations. Several resource-rich countries have fared extremely well, indicating that resource wealth is no barrier to success. On the contrary, it has been stated that the United States of America outpaced the United Kingdom in the nineteenth century because of richly blessed natural wealth. Other examples include Canada and Norway. Scholars of the industrial revolution in fact highlighted the great advantages that natural resources bestowed on a nation. Moreover, several authors refute the claim that natural resource wealth has adverse implications on economic growth (Mikesell, 1997; Lederman and Maloney, 2003; Ding and Field, 2005; Brunnschweiler and Bulte, 2008; Alexeev and Conrad, 2009).

While the bulk of the literature has continued to focus on the relationship between natural resources and income growth or other measures of economic performance, a new line of research lies in studying the impact of the resource curse from a broader point of view. Bulte et al. (2005) find that the resource curse seems to extend from economic growth to a broader set of human development indicators. Carmignani and Avom (2010) find that natural resource dependence has adverse effects on social development, measured by a combination of health and education outcomes. De Soysa and Gizelis (2013) even link the resource curse to the spread of HIV/AIDS. Several authors have established an important association between natural resource wealth and income inequality (Gylfason and Zoega, 2002; Goderis and Malone, 2011). The relationship between natural capital and human capital accumulation has received particular interest as well. Gylfason et al. (1999) and Gylfason (2001) demonstrate that school enrolment tends to be inversely related to the ratio of natural capital to total national wealth, and Kronenberg (2004) shows that this holds for a sample of transition countries as well. Stijns (2006) similarly reports negative correlations for a number of measures of resource abundance and human capital accumulation. Cabrales and Hauk (2011) present empirical evidence that suggests that the impact of natural capital on schooling is conditional upon institutional quality. Blanco and Grier (2012) find that the dependence on petroleum exports appears to have a negative effect on human capital stocks in Latin America. Shao and Yang (2014) provide a theoretical rationale for the crowding-out effect on human capital in resource-rich settings. The authors state that the expansion of resource-based industries tends to lower the demand for high-skilled labor and education. They further argue that the associated economic volatility might induce psychological uncertainty, causing households to prefer current consumption rather than education investment. Sarr and Wick (2010) demonstrate an adverse effect of natural resources on the availability of physical and social infrastructure. Bhattacharyya and Collier (2013) argue that while resource revenues provide an opportunity for developing countries with vast natural capital reserves to invest in much-needed public capital, there is clear evidence that natural resource rents are on the contrary associated with reduced public capital stocks. Finally, Cockx and Francken (2014) find that natural resources are linked with lower public health expenditures.

This chapter investigates the existence of a natural resource curse in the Middle East and North Africa (MENA), with particular attention to the role of resource revenues in shaping political outcomes and the choice of developmental policies. The first section will give an overview of the general literature on the resource curse and its proposed transmission channels. The second section will provide a short discussion of the oil sector and oil regimes in the MENA region, as well as a review of the existing evidence of a resource curse in MENA countries, and shed light on the discrepancy between the region's vast natural resource wealth and the relatively low spending on human development. Finally, the third section consists of concluding remarks and policy recommendations.

Understanding the Natural Resource Curse

There are many theories that provide a rationale for the existence of the natural resource curse. The following paragraphs will briefly discuss some of the most frequently cited causal mechanisms.

Economic and Fiscal Explanations

One of the main economic theories to account for the occurrence of a resource curse effect on growth is the "Dutch Disease." The phrase "Dutch Disease" was introduced to reflect the difficulties experienced by the Netherlands in the aftermath of the discovery of vast natural gas reserves (Stevens, 2003).This model specifies that sudden windfall gains from natural resource extraction can appreciate the real exchange rate. This in turn brings about a dynamic that gives primacy to the natural resource and non-tradable sectors. As a result, the manufacturing sector—that is argued to be more conducive to growth thanks to positive externalities (van Wijnbergen, 1984; Matsuyama,

1992)—tends to shrink. Moreover, the increased prosperity resulting from the natural resource boom can result in a spending effect, leading to a hike in prices. Sachs and Warner (1995) confirm this hypothesis of a slow-down of the growth of the non-resource sector in natural-resource-intensive economies. Collier and Goderis (2007), on the other hand, look into the exchange rate channel of this Dutch Disease model and estimate that the Dutch disease explains around 11 percent of the overall resource curse effect.

On top of that, it has been stated that resource-rich countries tend to adopt policies to cope with the Dutch disease, which incidentally lead to lowered economic growth. Auty (1994) also suggests that Latin America may have become worse off due to trade restrictions that were implemented as a result of extensive resource access.

Additionally, natural resource wealth can be argued to give rise to particularly volatile revenues. Van der Ploeg and Poelhekke (2011) demonstrate that the main effect of natural resource abundance on long-term economic growth operates through increasing growth volatility. Revenue volatility can lead to uncertainty over future financing, which tends to complicate longer term planning and increases the possibility of costly errors. This uncertainty will, in turn, create liquidity constraints that could potentially harm innovation and growth, especially with badly functioning financial systems. Volatility is also argued to hamper investment, and underinvestment is often hypothesized as an important transmission channel for the resource curse. Gylfason and Zoega (2006), for example, find evidence that the resource curse on economic growth can in part be explained by reduced savings and investment.

Political and Institutional Mechanisms

Next to adverse economic effects, vast natural resource endowments seem to generate an incentive structure that tends to weaken the state and its institutions. A vast body of literature discusses the linkages between natural resource wealth, political incentives, and institutions.

Natural resource revenues are one of the main sources of "unearned state income" that entails little "organizational and political effort in working with citizens" and is argued to give rise to a certain degree of state autonomy. This disconnect between governments and their citizens could lead to diminished state accountability. In the presence of a guaranteed source of income, there are few incentives for a government to be responsive to its citizen's needs. Moreover, unearned state income is associated with a less efficient civil service, as the incentive to develop a bureaucratic apparatus to raise taxes is diminished (Moore, 2001).

The fact that several high-income, resource-rich states—in particular, in the MENA region—have not become democratic has given rise to a substantial body of literature that investigates the hypothesis that natural resource wealth, and oil revenues in particular, impede democratization. Employing panel data covering more than 100 countries for the period between 1960 and 1995, Barro (1999) finds that democracy tends to fail in oil exporting countries. Ross (2001) reports evidence from 113 countries between 1971 and 1997 that demonstrates a robust negative relationship between oil and democracy. He further notes that the harmful impact of oil is by no means restricted to the Middle East, and that nonfuel mineral exports have similar effects. Additionally, Ross (2001) investigates three causal mechanisms that might explain the link between oil exports and autocratic regimes. The first of the three is the "rentier effect" that has been studied particularly in the context of the MENA region, and is related to the previously discussed concept of unearned income. The rentier effect has three components: a taxation, spending, and group formation effect. In the presence of large oil revenues, governments will be inclined to lower the burden of taxation and the citizens will, in turn, be less likely to demand accountability and representation. Moreover, oil revenues can be used for greater spending on patronage, which consecutively is expected to decrease pressure for democratization. With regard to the group formation effect in rentier states, the author suggests that government oil wealth impedes the formation of social capital and hence blocks the transition to democracy. A second proposed causal mechanism is the repression effect, as oil revenues can be used to finance increased internal safety and thus block democratic pressures. Finally, a third explanation can be derived from modernization theory, and starts from the hypothesis that resource-led growth doesn't produce the type of social change that is conducive to democratization, rising levels of education, and specialization. Jensen and Wantchekon (2004) present evidence from a panel of 46 sub-Saharan African countries between 1960 and 1995 suggesting that the unaccountability and autonomy associated with natural resource wealth tend to generate authoritarian governments or undermine democratic governance. Using exogenous variation in oil wealth for a sample of the top 65 oil countries, Tsui (2011) estimates that the discovery of 100 billion barrels of oil, which corresponds roughly to the initial endowment of Iraq, depresses the level of democracy by 20 percent below the existing trend.

In line with Tornell and Lane (1999), who propose a "voracity effect" that entails rapacious rent seeking in the presence of weak institutions and multiple powerful groups, to explain why countries experiencing a resource windfall might experience lower growth, Leite and Weidmann (1999)—and several other scholars—demonstrate the interrelationships between natural resource wealth, rent seeking, and economic performance (e.g., Leite and Weidmann, 1999; Ades and Di Tella, 1999; Robinson et al., 2006). It has been argued that natural resource wealth, especially in conjunction with vague property rights, imperfect markets, and an inefficient rule of law leads to a reallocation of effort and resources from productive activities toward rent seeking (Gylfason and Zoega, 2006). Torvik (2002) shows that income reduction as a result of this shift outweighs the additional revenues from natural resource extraction. Extensive rent seeking then again breeds corruption, thus distorting both economic efficiency and social equity. Sala-i-Martin and Subramanian (2003) argue that "waste and corruption from oil rather than the Dutch Disease have been responsible for poor economic performance in Nigeria." Moreover, the authors report evidence from a sample of 71 countries that shows that natural resources have a strong and negative impact on growth by impairing the quality of institutions. Once this indirect effect is controlled for, they find limited evidence of a resource curse. Beck and Laeven (2006) identify natural resource dependence as a major negative determinant of institution building in transition economies. Bhattacharyya and Hodler (2010) demonstrate that resource rents are positively correlated with corruption at low levels only in countries that lack sound democratic institutions.

The availability of natural resources has also been argued to make states more vulnerable to conflict. Collier and Hoeffler (2003) estimate that the effect of primary commodity dependence on the risk of civil conflict is nonlinear, peaking with exports at around thirty percent of GDP. Moreover, Ross (2003) argues that the relationship between natural resources and conflict might constitute a self-reinforcing mechanism. He argues that one of the reasons why conflict is more likely to occur in resource-rich countries is their poor economic performance due to the resource curse. This hypothesis however, is not unchallenged. Cotet and Tsui (2013) argue that simply controlling for fixed effects renders the relationship between oil wealth and civil conflict statistically insignificant.

Furthermore, vast natural resource endowments are commonly associated with myopic behavior in general. The availability of natural resources can also bring about more and aggressive challengers for political control, as the stakes are now higher. Adopting a short-term horizon may therefore be rational due to political instability, but will cause politicians to lose sight of important growth-promoting policies (Caselli and Cunningham, 2009).

Conditional Versions of the Resource Curse

Several scholars have stated that there exists no unambiguous general resource curse effect; rather there is a "conditional resource curse," whose existence depends on additional factors.

It has been argued that the effect of natural resources depends on the concentration of the production and revenue patterns. Natural resources are therefore generally subdivided in point-source natural resources and diffuse natural resources. The former can be defined as those resources that are extracted from a narrow geographic or economic zone, while diffuse natural resources are spread throughout the economy. This geographic pattern of production matters, because it determines to what extent the state can effectively control and obtain rents. Isham et al. (2005) find that "only countries dependent on point-source natural resources are subject to heightened economic and social divisions and weakened institutional capacity." Similarly, Van der Ploeg and Poelhekke (2009) note that the detrimental volatility associated with the resource curse mainly stems from point-source resources.

Mehlum et al. (2006) suggest that institutional quality determines whether natural resource wealth will represent a curse or a blessing for economic growth. The authors study cross-sectional data for 87 countries and find a significant interaction effect between the quality of institutions and the ratio of primary exports to GNP in 1970 on the average real GDP per capita growth between 1965 and 1990. Andersen and Aslaksen (2008) find that the effect of natural resources is conditional upon electoral rule, as the resource curse appears to exist in presidential but not parliamentary democracies. Baggio and Papyrakis (2010), Hodler (2006), and Fum and Hodler (2010) find that the effect of natural resource wealth on income is positive in ethnically homogeneous societies. However, it becomes increasingly negative as ethnic fractionalization intensifies. Bravo-Ortega and De Gregorio (2005) find that natural resources negatively affect growth only when human capital is low and Arezki and Van der Ploeg (2007) find that the resource curse effect is less harsh in countries with a high degree of trade openness.

How Can Countries Overcome the Natural Resource Curse?

So far, we have discussed the different problems associated with natural resource wealth and its overall impact on economic development. In this section, we look into different ways to turn the resource curse into a blessing.

A commonly proposed solution for overcoming the resource curse is the setting up of a "Natural Resource Fund." "Stabilization Funds" are intended to taper the effect of revenue volatility and smoothen consumption—as they reduce overspending and revenue can be transferred out of the funds to make up for budgetary shortcomings when prices fall. "Saving Funds" aim to safeguard part of the natural capital for future generations. The mere construction of a Natural Resource Fund however, does not lessen the need for sound fiscal policies, as there are strong political incentives not to follow the economically best expenditure path (Humphreys and Sandbu, 2007). It is therefore not surprising that the evidence on the impact of these funds is still mixed (Davis et al., 2003; Tsani, 2013).

While the establishment of a Natural Resource Fund might not be sufficient to tackle one of the main causal mechanisms behind the resource curse, the interruption of state-citizen accountability and the setting up of a system of direct distribution of natural resource revenues could, in theory, compensate for the negative effects of the breakdown in the social contract, as this will force the state to collect revenues through taxation, thereby increasing public demand for accountability and transparency as well as providing governments with clear incentives to improve public service delivery (Moss and Young, 2009). This approach has been widely advocated. However, one important concern is the political viability of this framework, as there are very limited incentives for politicians to give up their access to natural resource wealth.

Several international organizations attempt to tackle the political and institutional problems associated with the resource curse by directly promoting transparency and accountability with initiatives such as Publish What You Pay (PWYP) and the Extractive Industries Transparency Initiative (EITI). However, questions are rising about the effectiveness of these mechanisms in addressing the natural resource curse. Kolstad and Wiig (2009), for example, argue that the EITI overemphasizes the revenue-side and applies a narrow concept of transparency. Ölcer (2009) states that this focus combined with the limited minimum disclosure standards is not sufficient to provide sound information and enable scrutiny by the general public. Kasekende et al. (2014) report limited evidence on reduced corruption in EITI member countries and find no evidence of a change in corruption as a result of PWYP. Weinthal and Luong (2006) further argue that there are limitations to what external actors can achieve in building transparency, accountability, and public scrutiny.

To prevent the crowding out of the non-resource sector and protect the economy from shocks caused by commodity price volatility, resource-rich countries are often advised to use windfalls for investments in economic diversification. While the theoretical rationale for this policy prescription is particularly strong, there have been few success stories. Weinthal and Luong (2006) take this further and argue that governments' efforts to mitigate the Dutch Disease effect in resource-rich countries by transferring rents from the natural resource sector to the export sector have often entailed adverse economic effects. Attempts to encourage economic diversification have often given rise to inefficient investments, import substitution and protectionism, all of which are argued to further contribute to economic stagnation.

Weinthal and Luong (2006) claim that these traditionally proposed solutions may only help in boosting the economic performance if the right institutions are in place. In reality however, institutions that promote good governance and curtail rent seeking and corruption have been found to be weak or even absent in most developing countries. The authors further argue that "by taking resource rents out of the state's direct control, privatization simultaneously fosters the conditions under which governments have an incentive to build strong fiscal and regulatory institutions and creates a new set of societal actors with the potential to demand these institutions." In practice, however, the history of large-scale privatization has been characterized by failure. Stiglitz (2007), for example, argues that "it became abundantly clear that privatization does not eliminate scope for corruption, or more generally, eliminate agency problems and full privatizations of rights to oil and gas wealth have been marked by some of the worst abuses, with governments getting the worst deal." Lower prices will prevail because of limited competition and asymmetric information and there is also the problem of contract enforcement. Moreover, even if the privatization process is conducted correctly, the problem of the issue of government expenditure remains, as the privatization will still give rise to taxes and royalties and the actual sale proceeds (Palley, 2004). In sum, privatization without a developed institutional infrastructure just as easily fails as other proposed policies that actively involve the government

Natural Resources in MENA Countries: Curse or Blessing?

The MENA region is of strategic significance for the industrialized and emerging economies because the region possesses nearly 55 percent of global oil reserves and contributed to over 35 percent of world oil production in 2013 (BP, 2014). As natural resources can be considered the main source of revenue and wealth in the region, it provides an interesting opportunity to assess the consequences of the availability of vast natural capital endowments.

Given the presence of some of the world's largest oil exporters in this region, the first part of this section on the natural resource curse in MENA countries entails a brief discussion of the oil sector and oil regimes. The second part will provide a review of the existing literature on a resource or oil curse in this particular region, and, finally, the third part will investigate the resource curse in MENA countries from a broader point of view by looking into the impact of resource and oil dependence on government social spending.

Oil Sector and Oil Regimes in MENA

By studying the empirical analysis conducted by the Energy Information Administration (EIA, 2011) and the Organization of Petroleum Exporting Countries (OPEC, 2011), O'Sullivan et al. (2011) and Hvidt (2013) distinguish the following five periods in oil price regimes: from 1990 to 1997, from 1997 to 2003, from 2003 to 2009, from 2009 to 2013, and from 2014 until the present day.

In 1990, Iraq invaded Kuwait, which irked the oil prices and marked the first oil price regime through the Gulf War. As an effect of the Gulf War, oil prices were $14.74 per barrel in 1994, which depicted a great decline. Following a rise in oil consumption, the oil price increased again by 1997, along with the Asian currency crisis (OPEC, 2010). Therefore, the period between 1990 and 1997 can be considered as the first oil price regime.

By 1998, OPEC countries had increased production while consumption was low and oil prices fell again. OPEC eventually slowed down its production in 2001 because of the downward pressure on oil prices, mainly as a consequence of the sluggish US economy and the production of oil by non-OPEC members. It continued until 2002, with an increase to $25 per barrel. In 2003, the U.S. invasion of Iraq marked the end of the second oil price regime.

Erosion of the excess oil production capacity happened because of several factors such as low oil inventories among developed economies, rising demand for oil, and the damaged production capacity in Iraq. Oil prices reached record highs by July 2008, as oil prices surged from January 2007 to July 2008 by more than 150 percent. By June 2009, prices came down dramatically due to the global recession with a record 75 percent decline. Therefore, the third oil price regime ranged from 2003 to 2009.

After the recovery from the global recession, the economy started to bounce back in 2010. In 2011, oil prices rose (OPEC 2011), which continued until 2012 (OPEC, 2012). Several factors contributed to the increasing price; such as disturbance in supply in the North Sea, in West and East African countries, and geopolitical tensions that gave rise to supply fears. In mid-2012, oil prices fell below $100 again and prices rose in the fourth quarter, which marked the fourth oil price regime from 2009 to 2013.

By mid-2014, international oil prices dramatically fell down. In June 2014, Brent crude oil was around 116 dollars per barrel. At the end of January 2015, it had fallen to reach 49 dollars per barrel. Political and economic considerations have been evoked. This period is therefore the fifth oil price regime.

A Resource Curse in MENA

Arezki and Nabli (2012) study the economic performance of resource rich countries in MENA over the past 40 years and conclude that they have been characterized by reasonably low, non-inclusive, and highly volatile economic growth. Bjorvatn and Farzanegan (2013) also find that natural resource wealth reduces the capacity of the economy in MENA to productively absorb the labor market entry of young people. Al-Rawashdeh et al. (2013) confirm the existence of an adverse association between dependence on oil and gas exports and GDP per capita growth between 1971 and 2010 in MENA countries. Moreover, the authors find a significantly positive relationship between resource dependence and corruption and a lack of democracy, coupled with the need for excessive military spending. Bjorvatn, Farzanegan and Schneider (2012) stress the importance of the political power balance in oil-rich countries as a determinant of the efficient use of resource rents. Apergis and Payne (2014) provide results for the resource-rich labor abundant MENA countries[1] that demonstrate uniform support for the oil curse hypothesis over time, as the coefficient of oil reserves is negative throughout the period between 1990 and 2013. For the resource-rich labor importing country group, on the other hand, the coefficient is positive beyond 2003. The authors hypothesize that these results may reflect that the need to import labor provides additional incentives to create a favorable business climate to the international community.

Natural Resource Wealth and Social Spending in MENA

As became abundantly clear from the start of this chapter, beyond economic outcomes, natural resources may also shape political outcomes as well as the choice of developmental policies. The remainder of this chapter will therefore focus on a broader concept of the resource curse and will investigate in particular the discrepancy between the vast natural resource wealth and relatively low spending on human development in the MENA region.

Even though the Human Development Index (HDI) shows that development levels are relatively high in resource-rich MENA countries, Table 3.1 illustrates that most MENA resource-rich countries have large negative values for GDP per capita rank minus HDI rank, which seems to suggest that these countries have failed to translate their natural-resource fueled economic prosperity into improved standards of living. Comparable observations have been made by other authors like, for example, Aoun (2013).

Akkari (2004) similarly points to a negative difference between income and the Oxfam Educational Performance Index ranking for several resource-rich Middle Eastern countries, again leading to the conclusion that resource wealth wasn't converted into extended opportunities for education. Ross et al. (2011) conclude that even though education spending is generally high in the region, a number of resource-poor countries appear to be doing better. Arezki and Nabli (2012) note that while health and education outcomes have significantly improved over the past decades, resource-rich countries have by no means outperformed their resource-poor counterparts. The World Bank (2013) further states that health systems in MENA countries are not delivering results commensurate with wealth levels, and low public financing for health compromises access and quality.

These findings from the MENA region are in line with the idea that "natural resources may in general hinder the process of human capital creation that is the basis of long term growth" (World Bank, 2011). Even though, in theory, large natural capital endowments provide an

Table 3.1 Gross National Income (GNI) and Human Development Index (HDI) rankings of MENA countries

	GNI per capita rank	HDI rank	Difference
Algeria*	83	93	-10
Armenia	111	87	24
Azerbaijan*	71	76	-5
Bahrain*	31	44	-13
Cyprus	37	32	5
Djibouti	145	170	-25
Egypt, Arab Rep.	94	110	-16
Iran, Islamic Rep.*	79	75	4
Iraq*	77	120	-43
Israel	34	19	15
Jordan	89	77	12
Kuwait*	3	46	-43
Lebanon	69	65	4
Libya*	50	55	-5
Morocco	115	129	-14
Oman*	18	56	-38
Qatar*	1	31	-30
Saudi Arabia*	12	34	-22
Sudan	143	166	-23
Syrian Arab Republic*	123	118	5
Tunisia	93	90	3
Turkey	60	69	-9
United Arab Emirates*	8	40	-32
West Bank and Gaza	–	–	–
Yemen, Rep.*	140	154	-14

Source: UN statistics 2014.
Note: * Resource-rich MENA countries.

opportunity to build human capital with the revenues serving as a new source of finance, as mentioned above, several authors suggest that natural capital crowds out human capital (Blanco and Grier, 2012; Cabrales and Hauk, 2011; Gylfason et al., 1999; Gylfason, 2001; Shao and Yang, 2014). Moreover, Gylfason (2001) and Stijns (2006) find that several indicators of natural resource wealth are negatively correlated with public education spending, and Cockx and Francken (2014) provide robust evidence of an inverse relationship between natural resource wealth and public health spending.

Even compared to the developing countries' average, MENA countries on average had worryingly low levels of government spending on health care during the last 15 years (see Figure 3.1). Government health spending in this region hasn't even reached the 5 percent level,

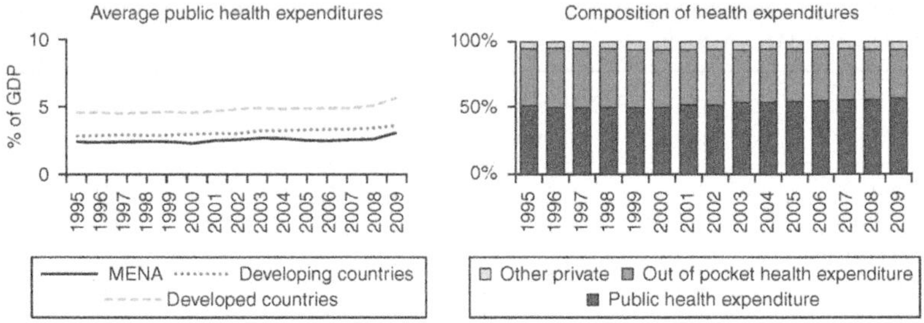

Figure 3.1 Health expenditures in MENA.
Source: World Bank, 2015.

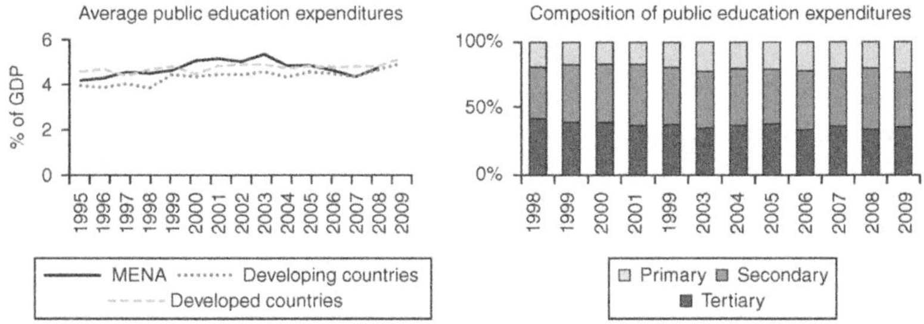

Figure 3.2 Public spending on education in MENA.
Source: World Bank, 2015.

suggested as an indicator by the WHO (Savedoff, 2007). Moreover, the composition of health expenditures has remained relatively constant over time, with household out-of-pocket spending accounting for nearly half of total health expenditures, indicating that many individuals lack financial protection or insurance against illness. Consequently, the financial burden of health care is likely to force part of the population into poverty, or forgo health care altogether.

Government spending on education, on the other hand, is relatively high (see Figure 3.2). There are however, some concerns about the equity of the distribution of education expenditures across different levels of education, with a bias toward investment in tertiary education, in particular, in the Gulf countries (Tansel and Kazemi, 2000).

There are various explanations as to why natural resource wealth could negatively affect public spending on health and education. First of all, as mentioned above natural resource revenues have been argued to represent an important source of "unearned state income" that allows for a certain degree of state autonomy and unaccountability.

This disconnect could decrease the need to gain citizens' support, which consequently diminishes incentives to be responsive to citizens' needs and provide public goods such as health and education. Bornhorst et al. (2009) find that large natural resource endowments reduce domestic revenue efforts. McGuirk (2013) corroborates these findings and hypothesizes that "in the presence of high natural resource rents, leaders lower the burden of taxation in order to reduce demand for democratic accountability." Similarly, Collier (2006) states that lower domestic tax effort in resource-rich countries diminishes the incentive for public scrutiny by the government. Bellin (2004) notes that access to rentier income from natural resource extraction in MENA countries has allowed the state to "pay itself first" and prioritize military and security spending while education expenditures remain flat. Ross et al. (2011) similarly conclude that throughout history, a number of MENA countries have fit this description of "rentier states" and that an abundant source of non-tax revenues may lead to governments indulging in increased military spending that detracts from resources available to other sectors and facilitates repression of the population. Al-Rawashdeh et al. (2013) find that, compared to the global average, almost all Gulf States, in fact, consistently overspend on their militaries.

Second, Gylfason (2001) argues that natural resource wealth gives rise to a disregard for human capital development and myopic behavior. Papyrakis and Gerlagh (2004) similarly claim that natural resource wealth creates a false sense of security and weakens the perceived need for growth-promoting strategies such as investment in health and education.

Finally, the large fluctuations in commodity prices render government revenues in resource dependent countries highly volatile. Arezki and Nabli (2011) find that over the last five decades, macroeconomic volatility in resource-rich MENA countries was twice as high as in resource-poor countries in the region. Such volatility contributes to poor planning and leads to booms and busts in public spending (Lane, 2003; van der Ploeg and Poelhekke, 2009).

Ongoing research by Cockx et al. (2015) shows that natural resource dependence in MENA has a significantly negative effect on public health and education expenditures, relative to GDP. Results from a panel data analysis covering the period from 1995 to 2009 demonstrate that the adverse effect of natural resource dependence, measured as the ratio of natural capital to total national wealth, is highly significant and robust to controlling for the effects of income, aid, the age structure of the population, and the quality of institutions.

According to these estimations, keeping all other factors constant, a 10 percent increase in the share of natural capital in total national wealth, which corresponds, for example, to the difference between Bahrain (41.45%) and Algeria (52.28%) in 2005, is associated with an average decrease of public health and education expenditures of approximately 0.16 and 0.29 percent of GDP, respectively.

As mentioned above, MENA is a particularly oil-rich region. Cockx et al. (2015) therefore also consider the existence of an education and health spending oil curse in the MENA region. The results indicate that even after controlling for all previously mentioned additional covariates, the effect of oil dependence is highly significant. Moreover, compared to the previously established effect of resource dependence in general, oil dependence has a considerably larger impact on public health and education expenditures. Keeping all else equal, a 10 percent increase in the share of oil wealth in total national wealth, which corresponds roughly to the difference between the United Arab Emirates (26.35%) and Oman (36.31%) in 2005, is on average associated with a decline of public health and education spending of approximately 0.26 and 0.36 percent of GDP, respectively.

Final Notes and Policy Implications

A considerable body of literature documents the adverse association between natural resource, or more specifically, oil wealth, and economic growth. The present chapter demonstrates that most of the research points to the importance of political and institutional mechanisms. Additionally, lower investments in human capital and the Dutch Disease contribute to the existence of the resource and oil curse.

This chapter has paid particular attention to the existence of a resource and oil curse in MENA. Our results in Cockx et al. (2015) confirm the existence of a health and education spending resource curse in this region, as natural resource rents appear to generate adverse incentives for politicians, leading to a reduction in public investment in human capital development. The robust and strong adverse association between natural resource and oil dependence and public health expenditures is especially worrying given the already exceptionally low average levels of government health spending in this region. Moreover, it is expected that due to the large population growth—that may well outperform economic growth rates—MENA countries in particular, will face increasing upward pressures on health spending. In addition, human capital building in general could substantially contribute to much-needed economic diversification in the region, which in turn could mitigate the adverse effects of macroeconomic volatility.

The establishment of the existence of a resource curse effect on public social spending underlines the importance of government accountability and transparency with regard to natural resource wealth. Governments should be made accountable for resource wealth, not only through transparent declaration, but also correct taxation and the redistribution of natural resource capital, with particular attention to the health and education sectors (Cockx and Francken, 2014). We note however, that governments in MENA countries appear to be particularly reluctant to increase transparency and accountability about natural resource revenues, as only two countries in the region—Iraq and Azerbaijan—currently adhere to the EITI Standard.

More generally, the resource-rich countries in the MENA region should focus on allocating resource revenues in such a way that it helps recover growth-oriented economic policies (Askari and Jaber, 1999). RRLA (Resource Rich–Labor Abundant) country groups are also recommended to lessen market stiffness, which will ease labor markets and lead to job creation.

NOTE

1. Countries in the MENA region are often subdivided into three groups. The Resource Poor Labor Abundant group includes countries that possess less oil resources relative to their overall size, while the population and labor force are abundant, like Djibouti, Egypt, Jordan, Lebanon, Morocco, and Tunisia. The Resource Rich Labor Abundant group covers countries like Algeria, Iran, Iraq, Syria, Libya, and Yemen. And lastly the Resource Rich Labor Importing group includes those countries that possess oil resources in abundance while the population and labor forces are scarce, such as the Gulf Cooperation Council (GCC) nations, including Saudi Arabia, the United Arab Emirates, and Qatar (World Bank, 2007; Arezki and Nabli, 2012; Apergis and Payne, 2014).

REFERENCES

Ades, A. and Di Tella, R. (1999). Rents, competition, and corruption. *American Economic Review*, 89 (4): 982–93.

Akkari, A. (2004). Education in the Middle East and North Africa: The Current situation and future challenges. *International Education Journal*, 5 (2): 144–153.

Alexeev, M. and Conrad, R. (2009). The elusive curse of oil. *The Review of Economics and Statistics*, 91 (3): 586–598.

Al-Rawashdeh, R., Al-Nawafleh, H., and Al-Shboul, M. (2013). Understanding oil and mineral resources in a political economy context: the case of the Middle East and North Africa (MENA). *Mineral Economics*, 26 (1–2): 13–28.

Andersen, J. J. and Aslaksen, S. (2008). Constitutions and the resource curse. *Journal of Development Economics*, 87 (2): 227–246.

Aoun, M.C. (2013). "Oil and Gas Resources of the Middle East and North Africa: A Curse or Blessing," in *The New Energy Crisis: Climate, Economics and Geopolitics*, edited by J. M. Chevalier. Basingstoke: Palgrave Macmillan.

Apergis, N. and Payne, J. E. (2014). The oil curse, institutional quality, and growth in MENA countries: Evidence from time-varying cointegration. *Energy Economics*, 46 (1): 1–9.

Arezki, R. and Nabli, M. K. (2012). Natural resources, volatility, and inclusive growth: Perspectives from the Middle East and North Africa. *IMF Working Paper*, No. 111–12. Washington, DC: International Monetary Fund.

Arezki, R. and van der Ploeg, R. (2007). Can the natural resource curse be turned into a blessing? The role of trade policies and institutions. *IMF Working Paper*, No. 07–55. Washington, DC: International Monetary Fund.

Askari, H. and Jaber, M. (1999). Oil exporting countries of the Persian Gulf: What Happened to all that money? *Journal of Energy Finance and Development*, 4 (2): 185–218.

Auty, R. (1994). Industrial policy reform in six newly industrializing countries: The resource curse thesis. *World Development*, 22 (1): 1165–1171.

Baggio, J. A. and Papyrakis, E. (2010). Ethnic diversity, property rights, and natural resources. *The Developing Economies*, 48 (4): 473–495.

Barro, R. (1999). Determinants of Democracy. *Journal of Political Economy*, 107 (6): S158–S183.

Beck, T. and Laeven, L. (2006). Institution building and growth in transition economies. *Journal of Economic Growth*, 11 (2): 157–186.

Bellin, E. (2004). The robustness of authoritarianism in the Middle East: Exceptionalism in comparative perspective. *Comparative Politics*, 36 (2): 139–157.

Bhattacharyya, S., and Hodler, R. (2010). Natural resources, democracy and corruption. *European Economic Review*, 54 (4): 608–621.

Bhattacharyya, S. and Collier, P. (2013). Public capital in resource rich economies: is there a curse? *Oxford Economic Papers*.

Bjorvatn K. and Farzanegan, M. R. (2013). Demographic transition in resource rich countries: A blessing or a curse? *World Development*, 45 (1): 337–351.

Bjorvatn, K., Farzanegan, M. R., and Schneider F. (2012). Resource curse and power balance: Evidence from oil-rich countries. *World Development*, 40 (1): 1308–1316.

Blanco, L. and Grier, R. (2012). Natural resource dependence and the accumulation of physical and human capital in Latin America. *Resources Policy*, 37 (3): 281–295.

Bornhorst, F., Gupta, S., and Thornton, J. (2009). Natural resource endowments and the domestic revenue effort. *European Journal of Political Economy*, 25 (4): 439–446.

BP. (2014). Statistical Review of World Energy June 2014. Available at: http://www.bp.com/en/global/corporate/about-bp/energy-economics/statistical-review-of-world-energy.html.

Bravo-Ortega, C. and De Gregorio, J. (2005). The relative richness of the poor? Natural resources, human capital, and economic growth. Natural Resources, Human Capital, and Economic Growth. *World Bank Policy Research Working Paper*, No. 3484. Washington, DC: World Bank.

Brunnschweiler, C. N. and Bulte, E. H. (2008). The resource curse revisited and revisited: A tale of paradoxes and red herrings. *Journal of Environmental Economics and Management*, 55 (3): 248–264.

Bulte, E., Damania, R., and Deacon, R. (2005). Resource intensity, institutions, and development. *World Development*, 33 (7): 1029–1044.

Cabrales, A. and Hauk, E. (2011). The quality of political institutions and the curse of natural resources. *The Economic Journal*, 121 (551): 58–88.

Caselli, F., and Cunningham, T. (2009). Leader behaviour and the natural resource curse. *Oxford Economic Papers*, 64 (4): 628–650.

Carmignani, F. and Avom, D. (2010). The social development effects of primary commodity export dependence. *Ecological Economics*, 70 (2): 317–330.

Cockx, L. and Francken, N. (2014). Extending the concept of the resource curse: Natural resources and public spending on health. *Ecological Economics*, 108 (1): 136–149.

Cockx, L., Francken, N. and Ben Ali, M. S. (2015). Natural resource wealth and public social spending in the Middle East and North Africa. *Forthcoming.*

Collier, P. (2006). Is aid oil? An analysis of whether Africa can absorb more aid. *World Development* 34 (9): 1482–1497.

Collier, P. and Goderis, B. (2007). Commodity prices, growth, and the natural resource curse: reconciling a conundrum. *Centre for the Study of African Economies Working Paper*, No. 274. Oxford.

Collier, P. and Hoeffler, A. (2003). Aid, policy, and peace: Reducing the risks of civil conflict. *Defense and Peace Economics*, 13 (6): 435–450.

Cotet, A. M. and Tsui, K. K. (2013). Oil and conflict: What does the cross country evidence really show? *American Economic Journal*, 5 (1): 49–80.

Davis, G. A. (2013). Replicating Sachs and Warner's working papers on the resource curse. *Journal of Development Studies*, 49 (12): 1615–1630.

Davis, J., Ossowski, R., Daniel, J., and Barnett, S. (2003) Stabilization and Savings Funds for Nonrenewable Resources. In *Fiscal Policy Formulation and Implementation in Oil-Producing Countries*, Davis, J., Ossowski, R., Fedelino, O. (Eds).

de Soysa, I., and Gizelis, T. I. (2013). The natural resource curse and the spread of HIV/AIDS, 1990–2008. *Social Science and Medicine*, 77 (1): 90–96.

Ding, N. and Field, B. C. (2005). Natural resource abundance and economic growth. *Land Economics*, 81 (4): 496–502.

EIA (2011). *Market Prices and Uncertainty Report.* EIA Publication: Washington, D.C.

Fum, R. M. and Hodler, R. (2010). Natural resources and income inequality: The role of ethnic divisions. *Economics Letters*, 107 (3): 360–363.

Goderis, B. and Malone, S. W. (2011). Natural resource booms and inequality: Theory and evidence. *The Scandinavian Journal of Economics*, 113 (2): 388–417.

Gylfason, T., Herbertsson, T. T., and Zoega, G. (1999). A mixed blessing. *Macroeconomic Dynamics*, 3 (02): 204–225.

Gylfason, T. (2001). Natural resources, education, and economic development. *European Economic Review*, 45 (4–6): 847–859.

Gylfason, T. and Zoega, G. (2002). Inequality and economic growth: do natural resources matter? *CESifo Working Paper*, 712 (5): 1–36.

Gylfason, T. and Zoega, G. (2006). Natural resources and economic growth: The role of investment. *The World Economy*, 29 (8): 1091–1115.

Hodler, R. (2006). The curse of natural resources in fractionalized countries. *European Economic Review*, 50 (6): 1367–1386.

Humphreys, M. and Sandbu, M. (2007)."The Political Economy of Natural Resource Funds,". in *Escaping the Resource Curse*, edited by M. Humphreys, J. Sachs, and J. Stiglitz. Columbia University Press: New York.

Hvidt, M. (2013). Economic diversification in GCC countries: past record and future trends. *Working Paper*, No. 27, Kuwait Program on Development, Governance and Globalisation in the Gulf States. London School of Economics and Political Science.

Isham, J., Woolcock, M., Pritchett, L., and Busby, G. (2005). The varieties of resource experience: natural resource export structures and the political economy of economic growth. *World Bank Economic Review*, 19 (2): 141–174.

Jensen, N. and Wantchekon, L. (2004). Resource Wealth and Political Regimes in Africa. *Comparative Political Studies*, 37 (7): 816–841.

Kasekende, E., Abuka, C., and Sarr, M. (2014). Extractive industries and corruption: An investigation into the effectiveness of EITI as a scrutiny mechanism. *Working paper for presentation at the Centre for African Economies Conference*, UK, March 2014.

Kolstad, I., and Wiig, A. (2009). Is transparency the key to reducing corruption in resource-rich countries? *World Development*, 37 (3): 521–532.

Kronenberg, T. (2004). The curse of natural resources in the transition economies. *Economics of Transition*, 12 (3): 399–426.

Lane, P. R. (2003). The cyclical behaviour of fiscal policy: evidence from the OECD. *Journal of Public Economics*, 87 (12): 2661–2675.

Lederman, D. and Maloney, W. F. (2003). Trade Structure and Growth. *World Bank Policy Research Working Paper*, No. 3025. Washington, DC: World Bank.

Leite, C. and Weidmann, J. (1999). Does Mother Nature Corrupt? Natural Resources, Corruption, and Economic Growth. *IMF Working Paper*, No. WP/99/85. Washington, DC: International Monetary Fund.

Matsuyama, K. (1992). Agricultural productivity, comparative advantage, and economic growth. *Journal of Economic Theory*, 58 (2): 317–334.

McGuirk, E. F. (2013). The illusory leader: Natural resources, taxation and accountability. *Public Choice*, 154 (3–4): 285–313.

Mehlum, H., Moene, K., and Torvik, R. (2006). Institutions and the resource curse. *The Economic Journal*, 116 (508): 1–20.

Mikesell, R. F. (1997). Explaining the Resource Curse, with Special Reference to Mineral-Exporting Countries. *Resources Policy*, 23 (4): 191–199.

Moore, M. (2001). Political underdevelopment: what causes "bad governance?" *Public Management Review*, 3 (3): 385–418.

Moss, T. and Young, L. (2009). Saving Ghana from its Oil: the Case for Direct Cash Distribution. *Center for Global Development Working Paper*, No. 186.

Neumayer, E. (2004). Does the resource curse hold for growth in genuine income as well? *World Development*, 32 (10): 1627–1640.

Ölcer, D. (2009). Extracting the Maximum from the EITI. *OECD Development Centre Working Paper*, No. 276. OECD, Paris.

O'Sullivan, A., Rey, M. E., and Mendez, J. G. (2011). Opportunities and challenges in the MENA region. *OECD Working Paper*, No. 11–2011. OECD, Paris.

OPEC. (2010). World Oil Outlook, 2010. Available at: www.opec.org.

OPEC. (2011). World Oil Outlook, 2011. Available at: www.opec.org.

Palley, I. (2004) Lifting the natural resource curse. *Foreign Service Journal*, 80: 54–61.

Papyrakis, E. and Gerlagh, R. (2004). The resource curse hypothesis and its transmission channels. *Journal of Comparative Economics*, 32 (1): 181–193.

Robinson, J. A., Torvik, R., and Verdier, T. (2006). Political foundations of the resource curse. *Journal of Development Economics*, 79 (2): 447–468.

Ross, M. L. (2001). Does Oil Hinder Democracy? *World Politics*, 53 (3): 325–361.

Ross, M. L. (2003). "The natural resource curse: How wealth can make you poor." in *Natural Resources and Violent Conflict*, edited by P. Collier, and M. Bannon. Washington, DC: World Bank.

Ross, M. L., Kaiser, K., and Mazaheri, N. (2011). The "Resource Curse" in MENA? Political Transitions, Resource Wealth, Economic Shocks, and Conflict Risk. *World Bank Policy Research Working Paper*, No. 5742. World Bank, Washington, DC.

Sachs, J. D. and Warner, A. M. (1995). Natural Resource Abundance and Economic Growth. *NBER Working Paper*, No. 5398. National Bureau of Economic Research.

Sachs, J. D. and Warner, A. M. (1997). Sources of Slow Growth in African Economies. *Journal of African Economies*, 6 (3): 335–376.

Sachs, J. D. and Warner, A. M. (2001). Natural Resources and Economic Development: The Curse of Natural Resources. *European Economic Review*, 45 (4–6): 827–838.

Sala-i-Martin, X. and Subramanian, A. (2003). Addressing the Natural Resource Curse: An Illustration from Nigeria. *IMF Working Paper*, No. WP/03. Washington, DC: International Monetary Fund.

Sarr, M. and Wick, K. (2010). Resources, conflict and development choices: Public good provision in resource rich economies. *Economics of Governance*, 11 (2): 183–205.

Savedoff, W. D. (2007). What should a country spend on health care?. *Health Affairs*, 26 (4): 962–970.

Shao, S. and Yang, L. (2014). Natural resource dependence, human capital accumulation, and economic growth: A combined explanation for the resource curse and the resource blessing. *Energy Policy*, 74 (1): 632–642.

Stevens, P. (2003). *Resource Impact: Curse or a Blessing? A Literature Survey.* Centre for Energy, Petroleum and Mineral Law and Policy, University of Dundee: Dundee.

Stiglitz, J. (2007). "What Is the Role of the State?," in *Escaping the Resource Curse*, eidted by M. Humphreys, J. Sachs, and J. Stiglitz. Columbia University Press: New York.

Stijns, J. P. (2006). Natural resource abundance and human capital accumulation. *World Development*, 34 (6): 1060–1083.

Tansel, A. and Kazemi, A. (2000). Educational expenditure in the Middle East and North Africa. *Middle Eastern Studies*, 36 (4): 75–98.

Tornell, A. and Lane, P. R. (1999). The voracity effect. *American Economic Review*, 89 (1): 22–46.

Torvik, R. (2002) Natural resources, rent seeking and welfare. *Journal of Development Economics*, 67 (2): 455–470.

Tsani, S. (2013). Natural resources, governance and institutional quality: The role of resource funds. *Resources Policy*, 38 (2): 181–195.

Tsui, K. K. (2011). More oil, less democracy: Evidence from worldwide crude oil discoveries. *The Economic Journal*, 121 (551): 89–115.

van der Ploeg, F. and Poelhekke, S. (2009) Volatility and the resource curse. *Oxford Economic Papers*, 61 (4): 727–760.

van der Ploeg, F. and Poelhekke, S. (2011). Natural resources: Curse or blessing? *Journal of Economic Literature*, 49 (2): 366–420.

van Wijnbergen, S. (1984). The "Dutch disease": A disease after all. *Economic Journal*, 94 (373): 41–55.

Weinthal, E. and Luong, P. (2006). Combating the Resource Curse: An Alternative Solution to Managing Mineral Wealth. *Perspectives on Politics*, 4 (1): 35–53.

World Bank (2007). *Middle East and North Africa Region: 2007 Economic Developments and Prospects. Job Creation in an Era of High Growth.* Washington DC: World Bank.

World Bank. (2011). *The Changing Wealth of Nations: Measuring Sustainable Development in the New Millennium.* Washington, DC: World Bank.

World Bank. (2013). *Fairness and Accountability: Engaging in Health Systems in the Middle East and North Africa: The World Bank Health Nutrition and Population Sector Strategy for MENA (2013–2018).* Washington, DC: World Bank.

World Bank. (2015). *World Development Indicators.* Available at: http://data.worldbank.org/data-catalog/world-development-indicators

4

Workers Remittances and Economic Development

Which Role for Education?

Eugenie W. H. Maïga, Mina Baliamoune-Lutz, and Mohamed Sami Ben Ali

In the past decades, international remittance inflows have significantly increased in developing nations. Their importance is being acknowledged due to their scale and growth, which makes them stand out on an aggregate and per capita basis; Adams (2011) reports that remittances make up 30 percent to 40 percent of household income in developing countries. Numerous developing countries receive international remittances (sent by family members that have emigrated) in volumes that exceed the volume of public aid, private capital flows, or foreign direct investment. Certified international remittances come after foreign direct investments as a major source of external finance, as they have grown from USD 3.3 billion to a staggering USD 289.4 billion between 1975 and 2007 (World Bank, 2009). This represents about twice the volume of official aid, in both absolute terms and as a share of GDP (Aggarwal et al., 2011), with the remittances ratio to GDP exceeding 1 percent in 60 nations (Bhaskara and Hassan, 2011). Some developing countries have had more international remittances than they do official development assistance (ODA) as well as foreign direct investments (FDI), and have, in 2010 alone, received over USD 325 billion in remittances (Ratha, 2003; Yang, 2011). These remittances are made up of transfers that involve migrants sending money back to their home nations. Remittance flow differs from other international financial flows, as it is purely a private household-level flow.

As stated by the World Bank (2006), the inclusion of informally sent remittances would result in the total remittances increasing by as much as 50 percent more than the official record. The attractiveness of the unofficial channels lies in the fact that they tend to be a cheaper way of transferring funds for some countries than through official channels. In the case of MENA, workers' remittances have come to be a progressively more noticeable financial source. Moreover, the part of the MENA region occupied by the Gulf Cooperation Council countries is considered as being the third most important labor-receiving region in the world (Adams 2009).

International remittances are important because of their relative stability and the way they grow in times of economic downturns and natural disasters (Yang, 2008). Rajan and Subramanian (2005) show how an outpouring of in inflows can eat away at the competitiveness of a country through the restriction of export performance, but remittances do not display such an adverse effect. Conversely, improving the income and living standards of the recipient family leads to workers' remittances directly alleviating the levels of poverty (Adams and Page, 2005; Siddiqui and Kemal, 2006; Gupta et al., 2009).

The impact of remittances on economic development is therefore worth studying. This chapter takes a step toward the study of the international remittances-economic development nexus, while focusing more on the role of education in this process.

Remittances and Economic Development: General Framework

Overview

Workers' remittances are existing private transfers that migrant workers send home and are distinguished through these three components: workers' remittances, migrants' transfers, and compensation of employees. There are limitations in record keeping on remittances because of classification difficulties, weaknesses in data collection causing unrecorded flows, or because of informal channels.

The literature identified three main reasons for why workers remit. Rapoport and Docquier (2006) proposed altruism, insurance, and investment as the main reasons for workers' remittances. Migrant workers may want to help family members that remained at home, thus displaying altruism. Migrant workers may wish to insure their family against adverse risks and shocks by sending remittances that would serve as coping mechanism in case of shock. Migrant workers can remit to invest in activities at home or to receive potential family bequests. It is worth noting that not every remittance payment is tied to particular uses. Money can be sent for an intentional use, but since the sender cannot monitor the recipient, a moral hazard could take place, as remittance flows might have inadvertent negative consequences. Some such consequences include a dependency on transfer income, conspicuous consumption, and laziness (Chami et al., 2008).

Other literature focused on how these flows are spent or used. The economics literature on remittances points out three main perspectives, with the first showing that remittances are spent at the margin, without any specific purpose—like any other income. The second viewpoint claims that remittances can result in adverse behavioral deviations at the household level. A third and current view maintains a positive and optimistic influence, wherein it is argued that remittances add to investments in physical and human capital compared to other methods of household income generation.

In his review of the economic impact of remittances in developing countries, Adams (2011) points out four main methodological problems economic research on international remittances is faced with and six potential solutions to those problems. The methodological difficulties include simultaneity, reverse causality, selection bias, and omitted variable bias, all of which could cause endogeneity, and therefore identification of the impact of remittances on the outcome of interest is not guaranteed. The potential solutions are randomized experiments, natural experiments (exogenous change in policy or economic environment), panel data, construction of a counterfactual situation though propensity score matching, for instance, selection model (e.g., two-stage Heckman model), and instrumental variable methods. Adams (2011) critically reviewed recent papers on the economic impacts of remittances that used these approaches to try to identify the impact of remittances, more or less with success.

Remittances and Economic Development

Remittances, Investment, Savings, Consumption, and Economic Growth

Economic growth sources have been the topic of a longstanding discussion in empirical macroeconomics. Much work has been done on the impact of different factors on economic growth, but little consideration has been paid to workers' remittance flows as a prospective cause of economic growth in developing nations. This is true because these flows were considered as used for the purposes of consumption

(Chami et al., 2003), and therefore, having insignificant or no impact on investment. However, the empirical evidence suggests that such external monetary flows are employed in investment when the credit needs of local entrepreneurs are not met in the financial sector (Giuliano and Ruiz-Arranz, 2009), but also as a result of consumed remittances positively influencing growth because of their potential multiplier effect (Stahl and Arnold, 1986). In addition, Adams and Cuecuecha (2010) found that remittance-receiving households in Guatemala spend more at the margin on investment goods such as education and housing and less on consumption goods such as food. Yang (2008) found a positive impact of remittances on household expenditure on education in the Philippines.

The current literature on remittance economics takes into account both direct and indirect macroeconomic impacts of such funds. The first indirect influence is dependent upon a robust and negative connection between output growth and its volatility (Hnatkovska and Loayza, 2003), wherein the findings of the World Bank (2006) and IMF (2005) display remittances indirectly increasing the growth rate through the reduction of output volatility. Additional studies offer evidence arguing that remittances indirectly raise the growth rate through speeding up the development of the financial sector (Giuliano and Ruiz-Arranz, 2009; Aggarwal et al., 2011). Empirical results also specify that remittances might indirectly impact real exchange rates—resulting in the "Dutch Disease" phenomenon—with exchange rates appreciating in nations that possess huge remittances, which will then hurt economic growth (Lopez et al., 2007; Lartey et al., 2008; Acosta et al., 2009).

Studies that contemplate direct channels regressed the growth rate on remittances by employing a group of control variables. Many studies conveyed a positive correlation (Stark and Lucas, 1988; Taylor, 1992) while others showed that remittance flows have a negative impact (Chami et al., 2005) or possess no impact on growth (IMF, 2005). Remittances can similarly diminish participation rates in the labor market, since receiving households will live off the transfers they obtain from migrants rather than work. Additionally, the effect of remittances on growth and poverty could diminish the reasons for employing sound macroeconomic policy or instituting required structural reforms (Catrinescu et al., 2009).

The empirical evidence suggests that the way remittances contribute to economic growth is through their positive influence on savings, consumption, or investment. A number of studies provide support for the positive influence of remittances on fast-tracking investment in Morocco, India, Pakistan (Lucas, 2005), and in some Mediterranean nations as detailed in Glytsos (2002). Likewise, Leon-Ledesma and Piracha's (2004) results show the presence of such an association for 11 Eastern Europe transition economies, with remittances having a positive influence on employment and productivity—both directly and indirectly—through their impact on investment. A related study examines this in Nigeria and reports that a 10 percent growth in remittance income increases the probability of housing investment by 3 percent (Osili, 2004).

In a microeconomic framework, the empirical literature demonstrates that the investment channel is effective in fast-tracking economic growth in numerous nations. For example, Dustmann and Kirchamp (2002) find that the savings of returning migrants is a significant basis of the startup capital obtained by microenterprises. Massey and Parrado (1998), in a cross community setting, display that US workers' remittances offer an imperative basis for startup capital in 21 percent of new business establishments in 30 West-Central Mexico communities. The study by Woodruff and Zenteno (2001) states that remittances make up nearly 20 percent of the capital financed in microenterprises all through urban Mexico.

Remittances, Education, Health, and Poverty

Remittances may affect the long-term wellbeing of recipients by impacting human capital formation. Examining this is imperative, because the effects on health and educational results of the households receiving the remittances can be seen as supplementing the exploration of the monetary scopes of poverty. The net effect migration and remittances have on human capital accumulation is uncertain. On the one hand, migrant remittances can assist in overcoming borrowing constraints, but on the other, the migration of household members that comes before the receipt of remittances can have unsettling impacts on family life and, possibly, negatively influence the educational attainment of children. Furthermore, the returns from investments in education may be worse for those pursuing international migration. Likewise, migration can cause distortions in the labor market by increasing wages, because adults of working age have migrated. As a consequence, older children (15–19) would face the dilemma of whether to work or go to school. If the wages are attractive enough (and they would be if employers cannot find people to hire), the cost of not working (that is the cost of staying in school when they could be working and earning wages) rises. In any instance, the direction of the relationship between remittances and children's education would be contingent on the idiosyncratic features of each nation.

Current evidence on the effect of remittances on education is documented in numerous studies. Hanson and Woodruff (2003), for example, find that remittances are connected to greater educational attainment in rural Mexico, especially amid 10–15 year old girls with mothers with little education. Lopez-Cordova (2005) illustrates that greater remittance flows are connected to lower illiteracy rates in Mexican municipalities, but its impact on school attendance is varied. Also for Mexico, McKenzie and Rapoport (2006) display that children aged 16 to 18 from migrant households illustrate lower educational attainment levels, an effect that is more negative for those with mothers who have higher levels of schooling.

As for El Salvador, Cox-Edwards and Ureta (2003) demonstrate that offspring from remittance-recipient households are less prone to dropping out of school due to the slackening of budget restraints influencing underprivileged recipient households. Acosta (2006) shows that this outcome is stronger for younger boys and girls in El Salvador. Discrepancies in secondary enrollment rates are huge in the Latin America and Caribbean (LAC) region, extending from about 80 percent in Chile and Argentina to less than 50 percent in Mexico, El Salvador, the Dominican Republic, Nicaragua, Honduras, Guatemala, and Haiti. Excluding Mexico, children from remittance reporting households are more inclined to stay in school. The biggest differences are found in Nicaragua, Guatemala, and Honduras, where enrollment rates are between 12 and 17 percent higher for recipient households.

Yang (2008), using a natural experiment in the Philippines, found a positive impact of remittances on investment in education and on educational attainment of children from migrant households. Calero et al. (2009) found that remittances are associated with increased children's schooling attendance and reduced prevalence of child labor, with a stronger effect for females in Ecuador. Using data from the Nepal Living Standards Survey (NLSS), Bansak and Chezum (2009) investigate the impact of remittances on educational attainment of school-age children in Nepal, focusing on differences between girls and boys. They estimated an instrumental variable (IV) model of human capital investment, endogenizing the migration and remittance decisions, to examine if male and female children are currently enrolled in school. They found that young girls benefit relatively less from remittances, but suffer less harm from household disruption, when examining the impact on human capital formation.

Amuedo-Dorantes and Pozo (2010) used the Dominican data from the Latin American Migration Project Survey to study the impact of migrant remittances on educational attendance. Their findings indicate that remittance receipt by households improves school enrolment among children who were 7 to 18 years of age. While Medina and Cardona (2010) did not find any impact of remittances on school attendance for individuals between the ages of 5 and 30 years, they showed that income from remittances led to an increase of the share of spending on education by 10 percent.

Bredl (2011) used Cox proportional hazard model on data from the Latin American Migration Project to investigate the effect of migrant remittances on the educational outcomes of children between the ages of 6 and 25 years among poorer households in Haiti. They found a positive effect of remittances on educational outcomes.

Using data from the 1999 to 2000 Sri Lanka Integrated Survey, De and Ratha (2012) investigated the impact of remittances on household income, assets, and human capital. Their findings show showed that remittance income positively affects children's health and education outcomes, but alongside conspicuous consumption or asset accumulation.

Alcaraz et.al. (2012) showed that the decline in remittance flows to Mexico due to the recent US financial crisis led to an increase in child labor and a decline in school retention rates in Mexico.

Ngoma and Ismail (2013) investigated the impact of remittances on human capital in 89 developing countries using data from 1970 to 2010. They found that, on average, an increase in migrant remittance inflows by 1 percent is associated with a 2 percent rise in years of schooling at both the secondary and tertiary levels.

Using a dataset of 697 end users of remittances collected at money operating facilities in the country between the periods of March 2011 and December 2012, Fonta et al. (2014) found that the bulk of remittances to Nigeria are mainly used to subsidize the consumption, education, and health expenditures (74.3%) of households.

As previously mentioned, evidence from Mexico has suggested that the positive influence of remittances on schooling differ based upon the educational attainment of the children's parents, supporting the idea that the positive outcome of remittances on education has a habit of being higher when the schooling of the parents is low. (Hanson and Woodruff, 2003; McKenzie and Rapoport, 2006).

A small number of papers have examined the impact of migration and remittances on one's health. Most of these papers focused on children's health as measured by infant mortality. Using data from Mexico, Duryea et al. (2005) found a statistically significant positive impact of international remittances on child mortality in urban areas. They also identified two main channels though which international remittances help lower child morality. Remittances allow mothers to stay at home with their children and they allow for improved living conditions (access to tap water and refrigerator acquisition). Lopez-Cordova (2005) determines that bigger quantities of remittances and migrant households at the municipal level are linked to lower infant mortality rates. Further proof has been delivered by Hildebrandt and McKenzie (2005) for the Mexican case, with their results demonstrating that migrant households have reduced infant mortality rates and increased birth weights. They also found that migration advances maternal health knowledge, but that preventative health care appears to be less expected for kids from migrant households.

In terms of adult health, Stillman et al. (2006) conducted a randomized experiment to assess the impact of migration from Tonga to New Zealand on mental health. They compared people who were selected in the lottery and migrated to those selected but did not migrate and to those who were not selected. The findings show that migrants experienced better mental health with higher gains for women and Tongans starting out with low levels of mental health.

Turning to poverty, Adams (2011) cited a number of studies that looked at the relationship between remittances and poverty reduction. Adams and Page (2005) examined the impact of international remittances on poverty in 71 developing nations and found an impact of 3.5 percent reduction in poverty for a 10 percent increase in per capita remittances. One shortcoming of this study is that the authors did not account for selection bias in the receipt of remittances, which Acosta et.al. (2008) tried to correct by using a two-stage Heckman model to estimate the impact of remittances on poverty in ten Latin American countries. They found an impact of a 0.4 percent reduction in poverty for each percentage point increase in the share of remittances in GDP. Studies by Lokshin et al. (2010), Adams (2006), and Taylor (2005) focused on single countries—Nepal, Ghana, and Mexico, respectively—and found that remittances reduce poverty. These authors controlled for selection and reverse causality. Yang and Martinez (2006) used a natural experiment in the form of exchange rate shocks that occurred before and after the 1997 Asian financial crisis to identify the impact of remittances on poverty in the Philippines. They found a reduction of 2.8 percentage points in the probability of a migrant living in poverty for an increase of 10 percentage points in international remittance flows.

Adverse Effects of Remittances on Economic development

Considering the nature, magnitude, and evolution of remittances, it comes as no surprise that these play a vital role in supporting development in recipient countries. Remittances can maintain these efforts in two ways: remittances can flow to the most disadvantaged groups, directly contributing to poverty reduction, and remittances can add to greater investment in physical and human capital. For example, these flows may eliminate some of the financial restrictions encountered by households and small-scale entrepreneurs that hindered investment. Correspondingly, remittances can offer insurance, allowing households and entrepreneurs to pursue riskier asset accumulation plans. Through these higher rates of capital accrual, remittances may contribute to increasing the country's long-term growth potential. Unfortunately, these possible positive effects may be counterbalanced. If migration has significant costs, it stands to reason that migrants will not arise from the lowest quintiles of income distribution, and so remittances do not go to the most impoverished.

Domestic competiveness can be negatively affected by remittances through the lowering of the expected returns on capital. For instance, remittances can exert pressure on the exchange rate and result in a real appreciation, something that, when all else is held constant, would decrease the profitability of the tradable sector (Amuedo-Dorantes and Pozo, 2004). Likewise, remittances may increase reservation wages and adversely impact labor supply (Rodriguez and Tiognson, 2001). In these two instances, remittances would affect the investment incentives of households and entrepreneurs, and lessen the capital accumulation rate.

Given the potential counterbalancing impacts from an outpouring of remittances, it could be rather challenging to define the magnitude as well as the direction of those prospective impacts. It is difficult to predict the direction (positive or negative) and magnitude of the impact of remittances. Therefore, empirical evidence is needed, but currently, there is limited evidence from the existing literature.

There are several concerns that must be considered first. For one, since cross-country studies are likely to deliver global results, they do not exploit country dissimilarities that may impact the influence of remittances on development. If significant variances exist across countries and regions in migration patterns, then such results can be misleading. Moreover, cross-country studies underestimate migration costs and could therefore be overestimating remittance benefits. For instance, some cross-country analysis estimates propose that a 10 percent growth in per capita remittances might result in a 3.5 percent drop in poverty. This estimation is not overly realistic when one considers that with such elasticity and perceived growth rates in per capita remittances seen in the past 15 years (which is above 10%), the present level of poverty in 1990 should have been nearly halved by now solely due to the influence of remittances.

It should be noted also that remittances do not inevitably create economic growth and development in migrant-sending zones. This appears to be connected to the unfavorable investment climate, oppression and the absence of political stability and legal security in numerous sending nations. It is also connected to the constricting immigration policies of migrant receiving nations, which possess the willful influence to inspire undocumented migration and the enduring settlement of migrants while disturbing arrangements of circular migration (Massey et al., 1998; Harris, 2002; Newland, 2003; Tapinos, 2000).

On the other hand, the influence of migration is not always positive, as "brain drains" can occur—seeing as there is no way to stop the highly skilled and otherwise from migrating. Emigration countries who have tried to enact stay-at-home policies have solely succeeded in alienating migrants and discouraging them from contributing knowledge and skills back home. In this setting, Bhagwati (2003) maintained that governments of sending nations should encourage "brain gain" by allowing emigrants economic and political rights rather than punishing them.

Finally, as pointed out earlier, remittances, like any other capital inflow (e.g., foreign aid or FDI) can potentially cause the appreciation of the home currency and thus produce a negative effect on the country's export sector—a phenomenon known as the Dutch disease. As noted in Addison and Baliamoune-Lutz (2013), in theory, the impact of remittances tends to be ambiguous, since more remittances may lead to the increased consumption of non-tradable goods or to a reduction in the supply of labor (income effect.) Either effect would cause the relative price of non-tradable goods, relative to tradable goods, to rise and therefore lead to the appreciation of the home currency. On the other hand, greater inflow of remittances may result in an increase in savings and investment, which may lead to an increase in the relative price of tradable goods and thus enhance the recipient country's competitiveness.

REMITTANCES AND ECONOMIC DEVELOPMENT IN THE MENA REGION: WHICH ROLE FOR EDUCATION?

Remittances and Economic Development in the MENA Region

Between 1970 and 2010, international remittances received averaged USD 1.1 billion in the MENA[1] region (Maïga et. al, 2015), representing 2 percent of the GDP over the period. Wahba (2013) reports that the top remittance recipients in MENA in 2010 were Lebanon ($8.2 billion), Egypt ($7.7 billion), Morocco ($6.4 billion), Jordan ($3.8 billion), Algeria ($2.0 billion), Tunisia ($2.0 billion), the Republic of Yemen ($1.5 billion), and Syria ($1.4 billion). The MENA region has both some of world's top remittance-receiving (Lebanon, Morocco, Jordan) and remittance-sending countries (Saudi Arabia, Bahrain, Oman, Lebanon), making this region a "two-way traffic" area in terms of remittances (Naufal and Vargas-Silva, 2012; Wahba, 2013). This inflow of funds can positively influence growth if at least part of the funds is invested as shown by studies reviewed above.

Empirical evidence on the impact of remittances on economic development in the MENA region is mixed at best. Glytos et al. (2002) found that the effect of remittances on growth in Egypt, Greece, Jordan, Morocco, and Portugal fluctuates between positive and negative over time with the positive (boosting growth or moderating recession) outweighing the negative (restraining growth or accentuating recession). Berthomieu and Tykhonenko (2009) found a positive impact of remittance flow on per capita growth in Jordan, Lebanon, Morocco, the Syrian Arab Republic, Turkey, and Yemen, but no significant effect in Algeria, Egypt, Iran, Israel, Malta, Oman, and Tunisia. Ben Mim and Ben Ali (2012) found a significant effect of remittances on GDP growth in 15 MENA[2] countries with human capital formation being the main channel. Yaseen (2012) found that remittances affect economic growth through institutions and financial development in eight MENA[3] countries.

Some recent studies have focused on concerns that remittances into MENA countries may have adverse effects on the real exchange rate. Fayad (2010) finds that there is a complementarity between remittances and inward FDI in a group of MENA countries, and that FDI actually significantly reduce the potential Dutch disease effects of remittances through a productivity-enhancing depreciative effect. Similarly, using time series data, Addison and Baliamoune-Lutz (2013) examine the possibility that ODA may cause Dutch disease effects in Morocco and Tunisia, while controlling for the effects of remittances and FDI on exchange rates, and obtain empirical evidence in support of aid causing appreciation of the real exchange rate in Morocco—mostly over the long run—but no evidence of such an effect in the case of Tunisia. Interestingly, remittances were found to cause the depreciation of the Tunisian Dinar, but had no effect on the Moroccan dirham. The fact that remittances had a depreciative impact on the home currency in Tunisia suggests that remittances may have served a role similar to that of FDI (possibly as a substitute) while in Morocco, the authors find that remittances seem to complement FDI in the short term. This study also finds that real exchange rate appreciation in Tunisia causes an increase in remittance inflows.

Remittances, Education, and Public Spending on Education in the MENA Region

The impact of remittances on education is ambiguous. Remittances can have a positive impact on education by easing liquidity constraints that can lead to household investment in children's education. Another way remittances can positively influence education is by leading young people to invest in more education, if higher education increases their migration potential and leads to higher returns upon migration (Wahba, 2013). The same author argues that remittances can negatively impact education if migrant individuals leave their household with more work to be distributed among members, thus leading to children not attending school, or if young people decide to limit their education by migrating early because returns from migration are higher than returns from education.

The effect of remittances on education has been discussed in numerous studies. However, few studies have focused on the Middle East and North Africa. Maïga et al. (2015) focus on the impact of remittances on educational outcomes in the MENA region for the period 1970 to 2010. The MENA countries studied include Algeria, Iran, Sudan, Armenia, Iraq, Morocco, Syria, Israel, Tunisia, Jordan, Palestine, Turkey, Cyprus, Saudi Arabia, Egypt, and Yemen. Their study is in line with Ngoma and Ismail (2013), Becker (1960), Schultz (1961), and Poirine (1997). Becker (1960) and Schultz (1961) view education as an investment in human capital. They report that those who invest in education do so because they expect a return on their investment. Poirine (1997) views remittance as an informal credit market among migrant and nonmigrant households that funds investment in human capital of children and relatives left at home until they are skilled enough to emigrate. Therefore, remittances are used by recipients to invest in education, in the hope that their children become skilled enough for migration. As a consequence, education is a function of the levels of remittance receipts. In their study, Maïga et al. (2015) report that remittances interact with public spending on education to negatively affect years of education achieved. The results suggest that remittances and public spending on education are substitutes. Public spending on education has a positive but statistically insignificant impact on years of education achieved and represents 5 percent of GDP between 1970 and 2010 in the countries studied.

Yaseen (2012) found a positive and significant effect of human capital on economic growth and Ben Mim and Ben Ali (2012) identified human capital as a channel through which remittances affect growth in MENA countries. Chaaban and Mansour (2011) investigated the impact of remittances on education investment in three MENA countries: Jordan, Syria, and Lebanon. Their findings show that migrant remittance inflows have a positive effect on school attendance of the youth of ages between 15 and 17 years in those three countries. In addition disparities in the magnitude by gender is observed with the impact of the remittance on education outcomes being larger for males compared to females in Jordan and Syria, but lower in Lebanon.

Mansour et al. (2011) studied the impact of migrant remittances on human capital formation in Jordan. Their findings from the augmented human capital model used indicate that remittances received increase the likelihood of attending schools among males aged 18–24 years, but not among females of the same age. In addition, migrant remittances encourage both males and females aged 18–24 years to attain a higher level of education with a stronger effect among males. No impact of remittances on human capital investment for youth aged 15–17 years was found, and the authors attributed the result to compulsory education laws that subsidize secondary education.

Conclusion and Policy Implications

In this chapter, we examined the links between remittances and economic development, focusing in particular on the MENA countries. The chapter provided an overview of the relevant literature and discussed several channels through which remittance inflows may influence economic development and growth. A significant, and often neglected channel is that linking remittances and education in the

MENA region. The chapter noted the findings from the few existing empirical studies on this channel. Some studies have identified a positive impact of remittances on education in MENA countries, whereas Maïga et al. (2015) has also documented the presence of substitutability between remittances and public spending on education. This last result may possibly point to the fact that remittance-recipient households may opt for private schools instead of public ones, but it may also hint to a potential Dutch disease effect caused by remittances. However, recent studies have in general demonstrated the absence of remittance-induced Dutch disease effects in most MENA countries.

The relevant literature generally finds that remittances have a tendency to exert a positive influence on recipient economies. Remittances appear to reduce poverty levels, increase educational attainment, and add to improvements in health indicators. Policymakers then should be interested in increasing the amount of remittances flowing to their countries. Some studies, however, have found that remittances and public spending on education can be substitutes (Maïga et al., 2015), in which case policymakers may want to investigate the channels through which this substitution effect operate in the economy and try to identify policy instruments that would take advantage of such substitutability, especially during high budget deficit cycles.

From a policy standpoint, the positive impact of remittances on education may create a dilemma. On the one hand, the positive impact should be welcome and this should advocate for policies and policy reforms to encourage more remittance inflows. On the other hand, however, given that most MENA countries have been experiencing a steady outflow of skilled (especially highly skilled) labor to wealthier countries (including to the oil-exporting MENA countries), policymakers should at the same time implement better policy instruments that would encourage skilled workers to seek employment in domestic labor markets, otherwise the benefits of greater remittance inflows may be negated by a higher outflow of skilled workers.

One of the sectors that seems to have a significant impact on remittance inflows is the banking/financial sector. As the level of skills among migrant workers increases, so does their demand for more developed or sophisticated means of transferring money into their home countries. A more developed, streamlined (and offering services at a reasonable cost) financial system would contribute greatly to enhancing the flow of remittances. In this regard, electronic banking may offer a great opportunity for both banks and remittance senders to reduce their respective direct and opportunity costs.

NOTES

1. The MENA countries studied include Algeria, Iran, Sudan, Armenia, Iraq, Morocco, Syria, Israel, Tunisia, Jordan, Palestine, Turkey, Cyprus, Saudi Arabia, Western Sahara, Egypt, and Yemen.
2. Algeria, Egypt, Djibouti, Iran, Jordan, Lebanon, Mauritania, Morocco, Oman, Sudan, Syria, Tunisia, Turkey, West Bank and Gaza, and Yemen.
3. Algeria, Egypt, Jordan, Libya, Morocco, Oman, Syria, Lebanon and Tunisia.

REFERENCES

Acosta, P. (2006). Labor supply, school attendance, and remittances from international migration: The Case of El Salvador. *Policy Research Working Paper Series*, 3903. Washington, DC: The World Bank.

Acosta, P., Calderon, C., Fajnzylber, P. and Lopez, H. (2008) What is the impact of international remittances on poverty and inequality in Latin America? *World Development*, 36 (1), pp. *89remit.*

Acosta, P., Lartey, E., & Mandelman, F. (2009). Remittances and the Dutch Disease. *Journal of International Economics*, 79 (1): 102–116.

Adams, Jr., R. (2006) Remittances and poverty in Ghana. World Bank Policy Research Working Paper 3838, World Bank, Washington, DC.

Adams, Jr., R. (2009) "The Determinants of International Remittances in Developing Countries," *World Development*, 37 (1): 93–103.

Adams, Jr, R. (2011) Evaluating the Economic Impact of International Remittances On Developing Countries Using Household Surveys: A Literature Review, The Journal of Development Studies, 47 (6): 809–828.

Adams, Jr., R. and Cuecuecha, A. (2010) Remittances, household expenditure and investment in Guatemala. *World Development*, 38 (11): 1626–1641.

Adams, Jr., R., & Page, J. (2005). Do International Migration and Remittances Reduce Poverty in Developing Countries? *World Development*, 33 (10): 1645–1669.

Aggarwal, R., Demirguc-Kunt, A., & Martinez Peria, M. S. (2011). Do Workers' Remittances Promote Financial Development? *Journal of Development Economics*, 96: 255–264.

Addison, T. and Baliamoune-Lutz, M. (2013). Aid and Dutch Disease: Evidence from Moroccan and Tunisian time-series data. UNU-WIDER Working Paper No. 2013/132.

Alcaraz, C., Chiquiar, D., Salcedo, A. (2012). Remittances, schooling, and child labor in Mexico. *Journal of Development Economics* 97, 156–165

Amuedo-Dorantes, C., & Pozo, S. (2004). Workers' remittances and the real exchange rate: A paradox of gifts. *World Development*, 32 (8): 1407–1417.

Amuedo-Dorantes, C., & Pozo, S. (2010). Remittances and their Response to Portfolio Variables, CReAM Discussion papers Series 1021, Center for Research and Ananlysis of Migration (CReAM), Department of Economics, University College London

Bansak, C. and B. Chezum (2009). How Do Remittances Affect Human Capital Formation of School-Age Boys and Girls? *American Economic Review: Papers & Proceedings*, 99 (2): 145–148.

Becker, G. (1960). An Economic Analysis of Fertility, In: *Demographic and Economic Change in Developed Countries*, NBER Books, Columbia University Press.

Ben Mim, S. and Ben Ali, M. S. (2012). Through Which Channels Can Remittances Spur Economic Growth in MENA Countries? *Economics: The Open-Access, Open-Assessment E-Journal*, 6 (2012–33): 1–27.

Berthomieu, C., and A. Tykhonenko (2009). Macroeconomic implications of remittances in MENA and Mediterranean countries. Proceedings of the *29th annual meetings of the Middle East Economic Association*, January 2009, San Francisco, California, U.S.

Bhagwati, J. (2003). Borders beyond control. *Foreign Affairs*, 82: 98–104.

Bhaskara, B. R., & Hassan, G. M. (2011). A Panel Data Analysis of the Growth Effects of Remittances. *Economic Modelling*, 28 (1–2): 701–709.

Bredl, S. (2011). Migration, Remittances, and Educational Outcomes: the Case of Haiti. *International Journal of Educational Development* (31): 162–168.

Brockerhoff, M. (1990). Rural-to-Urban Migration and Child Survival in Senegal. *Demography*, 27: 601–616.

Calero C., Bedi A.S., & Sparrow, R. (2009) Remittances, liquidity constraints and human capital investments in Ecuador. *World Development*, 37 (6): 1143–1154.

Catrinescu, N., Leon-Ledesma, M., Piracha, M., & Quillin, B. (2009). Remittances, Institutions, and Economic Growth. *World Development*, 27 (1): 81–92.

Chaaban, J. and W. Mansour (2011). The Impact of Remittances on Education in Jordan, Syria and Lebanon, ERF report.

Chami, R., Fullenkamp, C., & Jahjah, S. (2005). Are Immigrant Remittance Flows a Source of Capital for Development? *IMF Staff Papers*, 52 (1): 55–81.

Chami, R., Barajas, A., Cosimano, T., Fullenkamp, C., Gapen, M., & Montiel, P. (2008). Macroeconomic consequences of remittances. *IMF Occasional Paper*, 259. Washington, DC: International Monetary Fund.

Chami, R., Fullenkamp, C., and Jahjah, S. (2003). Are Immigrant Remittance Flows a Source of Capital for Development?, IMF Working Papers 03/189 (Washington: International Monetary Fund).

Cox-Edwards, A., & Ureta, M. (2003). International Migration, Remittances, and Schooling: Evidence from El Salvador. *Journal of Development Economics*, 72 (2): 429–461.

De, P. and Ratha, D. (2012). Impact of remittances on household income, asset and human capital: Evidence from Sri Lanka, *Migration and Development*, 1:1, 163–179.

Duryea, S., Lopez-Cordova, E. and Olmedo, A. (2005) Migrant remittances and infant mortality: evidence from Mexico. Unpublished draft manuscript, Inter-American Development Bank, Washington, DC.

Dustmann, C., & Kirchkamp, O. (2002). The Optimal Migration Duration and Activity Choice after Remigration. *Journal of Development Economics*, 67: 351–372.

Fayad, _G. (2010). Remittances and Dutch Disease: A Dynamic Heterogeneous Panel Analysis on the Middle East and North Africa Region, Centre for the Study of African Economies (CSAE), University of Oxford (downloaded at: http://citeseerx.ist.psu.edu/viewdoc/download?doi=10.1.1.192.6185&rep=rep1&type=pd)

Fonta, W., Onyukwu, O. and Nwosu, E (2014) International Remittance Inflows and Household Welfare: Empirical Evidence from Nigeria, *Research Journal of Finance and Accounting*, 2 (3):140–149.

Giuliano, P., & Ruiz-Arranz, M. (2009). Remittances, Financial Development, and Growth. *Journal of Development Economics*, 90 (1): 144–152.

Glytsos, N. P. (2002). The Role of Migrant Remittances in Development: Evidence from Mediterranean Countries. *International Migration*, 40 (1): 5–26.

Gupta, S., Pattillo, C., and Wagh, S. (2009). Effect of Remittances on Poverty and Financial Development in Sub-Saharan Africa. *World Development*, 37 (1): 104–115.

Hanson, G. H., and Woodruff, C. (2003). *Emigration and Educational Attainment in Mexico.* Mimeo. University of California at San Diego.

Harris, N. (2002). *Thinking the Unthinkable: The Immigration Myth Exposed.* London: IB Tauris.

Hildebrandt, N. and McKenzie, D. (2005). The effects of migration on child health in Mexico. *Economia*, 6 (1), pp. *257f mig.*

Hnatkovska, V., & Loayza, N. (2003). Volatility and Growth. *World Bank Working Paper*, No. 3184. Washington, DC: World Bank.

IMF (2005). *World Economic Outlook.* Washington, DC: International Monetary Fund.

Kanaiaupuni, S., and Donato, K. (1999). Migradollars and Mortality: The Effects of Migration on Infant Survival in Mexico. *Demography*, 36: 339–353.

Lartey, E., Mandelman, F., and Acosta, P. (2008). Remittances, Exchange Rate Regimes, and the Dutch Disease: A Panel Data Analysis. *Federal Reserve Bank of Atlanta Working Paper*, No. 2008-12. Atlanta, GA.

Leon-Ledesma, M., and Piracha, M. (2004). International Migration and the Role of Remittances in Eastern Europe. *International Migration*, 42 (4): 65–83.

Lokshin, M., Bontch-Osmolovski, M. and Glinskaya, E. (2010) Work-related migration and poverty reduction in Nepal. *Review of Development Economics*, 14 (2): 323–332.

Lopez Cordova, J. E. (2005). Globalization, Migration, and Development: The Role of Mexican Migrant Remittances. *Economía*, 6 (1): 217–256.

Lopez, H., Molina, L., & Bussolo, M. (2007). Remittances and Real Exchange Rate. *World Bank Policy Research Working Paper*, No. 4213. Washington, DC: The World Bank.

Lucas, R. E. B. (2005). *International Migration and Economic Development.* Stockholm: Expert Group on Development Issues, Swedish Ministry for Foreign Affairs.

Maïga, E., Baliamoune-Lutz, M. and Ben Ali M. S. (2015) "Remittances and Education in the MENA Region," *Forthcoming.*

Mansour W., J. Chaaban, and J. Litchfield (2011), The Impact of Migrant Remittances on School Attendance and Education Attainment: Evidence from Jordan. *International Migration Review*, 45 (4): 812–851.

Massey, D., and Parrado, E. (1998). International Migration and Business Formation in Mexico. *Social Science Quarterly*, 79 (1): 1–19.

Massey, D. S., Arango, J., Hugo, G., Kouaouci, A., Pellegrino, A., and Taylor, J. E. (1998). *Worlds in Motion: Understanding International Migration at the End of the Millennium.* Oxford: Clarendon.

McKenzie, D., and Rapoport, H. (2006). Can migration reduce educational attainment? Evidence from Mexico. *World Bank Policy Research Working Paper*, No. 3952. Washington, DC: The World Bank.

Medina, C. and Cardona, L. (2010). The Effects of Remittances on Household Consumption, Education Attendance and Living Standards: the Case of Colombia, *Lecturas de Economía*, 72 (Enero-junio): 11–43.

Newland, K. (2003). Migration as a factor in development and poverty reduction. *Migration Information Source*, 1.

Naufal, G. and C. Vargas-Silva (2012). Migrant Transfers in the MENA Region: A Two-Say Street in Which Traffic is Changing, in Sirkeci, Cohen and Ratha: Migration and Remittances during the Global Financial Crisis and Beyond, The World Bank.

Ngoma and Ismail (2013). Do migrant remittances promote human capital formation? Evidence from 89 developing countries, *Migration and Development*, (1): 106–116.

Osili, U. (2004). Migrants and Housing Investments: Theory and Evidence from Nigeria. *Economic Development and Cultural Change*, 52 (4): 821–849.

Poirine, B. (1997), A theory of remittances as an implicit family loan arrangement. *World Development*, 25 (4): 589–611.

Rajan, R. G., & Subramanian, A. (2005). What Undermines Aid's Impact on Growth? *NBER Working Paper*, No. 11657. Cambridge, MA: National Bureau of Economic Research.

Rapoport, H. and Docquier, F. (2006) The economics of migrants' remittances, in: S. Kolm and J. Mercier-Ythier (eds) *Handbook on the*

Economics of Giving, Altruism and Reciprocity (New York: Elsevier-North Holland), pp. 1138–1195

Ratha, D. (2003). Workers' remittances: An important and stable source of external development finance. *Global Development Finance*: 157–175. Washington, DC: The World Bank.

Rodriguez, E., and Tiongson, E. (2001). Temporary Migration Overseas and Household Labor Supply: Evidence from Urban Philippines. *International Migration Review*, 35: 1185–204.

Siddiqui, R., and Kemal, A. R. (2006). Remittances, Trade Liberalisation, and Poverty in Pakistan: The Role of Excluded Variables in Poverty Change Analysis. *The Pakistan Development Review*, 45 (3): 383–415.

Ssengonzi, R., De Jong, G., and Stokes, C. (2002). The Effect of Female Migration on Infant and Child Survival in Uganda. *Population Research and Policy Review*, 21: 403–431.

Stahl, C. W., and Arnold, F. (1986). Overseas Workers' Remittances in Asian Development. *International Migration Review*, 20 (4): 899–925.

Stark, O., & Lucas, R. (1988). Migration, Remittances and the Family. *Economic Development and Cultural Change*, 36 (3): 465–481.

Stillman, S., McKenzie, D. and Gibson, J. (2006) Migration and mental health: evidence from a natural experiment. BREAD Working Paper 123, Bureau for Research in Economic Analysis of Development, Washington, DC.

Schultz, T. (1961). Investment in Human Capital, *The American Economic Review*, 51 (1): 1–17

Tapinos, G. (2000). Globalisation, regional integration, international migration. *International Social Science Journal*, 165: 297–306.

Taylor, J. E. (1992). Remittances and Inequality Reconsidered: Direct, Indirect and Intertemporal Effects. *Journal of Policy Modelling*, 14 (2): 187–208.

Taylor, J.E., Mora, J., Adams, Jr., R. & Lopez-Feldman, A. (2005) Remittances, inequality and poverty: evidence from rural Mexico. Working Paper 05idenc Department of Agricultural Economics, University of California, Davis, CA.

Wahba, J. (2013). "The Impact of Migration on Human Capital in MENA," Economic Research Forum, Policy Perspective No. 10.

Woodruff, C., & Zenteno, R. (2001). Remittances and Microenterprises in Mexico. *UCSD, Graduate School of International Relations and Pacific Studies Working Paper.*

World Bank (2006). The Development Impact of Workers' Remittances in Latin America, Vol. 2: Detailed Findings. (Chapter 3, Section V), Report No. 37026. Washington, DC: The World Bank.

World Bank (2009). *Global Development Finance*. Washington, DC: The World Bank.

Yang, D. (2008). International Migration, Remittances and Household Investment: Evidence from Philippine Migrants' Exchange Rate Shocks. *The Economic Journal*, 118: 591–630.

Yang, D. (2011). Migrant remittances. *Journal of Economic Perspectives*, 25 (3): 129–152.

Yang, D. and Martinez, C. (2006) Remittances and poverty in migrants home areas: evidence from the Philippines, in: C. Ozden and M. Schiff (eds) *International Migration, Remittances and the Brain Drain* (Washington, DC: World Bank), pp. 81–121.

Yaseen, H. (2012). The Positive and Negative Effects of Remittances on Growth in the MENA. *The Journal of International Management Studies*, 7 (1).

5

The Inflation-Central Bank Independence Nexus

Where Do MENA Countries Stand?

Mohamed Sami Ben Ali, Etienne Farvaque, and Muhammad Azmat Hayat

Inflation and its dynamics have been always capturing the attention of economic scholars and policymakers worldwide. Numerous theories in economic literature tried to define the concept of inflation by suggesting different sides of the phenomenon—by evoking the *cost-push* inflation side, the *demand-pull*, or both sides. Potential determinants of inflation discussed in the literature are diverse (see, e.g., Ben Ali and Ben Mim, 2011). The general consensus is to define inflation by its symptoms, as a persistent rise in the general price level in a given economy.

From a country setting and historical side as well, it's obvious that inflation rates are different across countries and over time. Different inflation periods had characterized both developed and developing countries, mainly in the mid-1970s and 1980s.

There has been a growing body of literature over many decades, asserting the damaging impact of high inflation levels on economic performance and social welfare (Fischer et al., 2002). As a result, policymakers set price stability as one of the main goals of their economic policies. More particularly, the importance given to the price stability in both developed and developing countries is seen as the prime challenge for central bankers committed to maintain prices under control. Given these harmful effects, why do some central bankers still have incentives to inflate? The answer can be embedded in the *time consistency* dilemma (Kydland and Prescott, 1977; Barro and Gordon, 1983). Monetary authorities may use lose short-term enhancing monetary policies by financing fiscal deficit and misusing a negative relationship between inflation and unemployment. Such policies, which are most likely to be pursued in developing countries lacking a sound institutional framework, cause inflation and, at the same time, problems of inconsistency. A monetary policy's reliability can mainly be proven by its ability to bring down inflation rates by instituting an efficient and credible framework based on greater central bank independence. Rogoff (1985) empirically shows that a loss function weighing the deviation of output and inflation from their socially optimal levels induces higher inflation rates. According to Rogoff, this loss could be reduced by the existence of a "conservative and independent" central banker, giving rise to a stable inflation rate. It is obvious also that from an economic point of view, stable growth can be achieved only by accelerating the progress of productivity and lengthening the investors' forecast. Inflation dynamics brings a slump in the extent of these two factors, introducing unpredictability in an economy's stability. For a policymaker, it is therefore crucial to capture the dynamics of inflation in order to craft a consistent macroeconomic situation.

After a relatively long period of price stability in the Middle East and North Africa, inflation has reemerged as a primary challenge for policymakers and academicians in this region and worldwide. This chapter thus addresses the relationship between inflation and central bank independence in MENA countries (considered here under an extensive definition).

Central Bank Independence and Inflation Redux

This section provides a brief introduction to the theoretical arguments on which the case for an independent central bank has been built, and to the way the degree of independence can be measured through de jure or de facto indices.

Why Is Central Bank Independence Desirable?

Understanding the case for central bank independence basically means finding an answer to the following question: why would politicians agree to delegate monetary policy to an authority that could stand beyond their reach (read influence)?

The most common answer to this question is that a central bank should be better insulated from fluctuations arising in the political world than the elected politicians can be. This argument, which can be traced down to the way American political philosophy justifies the independence of judges (Farvaque, 2007), is often given by central bankers themselves (see Blinder, 1998, for an example).

In modern literature, the argument dates at least back to Kydland and Prescott (1977), who study the case of a decision maker facing a potential tradeoff between inflation and unemployment. If one assumes that the inflation rate is higher than what had been expected, this implies that real wages decrease proportionally to the difference between actual inflation and expected inflation. All things being equal, this induces an increase in the labor demand of firms, and reduces unemployment. Manipulating the rate of inflation (by, for example, the emission of an extra quantity of money) then allows the decision maker to change the unemployment rate, even though, initially, this decision maker would have preferred a lower inflation rate. This example is a typical case of time inconsistency, and is explained by the reduced weight of the future (inflation) compared to the present (the increased employment level and its potential impact on the probability of re-election). Barro and Gordon (1983) show that, in such a theoretical framework, voters cannot be wrong all the time (an argument that is reminiscent of Lucas' own (Lucas, 1972). Hence, they know that the decision maker has an incentive to create inflation, which then negates any positive effect on wages and employment. As far as the incentives of the decision maker remain unchanged, any attempt to manipulate inflation can only result in a higher rate of inflation (the so-called inflationary bias) without any gain in jobs.

This problem of the time inconsistency of the preferences of elected officials has led the economic literature to propose a number of solutions, including granting independence (from the government) to central banks. We owe much to Rogoff (1985) for having shown that the need to balance the credibility of monetary institutions (in terms of low inflation) and their ability to respond to macroeconomic shocks can be satisfied through a central bank whose mandate is focused on the fight against inflation. In other words, if the central banker is "conservative," in the sense that their preferences reflect an aversion to higher inflation than in the average of the company, then the inflation bias can be reduced, and potentially eliminated.

This idea was then taken up and developed, including the analysis of contracts between the central banks and governments, in the context of inflation targeting regimes (as in Walsh, 1995), but also to understand the duration of the contracts between the central bankers. For example, in the model of Waller and Walsh (1996), the economy is composed of several productive sectors, whose desired inflation rates differ, while the government represents the preferences of the median voter. If, after each election, the newly elected government appoints a new central banker, the variability of voter preferences will be forwarded to the central bank's policy, monetary policy would become more difficult to predict, and therefore less credible. These authors show that the optimal duration of the mandate of the central bank is obtained by equating the marginal value of the reduction of economic fluctuations obtained by increasing the tenure of the central banker and the social cost of the difference between the central bank's preferences and those of the median voter. Then, if the median voter's preferences are relatively constant in time, and if the inflationary bias is relatively high, then the society's interest is to give the central banker a long term.

Another way to justify the independence of central banks and monetary policy mandates focused on price stability is based on the approach developed by Maskin and Tirole (2004), who compare the powers of elected decision makers—who are thus accountable to the electorate—to those of unelected decision makers (technicians or experts, the authors taking the case of judges as a leading example). They show that the delegation of policy to technicians or experts is preferable when the following three conditions are satisfied: (1) if the elected decision maker has little information on the optimal policy to implement; (2) if acquiring information on the topic is expensive; and (3) if it is not easy to check whether past decisions have had positive or negative effects. According to these authors, technical decisions are more likely to verify these conditions, and monetary policy is among those that justify the delegation.

The logic underlying these mechanisms is just one of a relatively long horizon contract between a society (and its decision makers) and the central bank. The distant horizon is enough to remove any incentive for the decision maker to play on the short-term trade-off between output (unemployment) and inflation, thereby reducing the money supply (and therefore, we have seen above, the level of future prices).

Measuring Central Bank Independence in Emerging Countries

We owe to Cukierman's(1992) famous book the method to measure the degree of central bank independence, using legal texts and coding them to weigh the relations the central bank has (or not) with the government. Cukierman's index has since been very frequently used as a proxy to measure central bank independence, providing a de jure measure of the choice a society has made to insulate itself from the upheavals of the political scene.

However, as stated already by Cukierman et al. (1992), and further argued by, for example, Fuhrer (1997), measuring central bank independence through legal texts relies on the assumption that they are enforced (at least, that the public believes that their implementation will have the expected impact). It also assumes that the institutional context does not matter, an argument that the literature has proven too far-fetched (Moser, 1999, Farvaque, 2002).

In fact, the real (de facto) degree of central bank independence can differ strongly from what a textual analysis would have implied in countries where the letter of the law is not fully enforced or believed. Hence, even though the empirical literature has tended to support the (negative) link between the degree of central bank independence and inflation (see, e.g., Eijffinger and de Haan, 1996, Berger et al., 2001), the relation seems to be driven by the situation in developed countries, where institutions are older and laws tend to be better respected. Moreover, even among the developed countries, it has been argued that the relationship is weaker than observed, due to either hidden factors (demography being a case in point, see Farvaque et al., 2010) or measurement issues (Forder, 1998). On econometric grounds, Brumm (2002; 2006) argues that the difference between the two types of measures (de jure and de facto) of central bank independence is due to measurement error, which can lead to anomalous, if not spurious, results, if they are not considered carefully.

As a consequence, especially for emerging and developing countries, and also to get a better view of the real degree of independence, scholars have come to another metric, based on the central banker's turnover rate. The idea here is that if the policymaker wants to use inflation to influence the economy, then they will put pressure on the central bank, either through bashing it (as in Waller, 1989), or by replacing the incumbent central banker with another one, more inclined to follow the politician's will. This measure has been used regularly, leading to results that lie in conformity with the expected results (i.e., a higher turnover, indicating a lower independence, is associated with higher inflation). For a recent example of a study using such data, see, for example, Crowe and Meade (2008). However, it has to be noted that using turnover rate as proxy for central bank independence may be a double-edged sword, as a higher turnover rate may depict the lack of independence of the central bank but, on the other hand, a very small turnover rate also indicates that central bank governor is never changed by the authorities and legal mandate is never respected.

It is worth noting that during the last two decades, many countries in the MENA region have undertaken significant efforts toward greater central bank independence after the waves of financial liberalization driven by financial institutions and the International Monetary Fund during the 90's. However, the level of independence of these banks in these countries is still much lower compared to developed countries.

The waves of reforms in this region were the most important in Tunisia and Morocco, and less pronounced in Egypt. These countries have introduced important amendments to the statutes of their central banks toward improving independence, such as the establishment of price stability as the primary objective of the central bank. The results of these reforms on the independence and, consequently, on inflation, were discernable in these two countries.

For example, the reforms undertaken in Tunisia to improve the transparency and independence of the Central Bank of Tunisia included the elimination of the supervision and control function of the Central Bank of Tunisia on other banks and replacing them by external audit procedures. These reforms have allowed the Central Bank of Tunisia to have more freedom in the choice of instruments to ensure price stability. Deeper and more structural reforms of the Central Bank of Tunisia have been introduced in the new constitution of 2014. Previously, the governor was appointed directly by the President. However, under the new constitution, the appointment and dismissal of the governor must be approved by Parliament.

In Morocco, following the Arab Spring, the central bank statutes were amended, with a noticeable improvement compared to the preceding 2006 amended legal framework. These reforms have mainly introduced some restrictions on the dismissal of board members, as well as the prohibition of governmental representation with voting power in the central bank board directory. In addition, the appointment of the Governor is assigned to a council with legislative and judicial representation. The central bank board has the power to choose the instruments to ensure stability. In addition, the control of the central bank on the financial sector has been lifted.

In Egypt, the most profound improvement in the statutes of the central bank is related to the objective of the institution: price stability is now the primary objective of the central bank. Independence, however, remains low, since the power of appointment and dismissal of the governor is still held by the government. The amendments to the constitution in 2012 and 2014 have brought a few insignificant changes to the independence of the central bank in Egypt.

CENTRAL BANK INDEPENDENCE AND INFLATION IN MENA COUNTRIES: EMPIRICAL ANALYSIS

In this section, we first analyze the degree of central bank independence in the MENA countries, before turning to the link it can have with inflation in these countries.

De Facto Indicators of Central Bank Independence for MENA Countries

Table 5.1 displays the data on the legal duration of the mandate of a central banker in the MENA countries, as enshrined in the local legislation, the number of years since the current central banker (i.e., in 2011, due to data availability, for consistency with what follows) has been in office, the difference between the two, as well as the polity score. The latter, collected and organized by the Center for Systemic Peace,[1] captures the democratic degree of a governing regime on a 21-point scale ranging from -10 (hereditary monarchy) to +10 (consolidated democracy). As can be seen, the difference is positive in many countries of the sample, indicating that the central banker has been in office for a length of time superior to the official length. This in itself would tend (i) to confirm the presumption of the literature about the (weak) relevance of legislation-based indicators of independence, and (ii) to highlight the need for a turnover-based indicator, which, although imperfect, would probably deliver a better-informed view of reality. In this case, this is confirmed by the polity score, which is quite low on average in these countries, inducing a legitimate suspicion that, with regard to monetary institutions, either they do not respect central bank laws or they repeatedly reappoint the central bank governor.

Table 5.2 contains this information, showing the turnover rate of the MENA countries' central bankers. We also show the irregular turnover, which, as argued by Hayat and Farvaque (2011), provides even better information—and probably a truer view of the way

Table 5.1 Length of mandates, MENA countries, 2011

Country	Time in office*	Legal duration	Difference	Polity Score
Algeria	10	7	+3	+2
Bahrain	6	5	+1	−8
Egypt, Arab Rep.	8	4	+4	−2
Iran, Islamic Rep.	3	5	−2	−7
Israel	6	5	+1	+10
Jordan	1	5	−4	−3
Kuwait	25	5	+20	−7
Lebanon	18	6	+12	+7
Libya	0	5	−5	0
Morocco	8	NA	NA	−4
Qatar	5	5	0	−10
Saudi Arabia	0	5	−5	−10
Syrian Arab Republic	6	NA	NA	−7
Tunisia	0	6	−6	−4
Average	6.86	5.25	1.58	

Source: Authors, update (2012) of Dreher et al. (2010). Polity score from Center for Systemic Peace (http://www.systemicpeace.org).

institutions are respected (or not)—than the turnover rate itself. It turns out that for four countries of the sample (namely, Iran, Israel, Jordan, and Libya), there is a difference between the two indicators, revealing that institutions are sometimes respected, sometimes not. For all the other countries, the absence of any difference between the two measures simply reveals that all the turnovers of central bankers have been irregular. Algeria, and then Egypt and Tunisia are typical cases in point, here, as can be seen in Table 5.2. In other words, more often than not, and never for most of the MENA countries, the replacement of a central banker has conformed to what had been enshrined in the legislation. Another important fact is also evident from Table 5.2 that some of the countries have not changed their central bankers even in a decade. For example, there was no turnover in Morocco and Qatar during 1990–1999, in Bahrain during 1980–1989, and in Kuwait during 1990–2011 (that is, in this case, for the last 22 years). This tendency also favors the argument already given that governments and decision makers in this region tend to reappoint the central bank governor.

Thus, in what follows, we will analyze the inflation—central bank independence nexus by relying on the de facto measure, as any other method would probably prove ineffectual.

Table 5.2 Central bankers' turnover and Inflation, MENA countries, 1980–2011

	1980–1989		1990–1999		2000–2011		Average		Inflation	
Country	Regular	Irregular	Regular	Irregular	Regular	Irregular	Regular	Irregular	Average	Maximum
Algeria	0	5	0	1	0	1	0.22	0.22	9.89	31.67
Bahrain	0	0	0	1	0	2	0.09	0.09	1.49	11.34
Egypt, Arab Rep.	0	3	0	1	0	2	0.19	0.19	11.72	23.86
Iran, Islamic Rep.	1	2	1	0	0	3	0.22	0.16	19.34	49.66
Israel	0	2	1	0	1	1	0.16	0.09	44.85	373.82
Jordan	0	2	0	1	1	1	0.16	0.13	5.28	25.71
Kuwait	0	2	0	0	0	0	0.06	0.06	3.45	10.58
Lebanon	0	1	1	1	0	0	0.09	0.06	64.40	487.57
Libya	1	2	0	2	3	0	0.25	0.13	5.04	15.52
Morocco	0	2	0	0	0	1	0.09	0.09	4.41	12.49
Qatar*	0	1	0	0	0	1	0.09	0.09	3.85	15.05
Saudi Arabia	0	1	0	0	0	2	0.09	0.09	1.43	9.86
Syrian Arab Rep.	0	2	0	2	0	1	0.16	0.16	11.43	59.48
Tunisia	0	3	0	1	0	2	0.19	0.19	4.81	8.90
Yemen **	NA	NA	0	1	0	1	0.13	0.13	18.62	55.08

*: 1989–2011

**: 1997–2011

Source: Author's calculations. See Table 5.1 for sources. Inflation data from IMF's *International Financial Statistics*.

Central Bank Independence-Inflation Nexus: The Empirical Facts

Figure 5.1 displays the relation between the central bankers' turnovers and the average inflation rate in the MENA countries. As can be seen, the relation is not really conform to what could be expected[2] and is, at first sight, globally negative. But a positive relationship between higher inflation and turnover appears if one removes Israel and Lebanon from the sample, as both countries have known episodes of very high inflation during this period[3], and whose inclusion delivers the negative trend. However, this unexpected relation (i.e., the negative relationship) vanishes once one uses the more relevant indicator, measuring irregular turnovers. As can be seen in Figure 5.2, once this indicator is considered (and removing the two outliers with regard to this dimension: Israel and Lebanon), the relation turns clearly positive, and thus lies much more in conformity with what the theory suggests.

Another interesting measure is the level of maximum inflation that each country of the group has known during the period under review (1980–2011). On this dimension (see Figures 5.3a and 5.4a), it is first interesting to note that the outliers are again Israel and Lebanon, which reveals that their average rate has been driven by the episodes of hyperinflation these countries have known (see also Table 5.2). Second, and interestingly, the relation between the central bankers' rates of turnover (overall and irregular) and the level

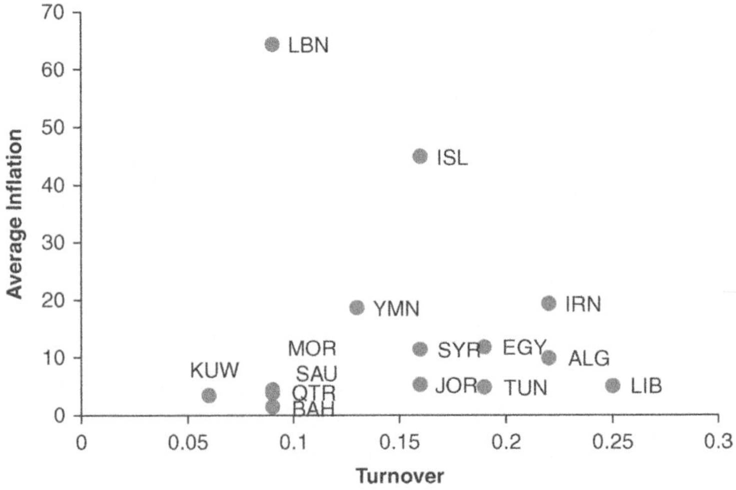

Figure 5.1 Overall turnover and average inflation.

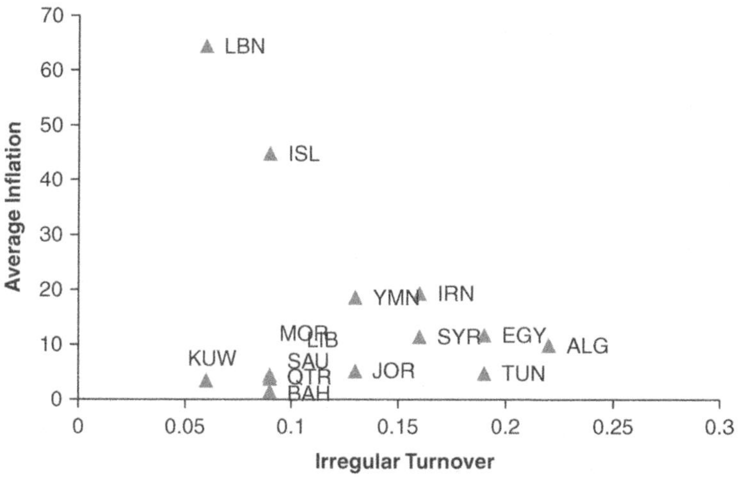

Figure 5.2 Irregular turnover and average inflation.

of maximum inflation is clear-cut, and positive, after removing the outliers (see Figures 5.3b and 5.4b). Once again, this confirms that de facto indicators of turnover provide a better assessment of central bank independence in these countries, and that the evidence tends to back the theory.

Finally, we look at the relationship between central bank independence and the variance of inflation, a measure of uncertainty that has been shown to matter for economic policy definition and macroeconomic performance, either theoretically (Ball, 1992), or empirically (see, e.g., Grier et al., 2004). Interestingly, while Alesina and Summers (1993) could exhibit a strongly negative relation between inflation uncertainty and central bank independence, for OECD countries, the relation is not so apparent, nor negative, in the case of the MENA countries. First, as can be seen from Figures 5.5 and 5.6, if we exclude the first outliers (Israel and Lebanon, as both have very high variances), two new outliers appear in the sample: Syria and Yemen have a large variance of their inflation rate as compared to other countries in the sample. Second, when considering the overall rate of turnover, and eliminating the four outliers (Lebanon, Israel, Syria, and Yemen), a positive relation can be observed (hence, the opposite of what can be observed in the OECD countries). Moreover, this is even reinforced when we use the measure of de facto independence based upon irregular turnovers. In this case, the slope of the relation seems even larger, and positive.

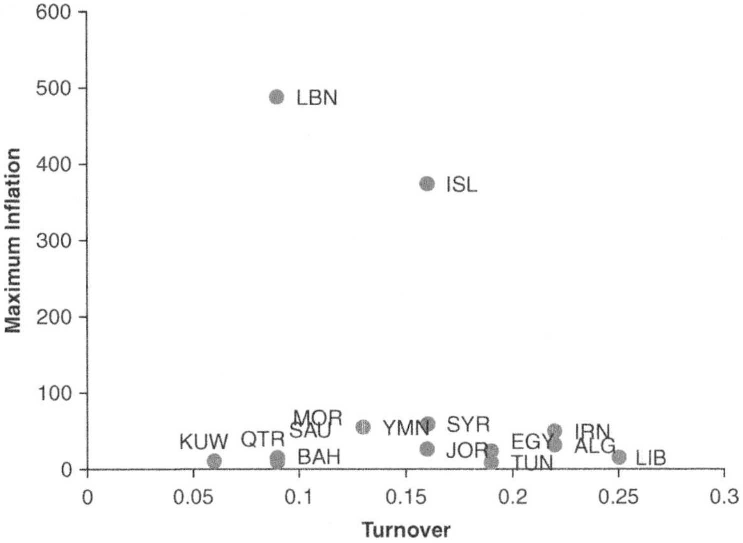

Figure 5.3a Overall turnover and maximum inflation.

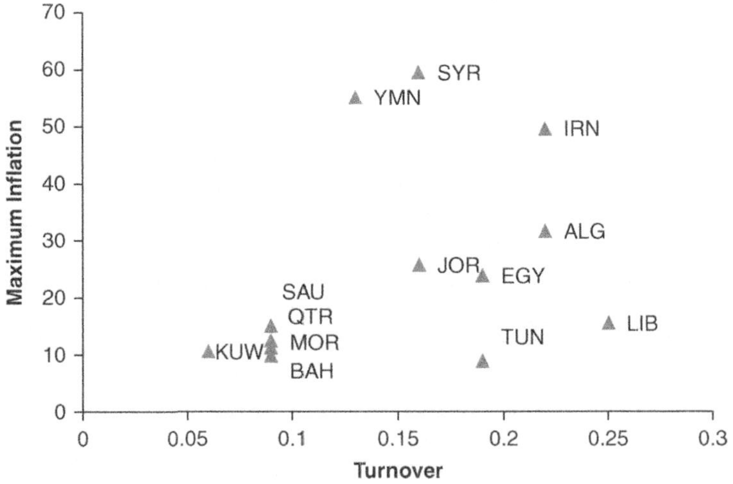

Figure 5.3b Overall turnover and maximum inflation (excluding Israel and Lebanon).

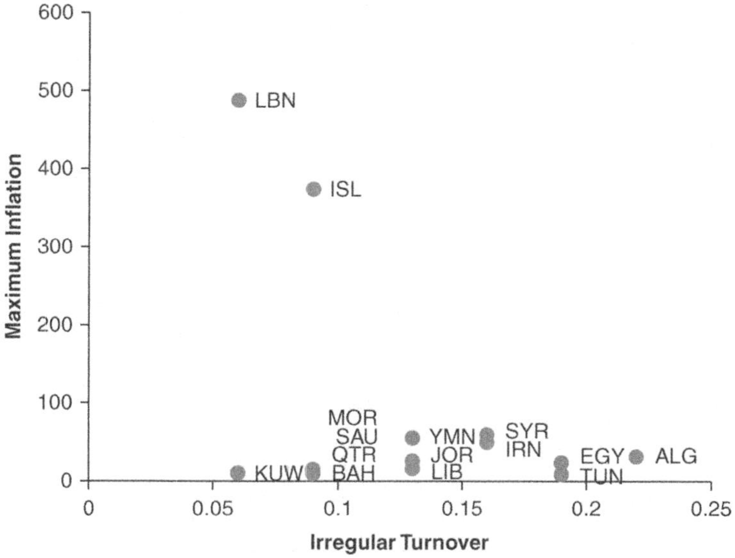

Figure 5.4a Irregular turnover and maximum inflation.

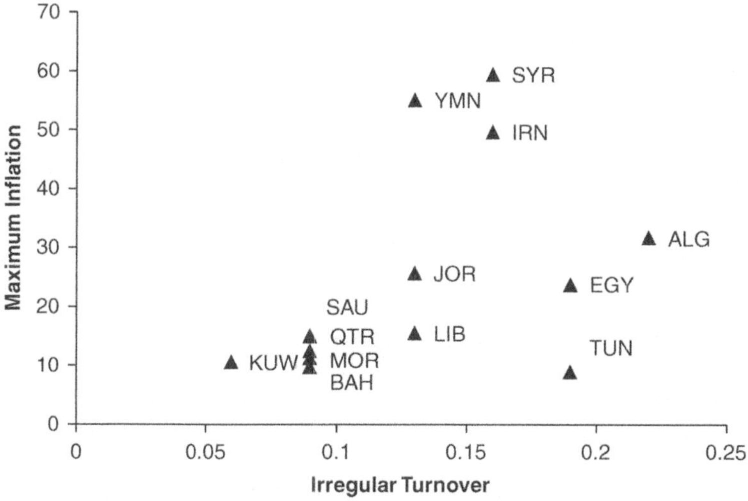

Figure 5.4b Irregular turnover and maximum inflation (excluding Israel and Lebanon).

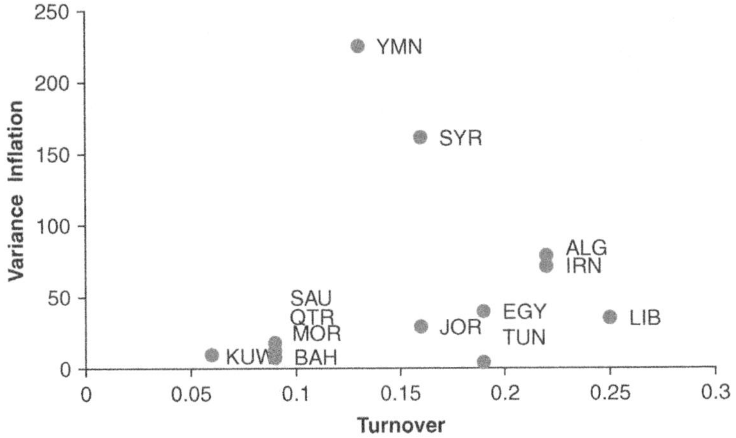

Figure 5.5 Overall turnover and inflation variance (excluding Israel and Lebanon).

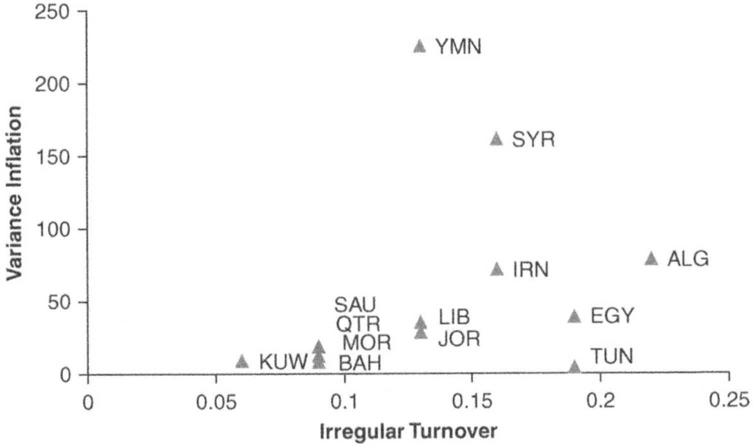

Figure 5.6 Irregular turnover and inflation variance (excluding Israel and Lebanon).

All in all, then, the evidence from the MENA countries tends to support the theoretical case for central bank independence. Given the low respect for legal dispositions in these countries, it is more relevant to use de facto measures of central bank independence. However, an even better view of the way these countries act comes from our measure of irregular turnovers. This measure is positively related to inflation, to the maximum level of inflation, as well as with the variance of inflation. This reveals, in our view, a weak (to say the least) degree of independence of the central banks in these countries, which induces a lack of control of inflation (as only Bahrain and Saudi Arabia have levels of average inflation over the period that can compare favorably with what OECD countries, for example, have known—see Table 5.2). This points to the need of reforms, although modifying the statutes will not be enough if the rulers themselves do not abide by their edicts.

Conclusion and Policy Implications

During the past two decades, the de jure independence of central banks in several countries in the MENA region, mainly in Tunisia, Morocco, and, to a lesser extent, Egypt, has greatly improved. For other countries in the MENA region, the independence of central banks remains very low, and heavily dependent on government decisions.

Based upon the empirical evidence examined in this chapter, it can be argued that it is even more important to ensure the de facto independence of the monetary authority. As official degrees of central bank independence (as enshrined in the legal texts) do not impact the performance of these countries, the real degree of independence of the monetary authority has to be assessed by making use of the turnover rate of central bankers. In addition, as could be expected, a high turnover appears to be related to higher inflation and inflation volatility.

MENA countries thus seem to possess important margins to improve their inflationary performance, conditional upon reforms of their central bank statutes and a stronger respect for the letter of the law. Such improvements would probably require a stable political base, an assurance of greater transparency in the process of appointment and dismissal of the central bank's executives, as well as a greater transparency in the management process, with clear and well-defined objectives and time horizons.

Notes

1. See http://www.systemicpeace.org/inscrdata.html.
2. For a similar analysis, although on a very different sample and period, see Alesina and Summers (1993).
3. See Fischer et al. (2002) for a global analysis and, for Lebanon in particular, Ayoub et al. (2008).

References

Alesina, A., and Summers, L. (1993). Central bank independence and macroeconomic performance: some comparative evidence. *Journal of Money, Credit and Banking*, 25 (2): 151–162.

Ayoub, H., Creel, J., and Farvaque, E. (2008). Détermination du niveau des prix et finances publiques: le cas du Liban, 1965–2005. *Revue d'économie du développement*, 16 (3): 115–141.

Ball, L. M. (1992). Why does high inflation raise inflation uncertainty? *Journal of MonetaryEconomics*, 29 (3): 371–388.

Barro, R., and Gordon, D. (1983). Rules, discretion and reputation in a model of monetarypolicy. *Journal of MonetaryEconomics*, 12 (1): 101–121.

Ben Ali, M. S., and Ben Mim, S. (2011). What drives inflation in MENA countries? *International Journal of Economics and Finance*, 3 (4): 119–129.

Berger, H., de Haan, J., and Eijffinger, S. C. W. (2001). Central bank independence: An update of theory and evidence. *Journal of Economic Surveys*, 15 (1): 3–40.

Blinder, A. (1998). *Central banking in theory and practice*. The MIT Press.

Brumm, H. J. (2002). Inflation and central bank independence revisited. *Economics Letters*, 77 (2): 205–209.

Brumm, H. J. (2006). The effect of central bank independence on inflation in developing countries. *Economics Letters*, 90 (2): 189–193.

Crowe, C., and Meade, E. E. (2008). Central bank independence and transparency: Evolution and effectiveness. *European Journal of Political Economy*, 24 (4): 763–777.

Cukierman, A. (1992).*Central Bank Strategy, Credibility and Independence*. MIT Press: Cambridge, MA.

Cukierman, A., Webb, S., and Neyapti, B. (1992). Measuring the independence of central banks and its effect on policy outcomes. *The World Bank Economic Review*, 6 (3): 353–398.

Eijffinger, S. C. W., and de Haan, J. (1996). *The Political Economy of Central-Bank Independence*. International Finance Section, Department of Economics, Princeton University: Princeton, NJ.

Farvaque, E. (2002). Political Determinants of Central Bank Independence.*Economics Letters*, 77 (1): 131–135.

Farvaque, E. (2007). Constitutional foundations of central bank independence. *Revue d'EconomieFinancière*, 87: 225–236.

Farvaque, E., Héricourt, J., and Lagadec, G. (2010). Central bank independence and ageing. *Applied Economics Letters*, 17 (12): 1167–1171.

Fischer, S., Sahay, R., and Végh, C. A. (2002). Modern hyper- and high inflations. *Journal of EconomicLiterature*, 40 (3): 837–880.

Forder, J. (1998).Central bank independence – conceptual clarifications and interim assessment. *Oxford Economic Papers*, 50 (3): 307–334.

Fuhrer, J. C. (1997). Central Bank independence and inflation targeting: Monetary policy paradigms for the next millenium? *New England Economic Review*: 19–36.

Grier, K. B., Henry, O. T., Olekalns, N., and Shields, K. (2004). The asymmetriceffects of uncertainty on inflation and output growth. *Journal of AppliedEconometrics*, 19 (5): 551–565.

Hayat, M. A., and Farvaque, E. (2011). When are central bankers removed? *Revue Economique*, 62 (3): 471–478.

Kydland, F., and Prescott, E. (1977). Rules rather than discretion: The inconsistency of optimal plans. *Journal of Political Economy*, 85 (3): 473–491.

Lucas, R. (1972). Expectations and the neutrality of money. *Journal of Economic Theory*, 4 (2): 103–124.

Maskin, E., and Tirole, J. (2004). The politician and the judge: Accountability in government. *American Economic Review*, 94 (4): 1034–1054.

Moser, P. (1999). Checks and balances, and the supply of central bank independence. *European Economic Review*, 43 (8): 1569–1593.

Rogoff, K. (1985). The optimal degree of commitment to an intermediate monetary target. *Quarterly Journal of Economics*, 100 (4): 1169–1190.

Waller, C. H., and Walsh, C. (1996). Central bank independence, economic behavior, and optimal term length. *American Economic Review*, 86 (5): 1139–1153.

Walsh, C. (1995). Is New Zealand's Reserve Bank Act of 1989 an optimal central bank contract? *Journal of Money, Credit and Banking*, 27 (4): 1179–1191.

6

Corruption and Economic Development

Mohamed Sami Ben Ali and Shrabani Saha

Corruption is believed to be widespread and it adversely affects countries at different intervals, in different degrees. Corruption scandals show that bribes are commonplace and that even societies that are supposedly free of corruption are affected by it. However, as highlighted in several studies, corruption influences countries' economic development in a manner in which the perception about rich countries is that they are less corrupt than poor nations. It is unclear, however, if increases in income reduce corruption across regions and income classification consistently. Researchers have often focused on the process of detection rather than exploring the degree to which the income level has an effect on corruption.

Concern about corruption has risen since the 1990s, mainly because of worries that a corrupt country would possibly influence other nations through the global economy. At a country level, the detrimental influence of corruption on growth and development is asserted in most cross-country empirical research. In this regard, policymakers and economists have highlighted the role of institutions in terms of political and economic freedoms in battling corruption (Saha and Gounder, 2013; Saha et al., 2009; Treisman, 2007; Graeff and Mehlkop, 2003; Bliss and Di Tella, 1997; Krueger, 1974). Although the majority of research confirms that increased economic freedom lessens corruption, studies found nonlinear effects of democracy on corruption (Saha et al, 2014; Rock, 2009; Montinola and Jackman, 2004; Mohtadi and Roe, 2003; Treisman, 2000; Ades and Di Tella, 1999). Addressing the issue is crucial from a policy perspective, as corruption control is a central concern, in particular, for developing nations.

THE CORRUPTION-ECONOMIC DEVELOPMENT NEXUS: GENERAL FRAMEWORK

What Is Corruption? How Is It Measured?

Transparency International defines corruption as an "*abuse of entrusted power for private gain.*"[1] Bardhan (1997) delineates corruption as the use of public offices for private enrichments, which can be in the form of bribery, embezzlement, fraud, wherein information is manipulated so as to further the personal goals of public officials, and allow favoritism and extortion too (Andvig and Fjeldstad, 2001). Corruption can be viewed as a major obstacle to good policymaking. Specifically, political corruption occurs when political decision makers carry out corrupt practices such as influencing policy formulation, and so on, through large bribes. Sometimes the concepts of governance and corruption are deemed as analogous; however, Blackburn and Forgues-Puccio (2009) characterize governance in much boarder terms, wherein poor governance nurtures corruption, which in turn undercuts quality of governance.

Estimation of corruption levels across nations is a daunting empirical challenge, since defining and measuring corruption is difficult due to its illegal and secret nature, the wide range of corrupt acts, and the differing expressions of corruption. In recent years, various corruption-related measures have been utilized. As detailed in Ben Ali and Sassi (2015), there are four vital and widely used indicators exhibit in the literature. The most popular corruption indicator assesses the probability of government officials demanding additional off-the-record payments or briberies. This indicator has been issued in the International Country Risk Guide and was initially employed by Knack and Keefer (1995) and Mauro (1995). The central downside of this indicator is that it only determines the political risk involved in corruption, not the corruption level of a country (Svensson, 2009). The second measure, by Transparency International, is the Corruption Perception Index. Control of Corruption Index is the third measure derived by Kaufmann et al. (2003) and is accessible through the World Bank. This index employs a strategy of aggregation of most cross-country indices. The fourth index, which was published by World Business Environment Survey (WBES), is employed in the literature for the purpose of measuring corruption at borders. It is constructed for each nation through interviewing businesses and averaging a country score. This measure is more appropriate when dealing with international trade issues.

Why Corruption Exists?

Legal theories relate a country's history to their current levels of corruption illustrating that the rule of law influences government attributes together with the control of corruption in a country. Other theories based on the colonial roots of corruption see previous British colonies, for example, as possessing finer civil service codes due to the effect of the British common law system. The civil servant in this system focuses on the bureaucratic facets of the law, in turn augmenting the competency of underlings and judges to test hierarchies in implementing the laws (Treisman, 2000).

Another hypothesis, one that has been scrutinized in previous literature, is the Protestant religion, which is less susceptible to abuses of power and corruption because it is less hierarchical than other religions. Accordingly, countries dominated by Protestants encounter corruption to a lesser degree. Also, there are theories that put forward that further ethnically fractionalized nations have a habit of being further corrupted (Mauro, 1995). The main cause of the inverse relationship may be the presence of substitute acquaintances and compliance with regard to the state. Societies that dissented ethnically, civil servants, and politicians abuse their stations and favor people from their own ethnic group. In addition, divided societies have a habit of underproviding public goods due to the dependence on special bonds to attain vital services from the government.

What Causes Corruption?

Three types of determinants can explain the occurrence of corruption. The focus of the first type is on the position of incentives and internal mechanisms inside the bureaucracy in monitoring corruption. The second stresses on the external mechanisms playing a role in checking corruption, while the final strand maintains the description of corruption by more indirect factors.

Internal controls contain all incentives and systems that govern corruption inside of the bureaucracy. In an administrative environment with an absence of explicit standards of performance, and where the single bureaucrat is poorly overseen, the belief is that corruption is high. Rauch and Evans (2000) claim that it is vital to ensure internal controls to oversee whether recruitments or promotions are founded on meritocracy or nepotism, and that a reduced amount of nepotism has a tendency to eliminate the chance of collusion of internal control among bureaucrats. The authors examine this by constructing an index made up of meritocratic recruitments and promotions, and the results show that it is significantly connected with corruption, particularly for developing nations. When it comes to accepting bribes, Van Rijckeghem and Weder (2001) assert that when public sector wages are low compared to the wages in the private sector, it increases incentives for bureaucrats on that front. The study shows that there exists an adverse correlation between the public sector wage and corruption, suggesting that the index is significantly associated with corruption in the less developed nations

The external control of corruption is primarily executed by the judicial power, and a sound court system effortlessly and effectively sues corrupt bureaucrats and in turn severely diminishes the prospective rewards from corruption. Other aspects of the society can play the part of external controller in nations with less established checks and balances. Rahman (1986) defines such a mechanism for Singapore, where citizen committees were put in place so as to allow citizens a voice in rectifying corrupt practices. In this regard, an empirical study by Chowdhury (2004) finds evidence that press freedom is an effective control for corruption.

Finally, the existing body of literature acknowledges culture and the amount of distortions in the economy as the indirect determinants of corruption. Lee (1986) and Tanzi (1994) both evoke culture. The former advises that a bureaucratic elitist culture may cause a disassociation between civil servants and the remainder of society, breeding corruption. The latter disputes that the lack of an arm's length relationship may cause systemic corruption. In addition, Shleifer and Vishny (1993) propose that more ethnically diverse states are more likely to face the damaging effects of corruption. A second indirect determinant is distortive policies, as Tanzi (1994) mentions government involvement in free markets generating rents and bringing about a severe escalation in corruption. Ades and Di Tella (1999) and Kaufmann (1997) also found evidence of the existence of these indirect determinants of corruption.

How Does Corruption Impact Economic Development?

It is argued that there is a link between corruption and a nation's active establishments and their economic development level. Studies done by Graeff and Mehlkop (2003) and Treisman (2000), for example, maintain that when it comes to corruption, the perception about rich countries, or countries with a high per capita income, is that they are less corrupt than underprivileged nations, or countries with low per capita income. Nevertheless, it is plausible that corruption reacts in a different way to comparable surges in income at different levels of economic development.

As a result of differences in income across nations, the costs of corruption are displayed differently from country to country. The anticipated cost of a corrupt act—be it in the form of moral, social, and/or economic costs—is weighed against the anticipated benefit, and since acting in a corrupt way can lead to losing one's job, it stands to reason that the higher one's salary is, the more costly corruption will be. Sandholtz and Koetzle (2000) discusses how the high value of money in poor countries leads to a higher incidence of both takers and givers of bribes, because of the extra income and benefits that can be obtained. Policymakers do not directly control the incidence of corruption, though because they control the measures that are directed at altering this incidence. These measures differ vastly in both their effectiveness and nature.

Two main hypotheses are discussed in the literature when dealing with corruption: the "grease" vs. the "sand" in the wheels. The grease side of the argument states that bribes may act as a way to save someone from trouble and advance the investment in and the economic growth of a state (Beck and Maher, 1986; Brunetti et al., 1998; Huntington, 1968; and Leff, 1964;). Corruption removes the constraint on production by greasing the wheels of bureaucracy for the firms that are weighed down by controls. Corruption then arguably enhances growth (Leff, 1964; Huntington, 1968; Friedrich, 1972; and Nye, 1989). Since low-income countries do not have the required income for paying bribes, an increase in income level allows people to offer bribes by increasing the affordability, and so the level of corruption will rise, especially in the early periods of growth (Saha and Grounder, 2013). Conversely, the "sand the wheel" side of the argument states that corruption can be harmful to growth through decelerating the bureaucratic process, being both costly and inefficient, and also through the transfering of resources to fruitless undertakings (Myrdal, 1989; Rose-Ackerman, 1997; Tanzi and Davoodi, 1997; and Mauro, 1998). Moreover, with a fragile rule of law and lacking government quality, growth in a country is slowed down immensely by corruption (Méon and Sekkat, 2005).

The first empirical study by Mauro (1995), reports that corruption negatively affects growth by lowering investment. Works done later by Pelligrini and Gerlagh (2004) and Mo (2001) highlight how human capital, political instability, and trade openness to be bonus channels through which corruption affects growth. They employed cross-sectional estimations, with the dependent variable being the average economic growth rate coupled with a set of economic and institutional controls. The issue of endogeniety in the growth-corruption relation is accounted for. While Mauro treats the endogeneity of corruption and investment separately, Pelligrini and Gerlagh (2004) and Mo (2001) consider them as exogenously determined. The conclusion arrived at by these studies is that corruption indirectly influences economic growth by depressing the investment, the stock of human capital, political instability, and openness. On the other hand, Swaleheen (2011) finds a nonlinear growth-corruption relation by employing a panel data technique and controlling the endogeniety of investment and corruption.

When it comes to human capital accumulation, it is generally recognized as an instrument of growth, as highlighted in the theoretical literature. Public officials may facilitate corruption through discretionary variations and/or implementation of the incentive system outlined in public policies. Firms disburse some endowments as bribes, in the pursuit of rent, or the evasion of rent annihilation, instead of spending money on research and development to expand human capital. Because of this, an adverse effect is noticed on the buildup of human capital, which lowers growth (Pecorino, 1992; and Murphy et al., 1991). Moreover, the growth inhibiting effect of corruption is greater with a low stock of human capital, usually in low-income countries (Ehrlich and Lui, 1999).

Furthermore, Kaufmann and Wei (2000) and Kaufmann (1998) discern that corruption may continually accelerate to ever-higher levels because, instead of productive work, managers allocate more time to dealing with public officials—specifically in economies where corruption is high. Although, Aidt (2003) highlights that the growth maximizing positive corruption is based on problematic assumptions, however, there would still be occurrences of corruption, but as a second-best option, since the deterrence of corruption by public officials requires costly close monitoring (Acemoglu and Verdier, 1998).

It is apparent that for low-income countries, the early phases of development do not produce adequate income, but when the income level rises, corruption can be enhanced because of bribes. By the time a country reaches the advanced point of development, a high-income level raises the cost of corruption to a great enough point that corruption is then deterred quite significantly (Saha and Gounder, 2013).

For assessing the direct impact of corruption on economic growth, Méon and Sekkat (2005) include an interaction term among corruption with government quality as an explanatory variable in a cross-sectional setting to identify the moderation effect of corruption and quality of governance on economic growth—in other words, to identify how corruption affects economic growth at various levels of government quality. The study finds that if there is poor governance, then increased corruption actually lessens the growth rate. With an improvement in the quality of governance though, it is noted that the negative effect of corruption turns out to be weaker. Therefore, corruption and the quality of governance are extremely interconnected with each other, and so the interaction between them can amplify the influence of corruption when there is high corruption and poor governance quality. The cost of reducing corruption is therefore highly dependent upon the construction of a sound institutional structure that can successfully and effectively fight corruption. For low and middle-income countries, the means to buildup such structures is of too great a cost, but that is not the case for countries in the mature stages of development, as they have the means to build strong institutional foundations and impose an anticorruption agenda.

Corruption and Economic Development in MENA Region

This section discusses economic, socioeconomic and political factors contributing to the corruption-growth nexus in the MENA region.

Economic, Socioeconomic and Political Outlook in MENA Region

The Middle East and North Africa (MENA) region comprises about 21 diverse countries. Taking into account the region's diversity, the World Bank (2014) classified the countries into three groups based on the population size and natural resources endowment:

1. Rich in natural resources and labor importing countries include Bahrain, Kuwait, Libya, Oman, Qatar, Saudi Arabia, and the United Arab Emirates (UAE). These countries produce and export oil and natural gas with a significant share of foreign residents among their total population.
2. Rich in natural resources and labor abundant countries comprise Algeria, Iraq, Syria, and Yemen. This group of countries produces and exports natural gas and oil and contains large percentages of their own native populations.

3. Countries poor in natural resources include Djibouti, Egypt, Jordan, Lebanon, Mauritania, Morocco, the Palestinian Authority, and Tunisia.

In recent years, the MENA region was under the spotlight of the international media, and attracted the attention of researchers due to the "Arab Spring" that started in 2011. The Arab Spring countries such as Egypt, Tunisia, and Yemen are currently encountering challenges to political transformations that impose a significant negative impact on economic growth and worsened macroeconomic imbalances. The World Bank (2014) estimates reveal that conflicts in Egypt, Libya, Syria, Tunisia, and Yemen with their spillovers into Jordan and Lebanon, cost the region approximately USD 168 billion over the period 2011–2013, which is equivalent to 19 percent of their combined gross domestic product (GDP). In particular, the real output in Syria shrinks by 40 percent compared to its pre-crisis level in 2010. The economic growth rates estimated by the growth of real GDP per capita of some selected countries in the region are shown in Figure 6.1. The figure illustrates that in 2011, the growth rates of all of these countries had declined, and the most affected countries in the region were Libya and Yemen. The per capita growth rate in these two countries decreases by 62 and 17 percent, respectively. Setting aside the Arab Spring of 2011, Bhattacharya and Wolde (2010) noted that despite the regions' immense endowment of natural resources, the growth performance has been rather disgruntling over the past two decades or so. This is evident from the 2004 growth rates in Figure 6.1.

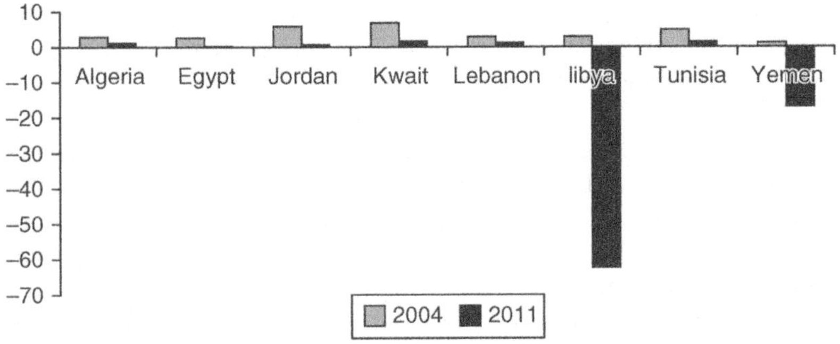

Figure 6.1 Economic growth in some MENA countries.

Source: WDI-World Bank.

In contrast, in spite of having undiversified economies and the problems of unemployment and skills mismatches, some of the oil-rich nations or monarchies (or both), have experienced moderate growth and macroeconomic stability (such as Saudi Arabia, where economic growth reached 6.6 percent in 2011). One of the major challenges face by MENA countries is the existence of a high rate of unemployment. In addition, it exists among the young and the most educated people. The youth unemployment (aged between 15 and 24) rate over the period 2004–2013 from the World Bank's World Development Indicators, shows a significantly higher unemployment, in particular, over 31 percent in Egypt; 36 percent in Iraq; 30 percent in Jordan; 30 percent in Saudi Arabia; 31 percent in Tunisia; and 28 percent in Yemen. The average youth unemployment rates are much higher in the resource–rich labor abundant countries, compared to the other two groups, although the unemployment rate increases quite significantly in the resource-rich labor-importing countries over the period 2004–2013 (Figure 6.2).

Although the Arab Spring of 2011 in the MENA region came about due to the youth bulge (ages between 15 and 24), there is no general agreement about the causes of the incidents. Anecdotal evidence demonstrates various reasons behind it, some of which are political. According to Freedom House, most of the MENA countries are characterized by less or no political freedom in terms of political and civil rights. The mean score of democracy indices combining political and civil liberties for the MENA countries during 1984–2013, is 2.6 out of the maximum score of 7, where the highest value indicates maximum

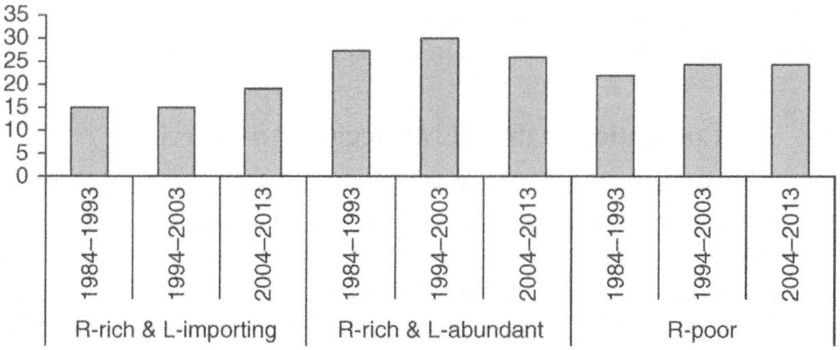

Figure 6.2 Average youth unemployment rates in percent in three groups of MENA countries.

Source: WDI-World Bank.

freedom (Table 6.1). The protests and demonstrations during the Arab Spring mostly manifest a greater demand for political and economic liberties and the end of the corrupted authoritarian regimes. For instance, demonstrations for toppling the long-ruling government in Egypt and Tunisia spread over the other neighboring countries in the region. In addition, the structural political reform cannot be isolated from economic reform. The lack of these freedoms poses challenges to the MENA countries in terms of pervasive corruption, overstuffed and inefficient public sectors, and weak governance in both public and corporate sectors. Transparency International (2008) noted that all countries in the region are ranked in the bottom half of the world with respect to public accountability.

The Bertelsmann Transformation Index (BTI) assesses the performances of countries in managing the process of democratization and market economy. The BTI produces the Status and the Management Indices to measure transformation processes and political management. The Status Index assesses the state of both political and economic transformation. The BTI Status Index (2014) ranked MENA countries below the world's median (out of 129 countries) with few exceptions. It is noted that Lebanon, Tunisia, Jordan, and Egypt perform better than Iraq, Syria, and Yemen. Moreover, in most cases, political transformation scores slightly lower than economic transformation. However, Tunisia and Egypt score better in political transformation than economic liberalization. On the other hand, the management index focuses on the quality of governance in terms of resource efficacy, consensus building, governance capability, and international cooperation. Countries such as Egypt, Jordan, Tunisia, and Yemen received very low ratings, overall, around 4.5 out of 10 being the highest performance, and Syria was ranked second from the bottom with little or no success in managing the changes.

Corruption in the MENA Region: An Overview

The general consensus is that the MENA region is characterized by widespread corruption, at both the petty and grand scales. One of the main causes of the high degree of corruption is entrenched in the institutional as well as political aspects of the states, such as dictatorships, monarchies, and oversized public sectors. The Corruption Perceptions Index (CPI) constructed by Transparency International shows that, with some degrees of variations, MENA countries are ranked below the world median. Moreover, comparing countries with similar income levels, MENA countries are ranked consistently lower. Corruption Perceptions Index (2014) illustrates that three out of the ten bottom countries are from the MENA region. According to the International Country Risk Guide (ICRG) corruption index produced by Political Risk Services, the average score for the period 1984–2013 for the MENA region is around 4 out of the maximum corruption score of 6 (Table 6.1). Interestingly, the low standard deviation value of the corruption index shows that corruption is very persistent throughout the region. In particular, the corruption level increases in most of the countries in the 2000s like, for instance, Iraq and Lebanon.

On the other hand, the Arab Human Development Report (2005) noted the Freedom Survey's (2004) report for five Arab countries (Algeria, Jordan, Lebanon, Morocco, and Palestine), which shows that 90 percent of the respondents considered that their society is contaminated with pervasive corruption. Furthermore, another international survey reports that 70 percent of the respondents alleged that their country is run by the few influential elites for their own benefit. In addition, BTI (2014) ranked all MENA countries poorly for control of corruption (included in the effective use of resources) with scores ranging from 2 (Syria and Yemen) to 5 (Egypt, Jordan, and Tunisia), where 10 indicates the maximum use of resources. Furthermore, the overwhelming majority of people think that favoritism is necessary for getting a public sector job.

The World Bank, in the world's most comprehensive company-level data provided by Business Enterprise Survey on the various constraints to business performance and growth covering over 130,000 businesses for the period 2002–2014 in 135 countries, reveals that

Table 6.1 Descriptive statistics about some corruption-related indices

	CORR ICRG Corruption Index	**AYS** Average Years of Schooling	**DEMO** Democracy Index	**EF** Economic Freedom	**ET** Ethnic Tension	**Growth** Real GDP Per Capita Growth Rate	**UNEM** Youth Unemployment
Mean	3.527	9.803	2.605	5.9918	1.834	1.495	24.087
Maximum	5.000	19.600	6.250	8.0689	6.000	102.777	53.100
Minimum	2.000	2.340	1.000	1.6250	0.000	–65.030	0.700
Std. Dev.	0.772	3.799	1.031	11.963	1.314	9.833	11.548
Observations	472	480	474	293	472	421	400

Sources: Data are extracted from ICRG (CORR), the Quality of Government Standard data set (AYS), Freedom House (DEMO), Heritage Foundation (EF); ICRG (ET), World Bank-WDI (Real GDP Per Capita Growth Rate); and World Bank-WDI (UNEM, Youth Unemployment, between 15–24).

public sector corruption imposes a major administrative and financial constraint on firms.[2] Enterprise survey provides three sets of indicators for corruption. The first set of indicators for overall corruption index reflects that the proportion of times a firm requires or expects to pay a bribe for six different public services, permits, or licenses, and the score is more than 20 percent for MENA countries. The second set of indicators show that over 40 percent of the firms are expected to provide gifts for securing government contracts. The third set of indicators for corruption focuses on bribes or informal payments for obtaining licenses or permits, and nearly 30 percent and 20 percent of firms in MENA countries are expected to provide gifts for construction permits and import licenses, respectively. In terms of country profile, Jordan and Lebanon perform much better (less corruption) than the average MENA country in all aspects, whereas Yemen experiences widespread and pervasive corruption in the region.

Bhattacharya and Wolde (2010) attempt to quantify the impacts of the various constraints on economic growth by using the World Bank's Business Enterprise Survey data in the MENA region, and the findings report that corruption constraint is statistically insignificant in explaining the region's growth performance. The explanation for the insignificant results put forward by the authors could be the informal mechanism to deal with this constraint over time, which creates a less binding effect on growth over the long run. The next subsection examines the corruption-growth association, considering other political and socioeconomic factors.

The Corruption-Growth Relationship in MENA Region

Various explanations have been provided for the incidence of corruption in different countries in the MENA region. These can be classified as economic, political, and socioeconomic factors. The economic category includes the stages of economic development, economic freedom, or the ease of doing business. Political aspects identify lack of democracy, governance processes, transparency, freedom of political associations, and ethnic tensions. For the socioeconomic perspective, educational levels and a large amount of unemployment have been regarded as key factors. The correlation coefficients of corruption with other economic, political, and socioeconomic factors are presented in Table 6.2.

The correlation coefficient between corruption and economic growth shows a positive sign, although not significant. The positive

Table 6.2 Correlation coefficients with corruption and various explanatory variables

	AYS	DEMO	EF	ET	Growth	Youth Unem
CORR	0.1206	−0.3839	−0.3542	0.0454	0.0642	0.2638
p-value	0.0589	0.0000	0.0000	0.3254	0.3152	0.0000

Sources: Data are extracted from ICRG (CORR), the Quality of Government Standard data set (AYS), Freedom House (DEMO), Heritage Foundation (EF); ICRG (ET), World Bank-WDI (Real GDP per capita growth rate); and World Bank-WDI (UNEM, Youth Unemployment, between 15–24).

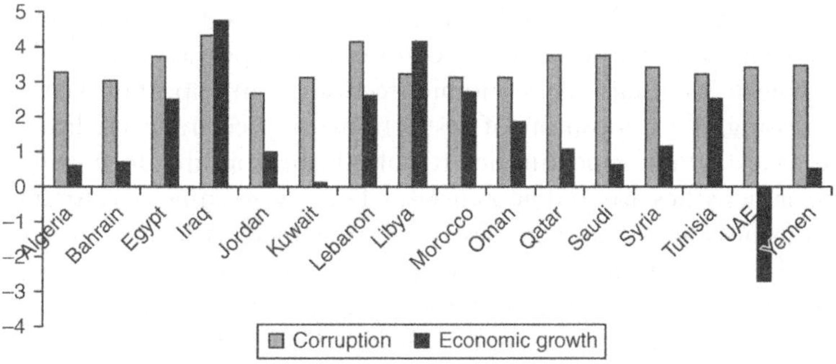

Figure 6.3 Corruption and economic growth in some MENA countries: Average for 1984–2013.

Source: ICRG (Corruption index), WDI-World Bank (Economic Growth).

sign indicates that economic growth and corruption grow together in the MENA region. The explanation could be that many countries in the region are rich in natural resources, which may lead to the greater potential gain to the public officials who set policy and allocate rights to exploit such resources, which in turn increases the corruption levels (Treisman, 2000; and Ades and Di Tella, 1999). Moreover, Al-Marhubi (2004) argues that natural resource abundance reduces the government's dependence on tax revenue collected from its citizens, which leads to the decrease in citizens' demand for government accountability and transparency. However, resource-poor countries may experience more corruption due to the low economic growth. The average corruption-growth relationship in some MENA countries for the period 1984–2013 in Figure 6.3 shows that countries like Iraq and Libya experience a higher GDP per capita growth in spite of having higher corruption (average corruption scores of these two countries are 4.5 and 3.3, respectively). In contrast, Algeria, Kuwait, UAE, and Yemen show higher corruption and lower economic growth.

The corruption-growth relationship in the MENA region illustrates the existence of a nonlinear corruption-income relationship (Figure 6.4). An increase in per capita income may increase corruption at a low level of economic development, and after a threshold point, an income increase lowers corruption. This pattern is consistent with Saha and Gounder (2013). In addition, the figure shows that resource-rich high-income countries experience a higher corruption level.

Economic freedom and ease of doing business is vital to attract FDI, external markets, and efficiency. Nonmarket resource allocation leads to corruption in every country that is pervasive throughout the world. As discussed, economic freedom is an important factor in addressing the imposition of restrictions on free trade via licenses, and taxes create opportunities to take bribes or/and to engage in similar activities for public officials. Thus, government restrictions on business activities increases rents in numerous forms, and public officials often indulge in varying degrees of corruption for higher rents (Krueger, 1974). In other words, the opening up a country's economy decreases its corruption level, which in turn eases of doing

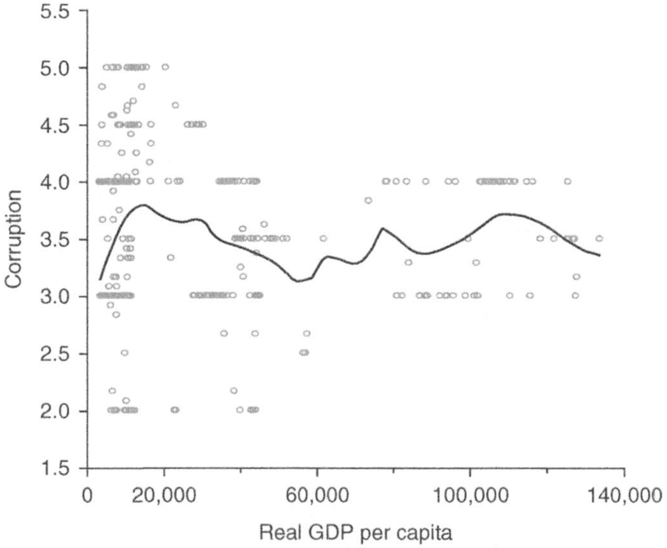

Figure 6.4 Corruption and real GDP per capita relationship: 1984–2013.

Source: Corruption (ICRG) and Real GDP per capita (World Bank-WDI).

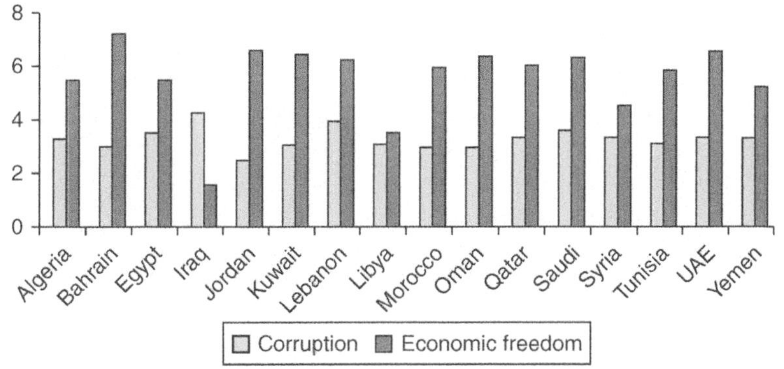

Figure 6.5 Economic freedom and corruption in MENA region: Average for 1984–2013.

Source: ICRG (Corruption index), Heritage Foundation (Economic freedom).

business and improves the economic performance of the country. Figure 6.5 shows the inverse relationship between economic freedom and corruption in some MENA countries for the period 1984–2013. On the one hand, Bahrain and Jordan experience a high level of economic freedom with a lower level of corruption. In contrast, less economic freedom enhances corruption in Iraq. The inverse relationship is supported by the negative and significant value of the correlation coefficient between CORR and EF (Table 6.2). The negative corruption-economic freedom association is consistent with current empirical literature (such as Saha et al., 2009). Furthermore, economic freedom shows a high level of variability in the region.

Likewise, many nations in the MENA region are described by increasingly high levels of corruption, and low or no real democratic process. The democratic structures of these nations have proved to be strikingly ineffective in restraining widespread corrupt practices (such as Syria). Democratic structures in MENA countries (Figure 6.6) are associated with high level of corruption with a lowering accountability and an absence of transparency (supported by the negative correlation coefficient between CORR and DEMO, Table 6.2).

In addition, ethnic tension (ET)—measured by the level of conflict within a country due to nationality, racial, or language rifts—has an influential impact on corruption in some MENA countries (Figure 6.7).

It is seen from the figure that ethnic tension increases over the period 2004–2013 in Syria in particular, along with a high corruption

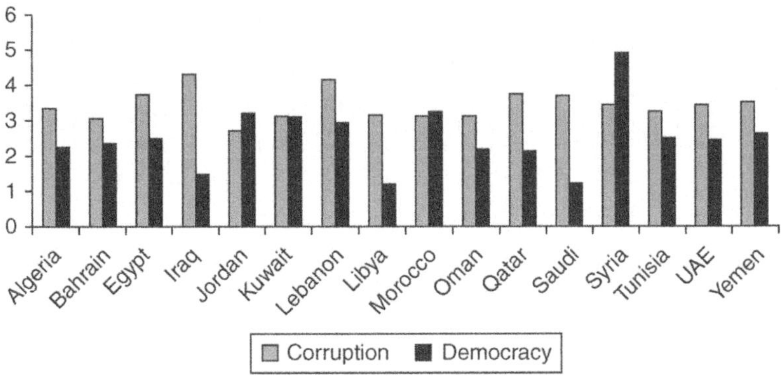

Figure 6.6 Democracy and corruption in MENA region: Average for 1984–2013.
Source: ICRG (Corruption index), Freedom House (Democracy index).

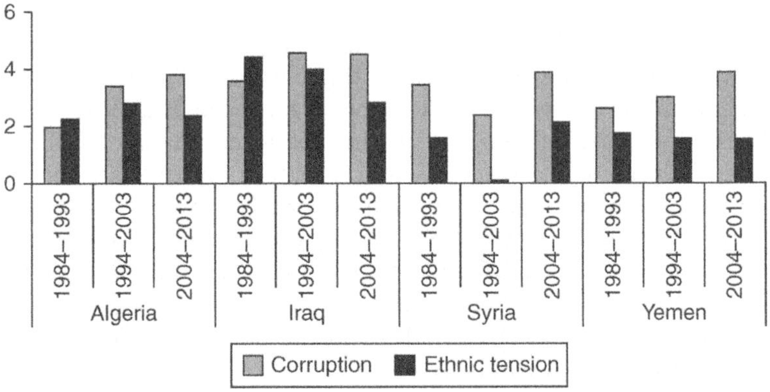

Figure 6.7 Ethnic tension and corruption in some MENA countries: Average for 1984–2013.
Source: ICRG.

level. Iraq also demonstrates a positive corruption-ethnic tension correlation since 1984.

Youth unemployment in the region has received new attention from researchers and policymakers in recent years. Studies have highlighted that labor-skill-mismatch and shortages are considered to be the largest factors contributing to the negative impact on growth in the MENA region (Pissarides and Véganzonés-Varoudakis, 2007; and Bhattacharya Wolde, 2010). These studies have argued that the existence of large public sectors distorts incentives of the private sectors due to the excessive government regulations. Furthermore, education systems in the MENA region are designed to fulfill the needs of the public sector and, as a result, private sectors experience a shortage of the acquired skill required for growth-enhancing activities. Excessive government regulations restrain private employers from recruiting and instructing skilled workers, which is a resultant factor of the existence of a high level of youth unemployment in MENA countries. Thus, excessive regulations, and the high level of corruption, increase unemployment among the educated youth in this region. Table 6.2 reflects a positive and significant correlation between corruption and youth unemployment, which is evident from the existence of high levels of youth unemployment and corruption in the region.

A higher youth unemployment level accompanies high corruption levels in Algeria, Iraq, Egypt, Jordan, Libya, Oman, Tunisia, and Yemen. On the other hand, Kuwait, Qatar, and UAE experience less constraint in terms of youth unemployment for economic growth (Figure 6.8). For example, a high unemployment level in Oman currently forced the Sultanate of Oman to assess its labor markets, educational system, and entrepreneurship sector as possible policy options to deal with the increasing number of youth who enter the education system and labor market. The government needs to create (40,000) employment opportunities a year to absorb youth with tertiary education. This initiative allows the Sultanate of Oman a temporary reprieve from the negative consequences of the Arab Spring of 2011,

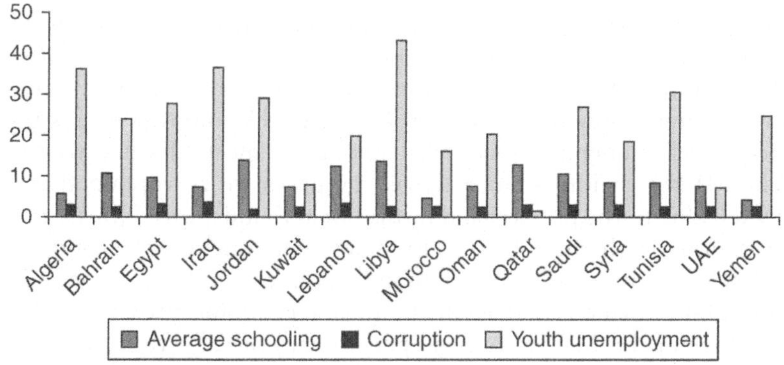

Figure 6.8 Corruption, average years of schooling, and youth unemployment in some MENA countries: Average for 1984–2013.

Source: ICRG (Corruption Index), The Quality of Government Standard data set (Average Years of Schooling), World Bank-WDI (Youth Unemployment).

by creating massive employment opportunities in the public sector and expanding higher education opportunities. However, these measurements dealt with the symptoms, but failed to help determine the main causes of the problems. The situation is similar across countries in the region. Corruption prevents the development of active private sectors that can play a crucial role in the economy and affects the transparency level required for a healthy business environment. Similarly, nepotism through the intensive uses of personal relationship to get access to information, contracts, and other economic activities that might have a negative impact on markets and competition as well as the quality of government bureaucracy and, in turn, on economic growth in the region.

Conclusion and Policy Implications

Estimating corruption levels is not an easy task because defining and measuring corruption is difficult. The literature has explored the possible reasons behind why corruption exists. There are three types of determinants that possibly explain the incidence of corruption, which involve internal and external control and indirect factors. The impact of corruption on economic development has been extensively studied, with differences being displayed from country to country. Some studies have concluded that corruption influences economic growth rate indirectly through investment, accumulation of human capital, political instability, and openness.

When it comes to assessing the corruption-growth nexus in the MENA region, the countries of this region are split up into resource-rich-labor-importing, resource-rich-labor-abundant, and poorly-resourced countries. Economic growth in the region has been quite disappointing, with some countries experiencing huge negative rates of economic growth. Another problem MENA countries face is the steep level of unemployment even among the most educated youths. The MENA region is characterized by pervasive corruption that is acutely due to the political and institutional foundations of this group of nations, with there being various explanations for corruption in MENA that are classified as economic, political, and socioeconomic. Several studies indicate that corruption and economic growth develop together in the MENA region. The corruption-growth nexus illustrates the potential presence of a nonlinearity amid corruption and income, wherein at a low level of economic development, a growth in per capita income may increase corruption, but after a threshold level, an income increase actually lowers corruption.

NOTES

1. See https://www.transparency.org/whoweare/organisation/faqs_on_corruption/2/ for details.
2. See http://www.enterprisesurveys.org/reports for details.

REFERENCES

Acemoglu, D., and Verdier, T. (1998). Property rights, corruption and the allocation of talent: A general equilibrium approach. *The Economic Journal*, 108 (450): 1381–1403.

Ades, A. and di Tella, R. (1999). Rents, competition and corruption. *American Economic Review*, 89 (4): 982–993.

Aidt, T. S. (2003). Economic analysis of corruption: A survey. *The Economic Journal*, 113 (491): F632–F652.

Al-Marhubi, F. (2004). The determinants of governance: a cross country analysis. *Contemporary Economic Policy*, 22 (3): 394–406.

Andvig, J. C. and Fjeldstad, O. (2001). *Corruption: a review of contemporary research* (CMI Report R 2001:7). Bergen: Chr. Michelsen Institute. http://www.cmi.no/publications/file/?861= corruption-a-review-of-contemporary-research. Accessed August 30, 2007.

Bardhan, P. (1997). Corruption and development: a review of issues. *Journal of Economic Literature*, 35 (3): 1320–1346.

Beck, P. J. and Maher, M. W. (1986). A comparison of bribery and bidding in thin markets. *Economics Letters*, 20 (1): 1–5.

Ben Ali, M. S. and Sassi, S. (2015). The Corruption-Inflation Nexus: Evidence from Developed and Developing Countries. *The B.E. Journal of Macroeconomics*. Forthcoming.

Bhattacharya, R. and Wolde, H. (2010). Constraints on growth in the MENA region. *IMF Working Paper*, WP/10/30. Washington: International Monetary Fund.

Blackburn, K. and Forgues-Puccio, G. F. (2009). Why is corruption less harmful in some countries than in others? *Journal of Economic Behavior & Organization*, 72 (3): 797–810.

Bliss, C., and Di Tella, R. (1997). Does competition kill corruption? *Journal of Political Economy*, 105 (5): 1001–1023.

Brunetti, A., Kisunko, G., and Weder, B. (1998). Credibility of rules and economic growth: evidence from a worldwide survey of the private sector. *The World Bank Economic Review*, 12 (3): 353–384.

Chowdhury, S. (2004). The effect of democracy and press freedom on corruption: An empirical test. *Economic Letters*, 85 (1): 93–101.

Ehrlich, I. and Lui, F. (1999). Bureaucratic corruption and endogenous economic growth. *The Journal of Political Economy*, 107 (6): S270–S293. Part 2: Symposium on the Economic Analysis of Social Behavior in Honor of Gary S. Becker.

Friedrich, C. S. (1972). *The Pathology of Politics: Violence, Betrayal, Corruption, Secrecy and Propaganda*. New York: Harper and Row.

Graeff, P. and Mehlkop, G. (2003). The Impact of Economic Freedom on Corruption: Different Patterns for Rich and Poor Countries. *European Journal of Political Economy*, 19 (3): 605–620.

Huntington, S. P. (1968). *Political Order in Changing Societies*. New Haven, CT: Yale University Press.

Kaufmann, D. (1997). Corruption: the facts. *Foreign Policy* (107): 114–131.

Kaufmann, D. (1998). "Research on Corruption: Critical Empirical Issues," in *Economics of Corruption*, edited by A. Jain. Dordrecht: Kluwer Academic Publishers.

Kaufmann, D. and Wei, C. S. (2000). Does grease money speed up the wheels of commerce? *IMF Working Paper*, WP/00/64. Washington, DC: International Monetary Fund.

Knack, S. and Keefer, P. (1995). Institutions and economic performance: Cross-country tests using alternative institutional measures. *Economics and Politics*, 7 (3): 207–227.

Krueger, A.O. (1974). The political economy of the rent-seeking society. *American Economic Review*, 64 (3): 291–303.

Lee, R. (1986). "Bureaucratic Corruption in Asia: The Problem of Incongruence between Legal Norms and Folk Norms." in *Bureaucratic Corruption in Asia: Causes, Consequences, and Controls*, edited by A. Carino. Quezon City: NMC Press.

Leff, N. (1964). Economic development through bureaucratic corruption. *American Behavioral Scientist*, 8 (2): 8–14.

Mauro, P. (1995). Corruption and growth. *Quarterly Journal of Economics*, 110 (3): 681–712.

Mauro, P. (1998). Corruption and the composition of government expenditure. *Journal of Public Economics*, 69 (2): 263–279.

Méon, P. and Sekkat, K. (2005). Does corruption grease or sand the wheels of growth? *Public Choice*, 122 (1): 69–97.

Mo, P.H. (2001). Corruption and economic growth. *Journal of Comparative Economics*, 29 (1): 66–79.

Mohtadi, H. and Roe, T. L. (2003). Democracy, rent seeking, public spending and growth. *Journal of Public Economic*, 87 (3): 445–466.

Montinola, G. R. and Jackman, R. W. (2004). Sources of corruption: A cross-country study. *British Journal of Political Science*, 32 (01): 147–170.

Murphy, K. M., Shleifer, A., and Vishny, R. W. (1991). Allocation of talent: Implications for growth. *Quarterly Journal of Economics*, 106 (2): 503–530.

Myrdal, G. (1989). "Asian Drama: An Inquiry into the Poverty of Nations," in *The Twentieth Century Fund, New York: Political Corruption: A Handbook*, edited by A. J.Heidenheimer, M. Johnston, V.T. Le Vine, Vol. 2. Oxford: Transaction Books, pp. 953–961 (Reprint in).

Nye, J. S. (1989). Corruption and political development: A cost benefit analysis. *American Political Science Review*, 61 (2): 417–427.

Pecorino, P. (1992). Rent seeking and growth: The case of growth through human capital accumulation. *Canadian Journal of Economics*, 25 (4): 944–956.

Pissarides, C. A. and Véganzonés-Varoudakis, M.-A. (2007). Labour Markets and Economic Growth in MENA Region, in *Explaining Growth in the Middle East*, edited by J. B. Nugent and Pesaron, H. Amsterdam and Boston, MA: Elsevier.

Pelligrini, L. and Gerlagh, R. (2004). Corruption's effect on growth and its transmission channels. *Kyklos*, 57 (3): 429–456.

Rahman, R. (1986). Legal and Administrative Measures against Bureaucratic Corruption in Asia, in *Bureaucratic Corruption in Asia: Causes, Consequences, and Controls*, edited by A. Carino. Quezon City: NMC Press.

Rauch, J. and Evans, P. (2000). Bureaucratic structures and economic performance in less developed countries. *Journal of Public Economics*, 75 (1): 49–71.

Rock, M. (2009). Corruption and democracy. *Journal of Development Studies*, 45 (1): 55–75.

Rose-Ackerman, S. (1997). The Political Economy of Corruption, in *Corruption and the global economy*, edited by K. A. Elliot. Washington: Institute for International Economics, 133–145.

Saha, S. Gounder, R. Campbell, N., and Su, J. J. (2014). Democracy and corruption: A complex relationship. *Crime Law and Social Change,* 61 (3): 287–308.

Saha, S. and Gounder, R. (2013). Corruption and economic development nexus: Variations across income levels in a non-linear framework. *Economic Modelling*, 31 (1): 70–79.

Saha, S., Gounder, R., and Su, J. J. (2009). The interaction effect of economic freedom and democracy on corruption: A panel cross-country analysis, *Economics Letters*. 105 (2): 173–176.

Sandholtz, W. and Koetzle, W. (2000). Accounting for corruption: Economic structure, democracy, and trade. *International Studies Quarterly*, 44 (1): 31–50.

Shleifer, A. and Vishny, R. W. (1993). Corruption. *Quarterly Journal of Economics*, 108: 599–617.

Svensson, L. E. (2009). Evaluating Monetary Policy. *NBER Working Papers,* No. w15385. National Bureau of Economic Research.

Swaleheen, M. (2011), Economic growth with endogenous corruption: An empirical study. *Public Choice*, 146 (1–2): 23–41.

Tanzi, V. (1994). Corruption, Governmental Activities and Markets. *IMF Working Paper*, 94/99. Washington, DC: International Monetary Fund.

Tanzi, V. and Davoodi, H. (1997). Corruption, Public Investment, and Growth. *IMF Working Paper*, WP/97/139. Washington, DC: International Monetary Fund.

The Arab Human Development Report (2005). United Nations Development Programme, Arab Gulf Programme For United Nations Development Organizations. Available at: http://www.arab-hdr.org/publications/other/ahdr/ahdr2005e.pdf.

Transparency International. (2008). Global corruption barometer. *Transparency International*, Berlin.

Treisman, D. (2000). The causes of corruption: A cross-national study. *Journal of Public Economics*, 76 (3): 399–457.

Treisman, D. (2007). What have we learned about the causes of corruption from ten years of cross-national empirical research? *Annual Reviews Political Science*, 10 (1): 211–244.

Van Rijckeghem, C. and Weder, B. (2001). Corruption and the rate of temptation: do low wages in the civil service cause corruption. *Journal of Development Economics*, 65 (2): 307–331.

World Bank. (2014). MENA Quarterly Economic Brief. Available at: http://www.worldbank.org/en/region/mena/publication/mena-quarterly-economic-brief.

7

The Finance-Growth Nexus

Which Factors Can Interfere?

Mohamed Sami Ben Ali, Nahla Samargandi, and Kazi Sohag

The financial sector's role in economic growth is heavily contested by economists. Some argue that economic growth is not caused by finance, but that it responds to changing demands, while others argue the positive effect of finance on economic growth (Robinson, 1952; Miller, 1998). Many researchers have concluded that ignoring the notion of the finance-growth link only restricts understanding of economic growth (Bagehot, 1873; Schumpeter, 1912; McKinnon, 1973).

To assess the finance-growth nexus, theoretical and empirical research are consulted. Financial systems could influence a number of different variables through financial arrangements that alter the motivations and restrictions facing economic agents. Literature studies the dynamic relations among finance and growth through the development of models where growth is affected by the financial system and transforms financial system operation. Additionally, an all-encompassing theoretical literature discusses the merits of different financial system types such as stressing the advantages of bank-based financial systems or highlighting the benefits of those that depend more on securities markets.

The Financial Development Economic Growth: Theory

The Importance of Financial Development for the Economy

The price of obtaining data, imposing contracts, and creating transactions incentivizes the appearance of specific financial agreements, markets, and intermediary types. Financial systems, in ameliorating market frictions, naturally impact resource allocation (Merton and Bodie, 1995). For example, financial contracts that increase the confidence of investors being paid back by firms will probably influence the way people distribute their savings.

Financial development occurs at the moment when financial market intermediaries ameliorate the effects of implementation, and transactions costs, doing better at providing the financial functions, as any one of these functions can affect savings and investment decisions and therefore economic growth. Due to the existence of many frictions and country differences over time, improvement has differing implications for the allocation of resources and welfare.

Evaluating firms, managers, and market conditions prior to decision making has large costs. Individuals may face high information costs when trying to obtain the necessary investment knowledge required to make an educated decision, and so this keeps capital from flowing to the most profitable uses and firms (Bagehot, 1873). These costs could be reduced when financial intermediaries interfere in this process, improving by the same the allocation of resources (Boyd and Prescott, 1986). Without these intermediaries, the fixed costs associated with evaluating all the necessary points investors have to evaluate would be associated with such a task and so, to undertake this costly process, financial intermediaries may be formed by groups of individuals.

The production of information may be stimulated by stock markets. The bigger and more liquid a market is, the greater the incentives to expend resources in obtaining such information on firms as it becomes easier to profit of said information (Holmstrom and Tirole, 1993). Liquid markets allow for information to be acquired more easily and to become disguised by agents and make money through trading it in the market. This will boost incentives to produce more worthy information and will therefore positively affect the allocation of capital (Merton, 1987).

Different market frictions could keep diffuse shareholders from efficiently exercising corporate governance, and therefore permits managers to chase their projects for their own self-interest. There is a large information asymmetry between managers and small shareholders, as the latter often does not possess the required expertise and incentives. In addition, the board may not embody the minority shareholder interests. Legal codes that protect these small shareholders' rights exist in many countries and help to create huge information and contracting charges that restrict diffuse shareholders from successfully exercising corporate governance. Having a large, concentrated owner has its own issues, even though such owners have greater incentives and power (Shleifer and Vishny, 1996; Stulz, 1988). Their presence creates an agency problem, as conflicts will arise amid controlling and other shareholders (Jensen and Meckling, 1976). Controlling owners are often powerful families that exert their power to control corporations and banks and partake in matters that benefit themselves (Claessens et al., 2002; Caprio et al., 2003). Highly focused ownership can interfere with corporate judgments and national policies by curtailing innovation, encouraging rent seeking, and stymieing economic growth.

A large strand of literature highlights how important well-functioning stock markets are in nurturing corporate governance (Jensen and Meckling, 1976). Publicly trading shares allows information on firms to be provided and links stock performance to managers' financial recompense, so as to line up managers' interests with owners' interests (Jensen and Murphy, 1990). Likewise, stock markets can stimulate improved corporate control through the simplification of poorly managed firm takeovers. There are several theoretical models that discuss how debt contracts could emerge and improve corporate governance or how it is well-functioning financial intermediaries that impact growth and improve corporate governance (Townsend, 1979; Boyd and Smith, 1994; Gale and Hellwig, 1985; Diamond, 1984). Bencivenga and Smith (1993) demonstrate how financial intermediaries enhance corporate governance through economizing and monitoring expenses so as to lessen credit regulation and increase productivity, accumulation of capital, and growth. Boyd and Smith (1992) provide a different perspective by showing that country dissimilarities in the financial intermediation quality have vast implications on international capital flows and economic growth rates as a result. Poor financial intermediation results in sub-optimal capital allocation.

Mobilization, otherwise known as pooling, is the pricey method of agglomerating capital from incongruent savers for the purposes of investment. This comprises of overcoming transaction costs and informational asymmetries as the presence of these connects to savings mobilization. As a result, many financial arrangements might arise to alleviate these frictions and assist in pooling. This could take place through several bilateral contracts among units generating capital as well as agents with surplus resources. Pooling may also take place through intermediaries that invest in many businesses (Sirri and Tufano, 1995). Economic development can be profoundly affected by financial systems with a more effective means of pooling savings.

It can enhance the allocation of resources and increase technological innovation. Numerous production methods would be limited to economically unproductive scales without the access to multiple investors, as one sole investor would usually not have the means (Sirri and Tufano, 1995). Bagehot (1873) discusses how England could mobilize resources more than poorer nations, and so projects did not fail due to a lack of capital. Mobilization also often creates small denomination instruments that allow households opportunities to diversify portfolios (Sirri and Tufano, 1995). When it comes to huge, indivisible projects, Acemoglu and Zilibotti (1997) display how financial arrangements that mobilize individual savings and invest them in diversified portfolios ease the investment reallocation to activities with higher returns and positively affect economic growth.

Financial arrangements that decrease transaction expenses can stimulate specialization, technological innovation, and growth. A study by Greenwood and Smith (1996) demonstrates the links concerning exchange, specialization, and innovation—with increased specialization requiring increased transactions. Considering the fact that transactions are costly, this means that any financial arrangements that lessen this cost will only lead to greater specialization. So, productivity gains are then encouraged through markets that stimulate exchange. Since there can also be feedback obtained from such gains, economic development can then spur financial market development.

The Effect of Finance on Growth

Financial development can augment economic growth through two different channels, such as capital accumulation channels and total factor productivity channels. Capital accumulation channels are known as quantitative channels, which are sketched from the "debt-accumulation" hypothesis of Gurley and Shaw (1955). Specifically, the main function of capital accumulation is to entice economic agents to save wealth from their disposable income. Consequently, financial development helps to channel these savings into productive sectors, as investment into projects. Thus, it leads to augment capital accumulation and a large scale of production. Goodhart (2004) states that a deepening financial infrastructure reduces the frictions in the market, such as decreasing the transaction and information cost, which fosters investment and economic growth. Moreover, the functional role of FD is to promote investment and economic growth by facilitating the best productive allocation of resources (Levine, 1997). In this process, the financial development helps to provide the liquidity to firms to explore new capacities in an efficient manner. Financial development thus promotes the establishment and expansion of institutions, financial instruments, and markets that enhance the investment and growth process. However, despite of the plausible role of financial development, the overall outcome from it cannot be generalized across the countries due to country specific economic structure and institutional quality (Al-Yousif, 2002; Law et al. 2013). A number of recent studies provide empirical evidence of the importance of institutional quality for economic performance, for example, see Rodrik et al. (2002), Hall and Jones (1999), and Knack and Keefer (1995), among others. Furthermore, in the context of financial development, empirical evidence suggests that the potential outcome from financial development is largely determined by quality of financial regulation and rule of law (Demetriades and Andrianova, 2004; Arestis and Demetriades, 1996). Thus, it has been immensely important to embed institutional quality in explaining the FD and growth nexus. It can be argued that a standard financial framework may not accrue the growth due to corruption in the banking sector or political intrusion that may distract credit to unproductive or even lavish activities.

A recent study by Ductor and Grechyna (2015) argued that financial development and real sector output are interdependent. Conducting a study on 101 developed and developing countries, they found that the effect of financial development on economic growth depends on the growth of private credit relative to the real output growth. However, if there were rapid growth in private credit not accompanied by growth in real output, then the impact of financial development would be negative.

A strand of empirical studies done on finance and growth evaluates the effect of financial system operations on economic growth, in terms of whether this influence is economically huge and involves specific components. Theory centers on specific financial sector functions and how these impact the allocation of resource decisions and economic growth. Likewise, while empirical studies concentrate on measures of bank or stock market size, Demirgüç-Kunt and Maksimovic (2001), and Fisman and Love (2003a; 2003b) display that businesses regularly play the role of financial intermediaries by offering trade credit to interconnected corporations.

Goldsmith (1969) aimed to evaluate whether finance exercises a causal impact on economic growth. This is done by compiling data on the significance of financial intermediary properties as a portion of economic output. Goldsmith (1969) did not take a stand on the topic in terms of whether financial development causes growth, but his work proposes several issues, since the investigation only involved 35 countries and did not control for the other elements that influenced economic growth. King and Levine (1993a) built upon Goldsmith's study by studying 77 states from 1960 to 1989 and avoided all the pitfalls that Goldsmith came up against. They discover consistent results along different indicators of financial development and, specifically in 1960, financial depth is a good predictor of this once several factors such as income and trade are controlled. While King and Levine (1993a) demonstrate how finance predicts growth, they fail to formally deal with the problem of causality (Shan et al., 2001).

La Porta et al. (2002) study the degree of public bank ownership across the globe. This measure provides direct proof of the link between economic growth and financial intermediary services. The researchers demonstrate that higher public ownership degrees are connected to decreased levels of banking development, while high public ownership levels of banks are connected to slower economic growth. This research does improve on past measures, but its sole focus is on banks. In addition, the indicators La Porta et al. (2002) employ do not evaluate the extent to which financial systems amend transaction and information costs. Levine and Zervos (1998) build various stock market development measures so as to evaluate the relation between economic growth, capital accumulation, and productivity growth in 42 countries. Their research expands upon the pioneering work of Atje and Jovanovic (1993). Levine and Zervos find that both initial stock market liquidity level and initial banking development level are positively and meaningfully interconnected with future economic growth, productivity growth, and capital accumulation rates over the next 18 years. This coincides with the outlook that stock market liquidity enables long-term growth (Bencivenga et al., 1995; Holmstrom and Tirole, 1993), but is inconsistent with models that stress the negative characteristics of stock market liquidity (Bhide, 1993).

However, there are some weaknesses to the approach taken by Levine and Zervos. Although they fail to locate a strong connection between economic growth and the capability of investors to internationally diversify risk, they possess exceptionally restricted information on international integration. Future research requires a more full assessment of the relationship between stock markets, banks, and economic growth.

Instrumental variables that clarify cross-country differences but are not related to economic growth beyond their connection with financial development and other growth determinants are necessary in the process of assessing whether the finance-growth bond is motivated by simultaneity bias. Levine (1998; 1999) and Levine et al. (2000) employ the La Porta et al. (1998) measures of legal origin as instrumental variables. Levine et al. spread out the King and Levine (1993a; 1993b) measures of financial intermediary development by deflating the financial development indicators and by adding a new financial development measure known as private credit, which is the value of credits by financial intermediaries to the private sector divided by GDP. Their results show a very strong link concerning the exogenous financial intermediary development component and long-term economic growth. Levine et al. (2000) have instrumental variable outcomes that also specify an economically great effect of financial development on growth. While they read their outcomes as suggesting that financial development increases steady-state growth, Aghion et al. (2005) contest that deduction. They discover that financial development fails to exercise a direct impact on steady-state growth.

Several studies on the finance-growth nexus are detailed in the literature. Levine et al. (2000) construct a panel for 77 countries from 1960 to 1995, incorporating the variability of the time-series dimension. The benefit of this, however, is that biases associated with cross-country regressions are avoided and more accurate estimates can be provided because instrumental variables for all regressors are used.

Levine et al. (2000) employ the system estimator to study the connection between financial intermediary development and growth, whereas Beck et al. (2000) study the relationship between the sources of growth and financial development. Their results signify there is a positive link between the exogenous financial development component and economic growth, productivity growth, and the accumulation of capital. Other recent research suggests the use of something other than linear models. Rioja and Valev (2004a; 2004b), for example, discover that finance improves growth in rich countries chiefly by accelerating productivity growth, while finance boosts growth in poorer nations chiefly by fast-tracking capital accumulation.

THE FINANCE-GROWTH NEXUS IN MENA COUNTRIES

The MENA countries have, in the past two decades, witnessed a wave of liberalization reform (Ben Naceur et al., 2008). This occurred in the financial sector and involved different features, like lifting government restrictions on bank systems through the interest rate ceiling, and directing credit programs and high reserve requests that enhance financial development and therefore boost economic growth. This study contributes to the literature by considering the potential role of institutional quality. Other than the quality of institutions, it is essential to consider the role of foreign direct investment in explaining the FD-growth nexus. Hermes and Lensink (2003), among others, argued for the link between FDI and FD, wherein the former considered how the influence of FDI on economic growth is conditional on the host country's financial market development. This is intuitive, as financial markets that are functioning well increase FDI inflow productivity through the reduction of risks involved in the investments made by local firms. As argued by Alfaro et al. (2004), the development of the financial market in the host country acts as a vital precondition for positively impacting economic development through FDI. Azman-Saini et al. (2010) reinforces this, arguing that it is a particular level of financial market development that acts as a prerequisite for this nexus.

The studies dealing with the influence of financial development on economic growth for MENA are not copious. The recent study by Samargandi et al. (2015) is a pioneer in the field. In this study, the authors examine the effect financial development has on economic growth by looking at the institutional quality and foreign direct investment of 21 MENA countries over the period of 1980 to 2012. The dependent variable was the gross domestic product per capita in real terms. For the financial development measures, the authors use common indicators—such as domestic credit to the private sector—as a percentage of GDP, as well as the financial sector's liquid liabilities as a percentage of GDP. The other variables consist of general government final consumption expenditure, trade openness, population growth rate per year, foreign direct investment, private investment and its fixed domestic assets, and institutional quality.

Financial Development and Economic Growth: Is There any Role for the Quality of Institutions?

The central point of the research by Samargandi et al. (2015) is the connection between financial development and economic growth. The authors clearly highlight that credit to the private sector (as an important measure of financial development) improves economic growth significantly in the long run. However, the authors reveal that the impact of credit is inconclusive in the short term. They show that the credit-growth nexus is consistent with Levine et al. (2000) and

Loayza and Rancière (2006), who found positive effects of credit on growth. This is a reasonable finding in light of most growth theories, as it is stated that if credit is allocated to an efficient private sector, it increases labor productivity, which is a prominent source of growth. Therefore, it is evident that those MENA economies benefit from credit distributed in the private sector. In the short run, it is shown that time is required for financial development to adjust and result in a positive impact on growth.

The authors measure the dynamic influence of money supply on economic growth and show that fixed capital formation plays a significant part in promoting economic growth in the short and long terms for MENA countries. The economic rationale for such a result is quite appealing. Fixed capital formation leads to an optimum combination of labor and capital, which in turn increases the productivity of labor—as argued in the classical Cobb-Douglas production function. Since most of these countries are characterized by a very inefficient financial sector that is unable to mobilize savings into capital, any addition to fixed capital formation will naturally lead to higher economic growth. Furthermore, none of these countries suffers from the problem of "*too much finance*," which may hamper the stability of economic growth (Arcand et al., 2012).

Regarding the impact of money supply, the authors report a negative and significant coefficient for M2, implying that money supply adversely affects growth in MENA countries. It would happen, as liquidity fosters inflation and return to investment, which leads to decreasing the precautionary saving (Wu et al., 2010). Moreover, to get an optimum outcome from M2, institutional quality is immensely important because of the interfering role it plays in the finance-growth nexus. Rodrik et al. (2002) and Knack and Keefer (1995), among others, have provided empirical evidence on the significance of institutional quality in the realm of economic performance. Due to corruption in the banking sector, a standard financial framework might not arguably accrue growth. For the MENA region, contextualizing institutional quality is vital in describing the FD-growth nexus.

Samargandi et al. (2015) show that as a proxy for financial development, domestic credit to the private sector is significantly enhanced by institutional quality, in the long run, but this is insignificant in the short run. They also display the dynamic influence of institutional quality on financial development in the long run, but not in the short run. The assumption about oil exporting countries is that the quality of governance is better and so with a financial sector that is well developed, a significant impact on economic growth can be witnessed.

Credit to the private sector is rooted in institutional quality and can encourage economic growth over the long term.

Financial Development-Economic Growth: Does FDI Promote This Nexus?

The role of foreign direct investment (FDI) in the FD-growth nexus is considered for several reasons. Numerous studies consider that the financial market and FDI are interlinked and they even argued that FDI is an important measure of financial development (Hermes and Lensink, 2003; Alfaro et al., 2004; Azman-Saini et al., 2010). For example, the model by Hermes and Lensink (2003) argues that the effect of FDI on economic growth is conditional upon the level of financial market development in the host country. The idea is very intuitive, since a well-functioning financial market increases the productivity of FDI inflow by reducing the risks inherent to the investment made by local firms as well as by multinational companies seeking to expand their businesses. Alfaro et al. (2004) argue that the development of the host country's financial market is an important precondition for augmenting the positive influence FDI has on economic development.

The study by Samargandi et al. (2015) shows that the interaction of credit to the private sector and FDI significantly promote economic growth in MENA in the long run. Additionally, when money growth is embedded with FDI, economic growth improves even more in the long run. At the same time, Azman-Saini et al. (2010) also show that a particular level of financial market development is a prerequisite for augmenting the positive impact of FDI on growth. The study argued that as long as the threshold level of development in the financial market does not take place, the positive effect of FDI on economic development becomes negligible. An increased efficiency of financial markets can augment a greater growth potential by providing allocation efficiency in channeling funds to the most desired parts of the economy. Therefore, what is measured is the FDI's effect while interacting with financial development and economic growth in MENA economies. Additionally, in the long run, when FDI is embedded with M2, it augments economic growth.

Conclusion

In this review study, the aim was to assess the significance of development in explaining economic growth in MENA countries. The study found that there is a divergence regarding the impact of financial development on growth, from theoretical and empirical perspectives. With a closer look, we observed that credit to the private sector significantly promotes economic growth in the long run, either in the presence or absence of institutional quality in the model. However, money supply (M2) hinders the long run economic growth in absence of institutional quality, while it promotes growth in the presence of institutional quality in the same model. This study also found that institutional quality enhances credit to the private sector and money supply. Interestingly, this investigation has shown that foreign direct investment augments economic growth through the development of financial markets in the MENA countries. This research provides a new realm of knowledge in the field studying the nexus between financial development and economic growth by considering the mediating role of institutional quality and FDI. However, the findings of this study have potential importance for policymaking, to foster economic growth by developing financial sector, institutional quality, and FDI in the context of MENA countries.

REFERENCES

Acemoglu, D. and Zilibotti, F. (1997). Was Prometheus unbound by chance? Risk, diversification, and growth. *Journal of Political Economy*, 105: 709–775.

Acemoglu, D., Aghion, P., and Zilibotti, F. (2003). Distance to frontier, selection, and economic growth. *NBER Working Paper*, No. 9066. National Bureau of Economic Growth.

Aghion, P., and Howitt, P. (1998). *Endogenous Economic Growth Theory.* Cambridge, MA: MIT Press.

Aghion, P., Angeletos, M., Banerjee, A., and Manova, K. (2004). *Volatility and Growth: The Role of Financial Development.* Mimeo. Department of Economics, Harvard University: Cambridge, MA.

Aghion, P., Howitt, P., and Mayer-Foulkes, D. (2005). The effect of financial development on convergence: Theory and evidence. *Quarterly Journal of Economics*: 323–351.

Alfaro, L., Chanda, A., Kalemli-Ozcan, S., and Sayek, S. (2004). FDI and economic growth: the role of local financial markets. *Journal of international economics*, 64 (1): 89–112.

Allen, F. (1990). The market for information and the origin of financial intermediaries. *Journal of Financial Intermediation*, 1: 3–30.

Allen, F. and Gale, D. (1997). Financial markets, intermediaries, and intertemporal smoothing. *Journal of Political Economy*, 105: 523–546.

Al-Yousif, Y. K. (2002). Financial development and economic growth: another look at the evidence from developing countries. *Review of Financial Economics*, 11 (2), 131–150.

Arcand, J. L., Berkes, E., and Panizza, U. (2012). *Too Much Finance?* International Monetary Fund: Washington, DC.

Arestis, P., and Demetriades, P. (1997). Financial development and economic growth: Assessing the evidence. *Economic Journal*, 107: 783–799.

Atje, R., and Jovanovic, B. (1993). Stock markets and development. *European Economic Review*, 37: 632–640.

Azman-Saini, W. N. W., Baharumshah, A. Z., and Law, S. H. (2010). Foreign direct investment, economic freedom and economic growth: International evidence. *Economic Modelling*, 27 (5): 1079–1089.

Bagehot, W. (1873). *Lombard Street*, 1962 ed. Homewood, IL: Irwin.

Beck, T., Demirgüç-Kunt, A., and Levine, R. (2000). A new database on financial development and structure. *World Bank Economic Review*, 14: 597–605.

Ben Naceur, S., Ghazouani, S., and Omran, M. (2008). Does stock market liberalization spur financial and economic development in the MENA region? *Journal of Comparative Economics*, 36 (4): 673–693.

Bencivenga, V. R. and Smith, B. D. (1993). Some consequences of credit rationing in an endogenous growth model. *Journal of Economic Dynamics and Control*, 17: 97–122.

Bencivenga, V. R., Smith, B. D., and Starr, R. M. (1995). Transactions costs, technological choice, and endogenous growth. *Journal of Economic Theory*, 67: 53–177.

Benhabib, J. and Spiegel, M. M. (2000). The role of financial development in growth and investment. *Journal of Economic Growth*, 5: 341–360.

Berle, A. A. and Means, G. C. (1932). *The Modern Corporation and Private Property*. New York: Harcourt Brace Jovanovich.

Bhattacharya, S. and Pfleiderer, P. (1985). Delegated portfolio management. *Journal of Economic Theory*, 36: 1–25.

Bhide, A. (1993). The hidden costs of stock market liquidity. *Journal of Financial Economics*, 34: 1–51.

Blackburn, K. and Hung, V. T. Y. (1998). A theory of growth, financial development, and trade. *Economica*, 65: 107–124.

Boyd, J. H. and Prescott, E. C. (1986). Financial intermediary-coalitions. *Journal of Economics Theory*, 38: 211– 232.

Boyd, J. H. and Smith, B. D. (1992). Intermediation and the equilibrium allocation of investment capital: Implications for economic development. *Journal of Monetary Economics*, 30: 409–432.

Boyd, J. H. and Smith, B. D. (1994). How good are standard debt contracts? Stochastic versus nonstochastic monitoring in a costly state verification environment. *Journal of Business*, 67: 539–562.

Cameron, R. (1967). "Conclusion," in *Banking in the Early Stages of Industrialization: A Study in Comparative Economic History*, edited by R. Cameron et al. New York: Oxford University Press, 290–321.

Cameron, R., Crisp, O., Patrick, H. T., and Tilly, R. (1967). *Banking in the Early Stages of Industrialization: A Study in Comparative Economic History*. New York: Oxford University Press.

Caprio, G. Jr., Laeven, L., and Levine, R. (2003). Governance and bank valuation. *NBER Working Paper*, No. 10158. National Bureau of Economic Research.

Claessens, S., Djankov, S., Fan, J., and Lang, L. (2002). Disentangling the incentive and entrenchment effects of large shareholdings. *Journal of Finance*, 57: 2741–2771.

de Gregorio, J. (1996). Borrowing constraints, human capital accumulation, and growth. *Journal of Monetary Economics*, 37: 49–71.

Demirgüç-Kunt, A. and Maksimovic, V. (2001). *Firms as Financial Intermediaries: Evidence from Trade Credit Data*. World Bank mimeo: Washington, D.C.

Devereux, M. B. and Smith, G. W. (1994). International risk sharing and economic growth. *International Economic Review*, 35: 535–550.

Diamond, D. W. (1984). Financial intermediation and delegated monitoring. *Review of Economic Studies*, 51: 393–414.

Diamond, D. W. and Dybvig, P. H. (1983). Bank runs, deposit insurance, and liquidity. *Journal of Political Economy*, 91: 401–419.

Diamond, D. W., and Verrecchia, R. E. (1982). Optimal managerial contracts and equilibrium security prices. *Journal of Finance*, 37: 275–287.

Ductor, L. and Grechyna, D. (2015). Financial development, real sector, and economic growth. *International Review of Economics & Finance.*

Fisman, R. J. and Love, I. (2003a). Trade credit, financial intermediary development, and industry growth. *Journal of Finance*, 58: 353–374.

Fisman, R. J., and Love, I. (2003b). Financial development and growth revisited. *NBER Working Paper*, No. 9582. National Bureau of Economic Research.

Gale, D. and Hellwig, M. (1985). Incentive-compatible debt contracts: The one-period problem. *Review of Economics Studies*, 52: 647–663.

Galetovic, A. (1996). Specialization, intermediation and growth. *Journal of Monetary Economics*, 38: 549–559.

Galor, O., and Zeira, J. (1993). Income distribution and macroeconomics. *Review of Economic Studies*, 60: 35–52.

Goldsmith, R. W. (1969). *Financial Structure and Development*. New Haven, CT: Yale University Press.

Goodhart, C. A. (Ed.). (2004). *Financial Development and Economic Growth: Explaining the Links*. Palgrave Macmillan: London, UK.

Greenwood, J. and Jovanovic, B. (1990). Financial development, growth, and the distribution of income. *Journal of Political Economy*, 98: 1076–1107.

Greenwood, J. and Smith, B. (1996). Financial markets in development, and the development of financial markets. *Journal of Economic Dynamics and Control*, 21: 145–181.

Grossman, S. J. and Hart, O. (1980). Takeover bids, the free-rider problem, and the theory of the corporation. *Bell Journal of Economics*, 11: 42–64.

Grossman, S. J., and Stiglitz, J. (1980). On the Impossibility of Informationally Efficient Markets. *American Economic Review*, 70: 393–408.

Guiso, L., Sapienza, P., and Zingales, L. (2002). Does Local Financial Development Matter? *NBER Working Paper*, No. 8922. National Bureau of Economic Research.

Gurley, J. G., and Shaw, E. S. (1955). Financial aspects of economic development. *American Economic Review*, 45: 515–538.

Haber, S. H. (1991). Industrial concentration and the capital markets: A comparative study of Brazil, Mexico, and the United States, 1830–1930. *Journal of Economic History*, 51: 559–580.

Haber, S. H. (1997). "Financial Markets and Industrial Development: A Comparative Study of Governmental Regulation, Financial Innovation and Industrial Structure in Brazil and Mexico, 1840–1940," in *How Latin America Fell Behind?*, edited by S. Haber. Stanford, CA: Stanford University Press, 146–178.

Hermes, N., and Lensink, R. (2003). Foreign direct investment, financial development and economic growth. *The Journal of Development Studies*, 40 (1): 142–163.

Holmstrom, B., and Tirole, J. (1993). Market liquidity and performance monitoring. *Journal of Political Economy*, 101: 678–709.

Holmstrom, B., and Tirole, J. (1998). Private and public supply of liquidity. *Journal of Political Economy*, 106: 1–40.

Jacoby, H. G. (1994). Borrowing constraints and progress through school: Evidence from Peru. *Review of Economics and Statistics*, 76: 151–160.

Jayaratne, J., and Strahan, P. E. (1996). The finance-growth nexus: Evidence from bank branch deregulation. *Quarterly Journal of Economics*, 111: 639–670.

Jensen, M., and Meckling, W. R. (1976). Theory of the firm, managerial behavior, agency costs and ownership structure. *Journal of Financial Economics*, 3: 305–360.

Jensen, M., and Murphy, K. (1990). Performance pay and top management incentives. *Journal of Political Economy*, 98: 225–263.

Jorgenson, D. W. (1995). *Productivity*. Cambridge, MA: MIT Press.

Jorgenson, D. W. (2005). Accounting for Growth in the Information Age, in *Handbook of Economic Growth*, edited by P. Aghion, S. Durlauf, Vol. 1A. Amsterdam: North-Holland/Elsevier.

King, R. G. and Levine, R. (1993a). Finance and growth: Schumpeter might be right. *Quarterly Journal of Economics*, 108: 717–738.

King, R. G. and Levine, R. (1993b). Finance, entrepreneurship, and growth: Theory and evidence. *Journal of Monetary Economics*, 32: 513–542.

Knack S, & Keefer P. (1995). Institutions and economic performance: cross-country tests using alternative institutional measures. *Economics and Politics*, 7: 207–227.

Kyle, A. S. (1984). "Market Structure, Information, Futures Markets, and Price Formation," in *International Agricultural Trade: Advanced Readings in Price Formation, Market Structure, and Price Instability*, edited by G.G. Storey, A. Schmitz, A. H. Sarris. Boulder, CO: Westview.

La Porta, R., Lopez-de-Silanes, F., and Shleifer, A. (2002). Government ownership of commercial banks. *Journal of Finance*, 57: 265–301.

La Porta, R., Lopez-de-Silanes, F., Shleifer, A., and Vishny, R. (1999). Corporate ownership around the world. *Journal of Finance*, 54: 471–517.

La Porta, R., Lopez-de-Silanes, F., Shleifer, A., and Vishny, R. (2000). Investor protection and corporate governance. *Journal of Financial Economics*, 58: 3–27.

La Porta, R., Lopez-de-Silanes, F., Shleifer, A., and Vishny, R. W. (1998). Law and finance. *Journal of Political Economy*, 106: 1113–1155.

Levhari, D. and Srinivasan, T. N. (1969). Optimal savings under uncertainty. *Review of Economic Studies*, 35: 153–163.

Levine, R. (1991). Stock markets, growth, and tax policy. *Journal of Finance*, 46: 1445–1465.

Levine, R. (1998). The legal environment, banks, and long-run economic growth. *Journal of Money, Credit, and Banking*, 30: 596–613.

Levine, R. (1999). Law, finance, and economic growth. *Journal of Financial Intermediation*, 8: 36–67.

Levine, R., and Zervos, S. (1998). Stock markets, banks, and economic growth. *American Economic Review*, 88: 537–558.

Levine, R., Loayza, N., and Beck, T. (2000). Financial intermediation and growth: Causality and causes. *Journal of Monetary Economics*, 46 (1): 31–77.

Loayza, N. V. and Rancière, R. (2006). Financial development, financial fragility, and growth. *Journal of Money, Credit and Banking*, 38 (4): 1051–1076.

McKinnon, R. I. (1973). *Money and Capital in Economic Development*. Washington, DC: Brookings Institution.

Merton, R. C. (1987). A simple model of capital market equilibrium with incomplete information. *Journal of Finance*, 42: 483–510.

Merton, R. C. and Bodie, Z. (1995). A Conceptual Framework for Analyzing the Financial Environment, in *The Global Financial System: A Functional Perspective*, edited by D. B. Crane et al. Boston, MA: Harvard Business School Press, 3–31.

Miller, M. H. (1998). Financial markets and economic growth. *Journal of Applied Corporate Finance*, 11: 8–14.

Morales, M. F. (2003). Financial intermediation in a model of growth through creative destruction. *Macroeconomic Dynamics*, 7: 363–393.

Morck, R., Stangeland, D., and Yeung, B. (2000). Inherited Wealth, Corporate Control, and Economic Growth: The Canadian Disease, in *Concentrated Corporate Ownershi*, edited by R. Morck. National Bureau of Economics Research: Cambridge, MA.

Obstfeld, M. (1994). Risk-taking, global diversification, and growth. *American Economic Review*, 84: 1310–1329.

Petersen, M. A. and Rajan, R. G. (1997). Trade credit: Some theories and evidence. *Review of Financial Studies*, 10: 661–692.

Ramakrishnan, R. T. S. and Thakor, A. (1984). Information reliability and a theory of financial intermediation. *Review of Economic Studies*, 51: 415–432.

Rioja, F. and Valev, N. (2004a). Finance and the sources of growth at various stages of economic development. *Economic Inquiry*, 42: 27–40.

Rioja, F. and Valev, N. (2004b). Does one size fit all?: A reexamination of the finance and growth relationship. *Journal of Development Economics*, 74 (2): 429–447.

Robinson, J. (1952). The generalization of the General Theory, in *The Rate of Interest and Other Essays*. London: MacMillan: 67–142.

Rodrik, D., Subramanian, A., & Trebbi, F. (2002). Institutions rule: the primacy of institutions over integration and geography in economic development. *IMF Working Paper*, No. 189.

Rousseau, P. L. (1998). The permanent effects of innovation on financial depth: Theory and US historical evidence from unobservable components models. *Journal of Monetary Economics*, 42: 387–425.

Rousseau, P. L. (1999). Finance, investment, and growth in Meiji-era Japan. *Japan and the World Economy*, 11: 185–198.

Rousseau, P. L. and Sylla, R. (1999). Emerging financial markets and early U.S. growth. *NBER Working Paper*, No. 7448. National Bureau of Economic Research.

Rousseau, P. L. and Sylla, R. (2001). Financial system, economic growth, and globalization. *NBER Working Paper*, No. 8323. National Bureau of Economic Research.

Saint-Paul, G. (1992). Technological choice, financial markets and economic development. *European Economic Review*, 36: 763–781.

Samargandi, N., Sohag, K., & Ben Ali, M. S. (2015). The Financial Development-Growth Nexus in MENA Countries: Which Role for Institutions and FDI? Forthcoming.

Scharfstein, D. (1988). The disciplinary role of takeovers. *Review of Economic Studies*, 55: 185–199.

Schumpeter, J. A. (1912 [1934]). Theorie der wirtschaftlichen Entwicklung, in *The Theory of Economic Development*, edited by Dunker and Humblot, Leipzig, translated by R. Opie. Cambridge, MA: Harvard University Press.

Shan, J. Z., Morris, A. G., and Sun, F. (2001). Financial development and economic growth: An egg and chicken problem? *Review of International Economics*, 9: 443–454.

Shleifer, A., and Vishny, R. W. (1996). Large shareholders and corporate control. *Journal of Political Economy*, 94: 461–488.

Sirri, E. R., and Tufano, P. (1995). The Economics of Pooling, in *The Global Financial System: A Functional Approach*, edited by D. B. Crane et al. Boston, MA: Harvard Business School Press, 81–128.

Stein, J. C. (1988). Takeover threats and managerial myopia. *Journal of Political Economy*, 96: 61–80.

Stiglitz, J., and Weiss, A. (1983). Incentive effects of terminations: Applications to credit and labor markets. *American Economic Review*, 73 (5): 912–927.

Stulz, R. (1988). Managerial control of voting rights: Financing policies and the market for corporate control. *Journal of Financial Economics*, 20: 25–54.

Townsend, R. M. (1979). Optimal contracts and competitive markets with costly state verification. *Journal of Economic Theory*, 21: 265–293.

Wu, J. L., Hou, H., and Cheng, S. Y. (2010). The dynamic impacts of financial institutions on economic growth: Evidence from the European Union. *Journal of Macroeconomics*, 32 (3): 879–891.

Xu, Z. (2000). Financial development, investment, and growth. *Economic Inquiry*, 38: 331–344.

8

Trade Diversification and Intra-Regional Trade in North Africa

Audrey Verdier-Chouchane, Mohamed Sami Ben Ali, and Charlotte Karagueuzian

Examination of the growth phases in developed and in developing countries and their involvement in international trade shows the importance of trade policies in these countries. In recent decades, many developing countries have made great efforts to liberalize their trade. North Africa is a developing region whose foreign trade plays an important and growing role in the economy. Many countries have established growth promotion policies driven by exports, evidenced by the signing of several bilateral and multilateral agreements.

Despite their openness and commercial signs of cooperation agreements, the geographical distribution of North Africa's foreign trade remains focused on Europe. Furthermore, regional trade integration in North Africa has essentially been a state-driven process, and governments have been reluctant to trust their neighbors and to liberalize their national economy. As a result, while having set ambitious targets for market integration schemes, North African countries have a dismal implementation record on regional integration measures as well as poor trade performances. The movement of goods in total exemption from duty and taxes within the region is still not achieved.

Geographical concentration of foreign trade is a risk and trade diversification is a foreground issue for these North African economies. The recent economic crisis in the euro zone and its spillover effects on the demand for North African products should act as an incentive to diversify markets and to stimulate exports to new destinations.

Moreover, regional trade integration is a response to the difficulties faced by these countries to remain competitive in an increasingly globalized world, as it fosters economies of scale, reduces production costs, increases access to markets, and improves transmission of technological innovations as well as value addition. Regional trade integration is also a means to foster peace and stability between neighboring countries through increased dialog and economic interdependencies. Moreover, in the post-Arab Spring context, regional trade integration has become an opportunity for North African states to boost their economy in order to address the social pressing demands.

This chapter intends to discuss the challenge of regional trade integration in North Africa in a changing political and economic context. We consider six North African countries as defined by the African Development Bank Group: Algeria, Egypt, Libya, Mauritania, Morocco, and Tunisia. The first section analyzes current trends, opportunities, and challenges of regional trade integration in North Africa as well as the unbalanced Euro-Mediterranean partnership. The second section formulates some key policy recommendations to accelerate the process of regional trade integration for the sake of North Africa's economic development. The last section is the conclusion.

Understanding Trade Performances in North Africa

North African countries belong to many different Regional Economic Communities (REC), but their most effective trade agreements have been signed on a bilateral basis with the European Union (EU). The first section reviews the deadlock of intra-regional trade from institutional and an economic points of view and considers Euro-Mediterranean integration as an unbalanced partnership with North Africa. The very strong links that North Africa has maintained with the EU are also an impediment to trade development within the region and with other trade partners. Finally, the section recaps the key constraints to trade integration within the region.

The Deadlock of Intra-Regional Trade in North Africa

Despite recurrent calls for ending the Arab Maghreb Union (AMU) deadlock, the situation has not changed much in the last two decades. From an institutional point of view, the trade integration process has been very slow, and is far more advanced between North African countries and other RECs than between AMU members. Furthermore,

North Africa is the least integrated region in the world, with little intraregional and international trade flows.

The Slow Regional Integration Process

The institutionalization of trade integration in North Africa has been a very slow process. North African countries have signed various regional economic agreements, mainly with the Arab world, the EU, and sub-Saharan Africa (see Figure 8.1). No single REC unites the six North African countries, with the exception of the Arab League

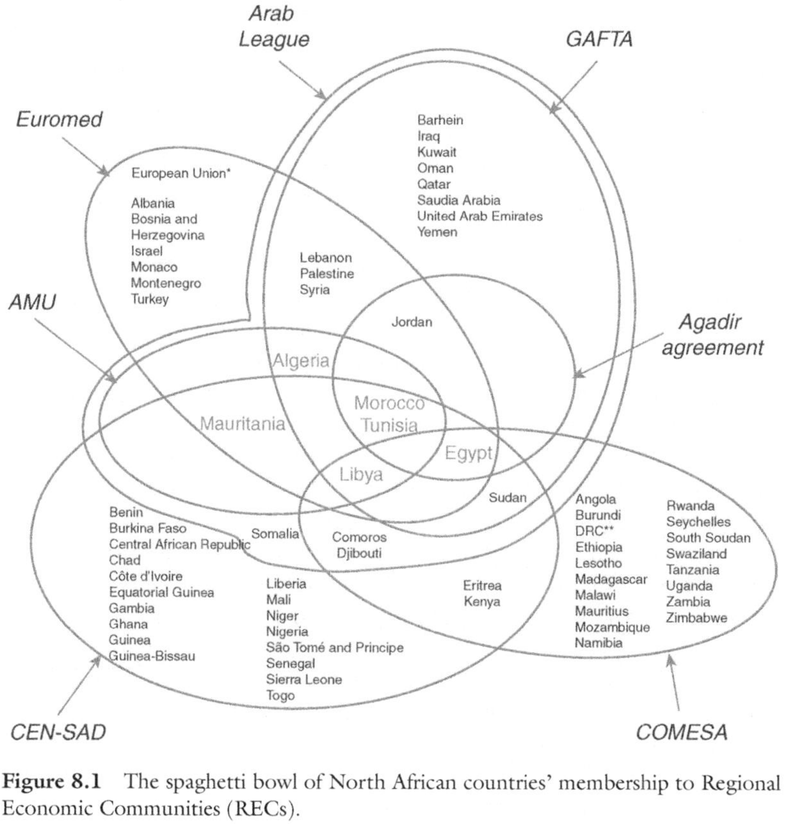

Figure 8.1 The spaghetti bowl of North African countries' membership to Regional Economic Communities (RECs).

* The European Union (EU) includes the following 28 member countries: Austria, Belgium, Bulgaria, Croatia, Cyprus, Czech Republic, Denmark, Estonia, Finland, France, Germany, Greece, Hungary, Ireland, Italy, Latvia, Lithuania, Luxembourg, Malta, Netherlands, Poland, Portugal, Romania, Slovakia, Slovenia, Spain, Sweden, and the United Kingdom.

** DRC: Democratic Republic of Congo.

Source: Authors.

created in 1945. The most important REC in the region is the Arab Maghreb Union (AMU) comprising all North African countries but Egypt (Egypt applied to join the AMU grouping in 1994 for permanent observer status and possible membership). Established in 1989, the AMU committed itself to the creation of a free trade area by removing both tariff and nontariff barriers, with the aim of gradually achieving full trade liberalization. Yet, in practice, progress toward the establishment of a common market with intra-AMU free movements of goods, services, and people—that was originally planned for 2000—is slow. Major reasons for the limited progress of the AMU's integration process are the political tensions. In this context, trade in AMU remains hampered by the numerous nontariff and regulatory barriers, a signal that governments are reluctant to liberalize trade with their immediate neighbors. The AMU hasn't organized a summit since 1994 and has been quasi-inactive since its creation. In 2010, although countries signed a new agreement to revive the free trade area process, to achieve food security, and to create the Maghreb Bank of Investment and External Trade (BMICE), these regional initiatives have been poorly implemented (UNECA, 2013).

In contrast, progress has been more relevant in other RECs to which North African countries belong. For instance, the Greater Arab Free Trade Area (GAFTA) established a Free Trade Area (FTA) for agricultural and industrial commodities in 2005 and improved customs clearance procedures between the 18 member countries. The average uniform tariff equivalent of all tariffs was reduced from 14.7 percent in 2002 to 5.9 percent in 2009 (Chauffour, 2010). The Arab League launched negotiations to liberalize services and investment and to upgrade GAFTA into a customs union by 2015. Indeed, due to regional differences in regulations as well as restrictions on the issues of movement of people and currency convertibility, it is currently easier for North African countries to operate outside the Arab region (Shui and Walkenhorst, 2010). Nonetheless, the labor market in the Arab countries is increasingly integrated at the regional level, and workers from labor-abundant countries such as Egypt, Morocco, and Tunisia move to resource-rich countries in the Gulf (World Bank, 2010). In COMESA, members have established a common market since 2000. Egypt, Jordan, Morocco, and Tunisia contracted the Agadir Agreement in 2004, which entered into force in 2007 and resulted in the liberalization of trade in agriculture and industrial products so far.

North Africa has also increasingly traded with the United-States, Algeria and Tunisia have signed Trade and Investment Facilitation

Agreements (TIFAs), while Egypt has embarked on the Qualified Industrial Zone (QIZ) with the United States (Al Khouri, 2008). Furthermore, in 2004, Morocco joined the United States-Middle East Free Trade Area (USMFTA) by signing a bilateral Free Trade Agreement (FTA) with the United States.

Nevertheless, the largest trading partner of North African countries remains the EU. Even if limited progress has been achieved with regard to the 1995 aim of the Euro-Mediterranean Partnership of creating a free trade area in the Mediterranean, North African countries have traded extensively with the EU within the frame of bilateral association agreements. On the one hand, the Barcelona process achieved the gradual removal of tariffs for manufactured goods. Trade facilitation measures, including on standards, conformity, and harmonized accumulation of origin, have been realized. On the other hand, the liberalization of agriculture, investment, and services has been limited. The establishment of the Mediterranean union in 2008, which aimed at reviving the integration process, in addition to expanding the partnership between 16 Mediterranean countries and the EU, has been suspended as a result of the 2008/2009 global financial crisis that strongly affected Europe.

In the case of North Africa, overlapping membership sometimes results as an impediment to further trade integration. It can be complicated in customs unions, since all members must align on a common external tariff and follow specific rules. For instance, the Agadir agreement performs well in the enforcement of obligations by member countries as it builds heavily on GAFTA and bilateral association agreements with the EU. However, key policy areas such as Rule of Origin (RoO) remain problematic, since some member countries of the Agadir agreement follow the Euromed accumulation of origin (which allows for accumulation of inputs among member countries to qualify for preferential tariffs), while others follow GAFTA's more restrictive RoO requiring that more than 40 percent of the commodity's added value come from a single other member country of the agreement to benefit from tariff relief. This rule has been created by GAFTA on a temporary basis, but no further negotiations have been undertaken to come up with less strict rules of origin (Brunel and Hufbauer, 2013). Also, the United States—Middle East FTA administers different systems of rules of origins and the United States insists that all countries in the region follow restrictive RoOs. These conflicting regimes are an impediment to trade harmonization prospects between North Africa and the Middle East. Familiarizing and complying with the "spaghetti bowl" of RoO is costly and burdensome for firms, especially for small and medium enterprises (SMEs) that have to pursue different production runs depending on export destination. It also prevents the creation of integrated supply chains for commodities whose inputs are originating from different countries.

However, no overlapping membership presents primary constraints to advancing regional integration in Africa (AfDB, 2014). This kind of issue can be resolved in the near future, and does not fully explain the very disappointing trade performances in North Africa.

Disappointing North Africa's Trade Performances

In addition to the AMU deadlock at the institutional level, North Africa is the least integrated region in Africa, together with the Central African region (UNCTAD, 2014). In 2012, AMU exported a total of USD 169.4 billion to the rest of the world, which represented 0.92 percent of total world exports (UNCTAD, 2014). Furthermore, the share of intra-regional trade within the AMU accounted for less than 4 percent over 1995–2012 (see Figure 8.2). As a comparison, in 2012, intra-regional trade in the MENA represented 13.6 percent and 61.8 percent in the EU. The economic cost of this "non-Maghreb" is huge, as many authors have evidenced. For Bchir et al. (2006), Santi

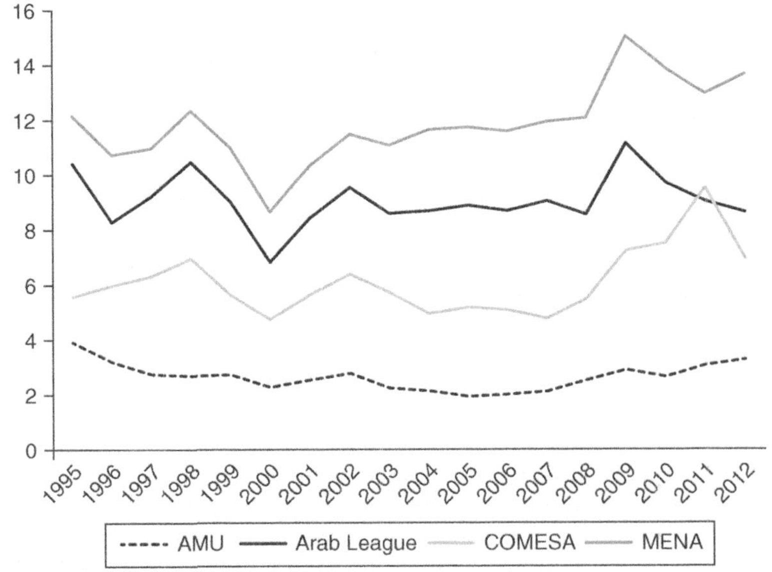

Figure 8.2 Intra-regional trade in selected RECs (%)—1995–2012.

Source: Authors based on UNCTAD (2014).

et al. (2012), as well as Oueslati and Brini (2013), the cost of this lack of regional integration has been estimated between 2 to 3 percent of GDP, with adverse consequences to employment.

As far as export diversification is concerned, North Africa performance is insufficient (see Figure 8.3). The region's main drivers are hydrocarbons (Algeria and Libya), industrial minerals (Mauritania) including phosphates (Morocco and Tunisia), as well as a relatively developed manufacturing sector in Morocco, Tunisia and, to a lesser extent, Egypt.

This lack of economic diversification is generally considered an impediment to increased trade in the region. Even in the most diversified economies, Havrylyshyn and Kunzel (2000) have empirically demonstrated that exporting the same products does not support intra-regional trade. The World Bank (2014) argues that economies similarly endowed in resources, production capabilities, and export structures have limited potential for regional trade as they cannot specialize in and diversify their exports. For De Wulf and Maliszewska (2009), the low level of complementarity in the region limits the accumulation prospects between North African countries. However, Chaponnière and Lautier. (2014) argue that the lack of complementarity is not a real constraint to regional trade in North Africa, pointing out the success of the Association of Southeast Asian Nations

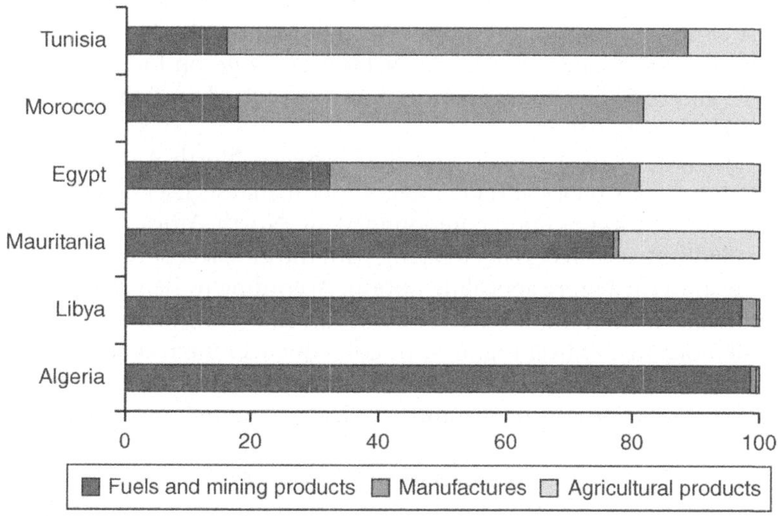

Figure 8.3 Export breakdown in 2013 (% merchandise exports).

Source: Authors based on UNCTAD (2014).

(ASEAN) model, which is based on intra-industry regional trade rather than inter-industry. Following this argument, North African countries would thus gain in developing an intra-industry regional trade made of more sophisticated items and, thus, greater value addition. According to the World Bank (2008), intra-industry trade is indeed a means to promote regional trade for countries with similar export structures. The main constraints to trade integration in North Africa are thus more related to political economy, to trade policy, and also to infrastructure deficits that hamper cross-border trade.

Key Constraints to Trade Integration in North Africa

The slow process of trade integration at the institutional level and the low intra-regional trade have been shaped by political tensions and distrust between North African countries, which has led to the upholding of protectionist trade policies at the national level. Furthermore, the lack of infrastructure, poor logistics, and cross-border trade facilitation have made regional trade a costly process and thus discouraged its development.

Political Considerations

Political tensions have certainly delayed the process of integration in North Africa. For example, since 1994, the 1,600-kilometer border between Algeria and Morocco has been closed for political reasons, including the dispute over the Western Sahara. It is one of the longest closed frontiers in the world. Algeria, Mauritania, Morocco, and Tunisia implemented the United Nations embargo on Libya between 1992 and 2003 and, in retribution, Libya boycotted the AMU (Brunel and Hufbauer, 2013).

The lack of trust and cooperation between North African states, which hampers regional trade integration, manifests itself in concerns over state "sovereignty," compounded by North African countries' decidedly mixed success in engaging with the global economy, making protectionism a more appealing option. According to Ben Ahmed and Othmani (2014), the absence of political will is attributed to a deficit of democratic political regimes. In consequence, the recent developments in the region could be seen as an opportunity to reinitiate the process and to better involve the civil society and the private sector.

Protectionism as a Trade Policy

The abuse of nontariff barriers and strong resistance to trade liberalization remains a major constraint to North African regional trade. For Ncube et al. (2015), countries face a timeframe challenge, as

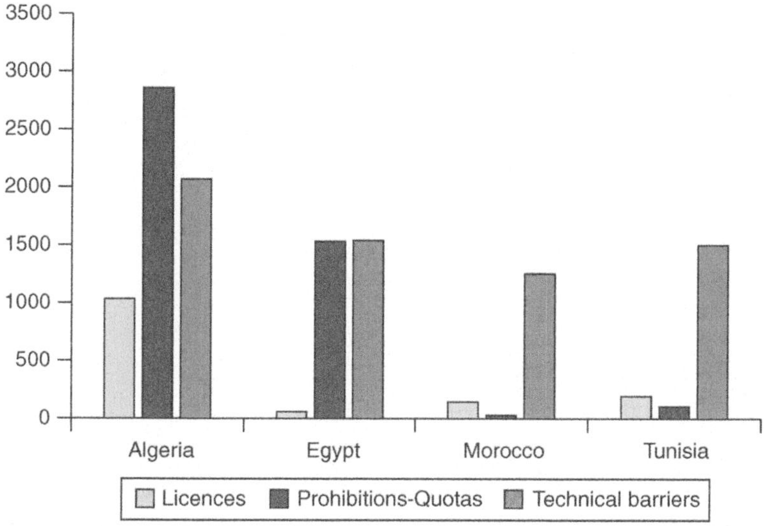

Figure 8.4 Non-tariff barriers in North Africa (number of products).
Source: Authors, based on World Bank (2012).

most of the benefits of regional integration accrue over the long run. However, the costs of regional integration are felt in the short term. Indeed, the removal of tariffs is immediately costly for member countries, as it leads to a loss of public revenue. Nonetheless, it allows regional trade agreements to be effective and beneficial in the longer term. North African countries still continue to apply a high level of protection between themselves in the form of customs tariffs but, even more acutely, nontariff barriers (Lopez-Calix et al., 2010). As shown in Figure 8.4, the two major nontariff barriers are technical measures—such as health, phytosanitary measures, and technical standards—and measures of quantity control—including import licenses, quotas, and prohibitions. All North African countries apply technical barriers, knowing that members of the Euromed Partnership align with the European standards.

Trade Infrastructure Issues

Another major impediment to regional trade in North Africa is the high cost of regional trade resulting from poor logistics, infrastructure, and trade facilitation at borders. North African countries have lower trade costs with the EU than between themselves. Figure 8.5 indicates that trade costs are twice as high from North Africa to the

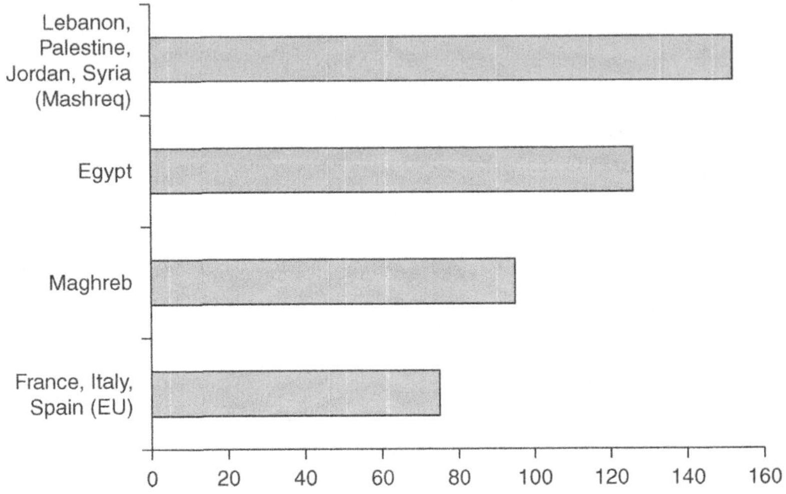

Figure 8.5 Trade costs for industrial products (%) from Maghreb to selected destinations.

Source: Authors, based on World Bank (2012).

Middle East than from North Africa to the EU. The World Bank (2010) argues that this is the result of the small road network in the region. Indeed, marine transport is predominating, while road and rail services are underdeveloped and costly.

According to the 2014 Enabling Trade Index (ETI) of the World Economic Forum (WEF, 2014), given their manufacturing base, Egypt, Morocco, and Tunisia tend to perform well in terms of availability of infrastructure, including transport infrastructure as well as transport services (referring to logistics quality and how easy and affordable it is to arrange international shipments). Morocco in particular has implemented an ambitious program to develop infrastructure in all modes (airports, ports, rails, and roads). In contrast, Algeria and Libya's transport infrastructure is still insufficient, whereas these two huge countries are in the middle of the North African region. With regard to customs modernization and other administrative procedures at the border, North African countries have undertaken important reforms since the 1990s. Morocco and Tunisia are more advanced on this issue as compared to other North African countries.

In conclusion, the key constraints to regional integration in North Africa reflect the importance of political economy considerations. Indeed, without the political will to effectively integrate within the region, liberalization measures and investment in infrastructure will not be implemented. North African countries have rather chosen to primarily trade with the EU, and in large volumes, and this has important implications for North African trade integration.

The Unbalanced Euro-Mediterranean Integration

Algeria, Egypt, Morocco, and Tunisia signed the Euro-Mediterranean Partnership on a bilateral basis in 2002, 2004, 2000, and 1995, respectively. The largest trading partner of North Africa represents on average nearly 60 percent of North Africa's exports and 55 percent of North Africa's imports (World Bank, 2014). However, as shown in Appendix A8.1, Euromed agreements have increased North African countries' imports from—rather than its exports to—the EU. With the exception of Algeria, whose exports to the EU are essentially fuels, the Euromed integration has led to trade balance deficits as well as to the diversion of North African countries' attention from regional initiatives.

The EU policy toward North African states has been often criticized, as it excludes the private sector from the integration process. Furthermore, while the European Neighborhood Policy tailored "action plans" between the EU and North African countries to promote economic reforms and liberalization in North Africa, the Union for the Mediterranean excludes these components, and is therefore even more state-focused (Kauch and Youngs, 2009). Notwithstanding a good financial and institutional background, Euromed did not focus on private sector development, thereby contributing to the region's weak export performance. Indeed, emerging markets like China, Mexico, Thailand, and Turkey experienced a more dynamic export performance to the EU than did North Africa, as measured by the number of new export categories and the share to total export (Ulgen, 2011).

This situation clearly calls for not only a rethinking of North Africa's partnership with the EU, but also within the region and with other partners, building on a more dynamic private sector. With the end of the predatorily dictatorial regimes in North Africa, the time has come to release the private economic strengths in order to foster regional integration.

RETHINKING NORTH AFRICA'S TRADE

There is a need to reactivate the North African integration effort as it offers a means to promote trade and economic growth and further diversifies the region's end markets. AMU could make trade less costly by developing infrastructure, harnessing regional financial integration, and supporting competitive regional and global value chains. The benefits of regional integration should be clearly acknowledged in a region where countries share a common language, history and culture, a high level of education, and the Mediterranean coastline. In light of the unwillingness among North African states to cede sovereignty to the regional level, the new regional integration agenda could be built upon the private sector initiative and the development of regional value chains. Given their generally poor trade performances at the regional level, North African countries should also diversify trade partners, look around for additional trade opportunities to the East and to the South, and reconsider their partnership with the North.

Involving the Private Sector

The slow progress of regional trade integration in North Africa under the leadership of the AMU has been increasingly criticized by economic actors in the region. A more integrated North African region doesn't need to be solely the initiative of states, it can also result from private sector initiatives. The private sector has been more and more "entrepreneurial," in terms of entering the debate and reviving the regional integration process—through a series of initiatives—at the institutional level, through a series of initiatives. It stands ready to enter regional value chains, to produce at a greater scale for a larger market, and to create productive employment. After the Arab Spring, public finances are in a critical situation in many North African countries and public employment is no longer an option to solve the unemployment issue, especially for young graduates.

Recent Initiatives from the Private Sector

The Maghreb Employers Union (UME) was created in 2007 by five North African employers' organizations in Algeria, Libya, Mauritania, Morocco, and Tunisia. The UME intends to effectively implement AMU policies, with a focus on infrastructure and market connectivity. It seeks to promote public-private partnerships, to remove trade barriers and resume dialog on the customs union. North African firms plead for the connecting of the customs authorities and simplifying the customs procedures through information and communications technology. The UME also wants the free movement of persons with the abolition of visas. More generally, the action plan adopted by the UME (Konsentio, 2013) to facilitate regional trade is aimed at influencing AMU's decision-making institutions and making administrative procedures more transparent.

More recent initiatives by the private sector include a roundtable summit held in October 2013, in partnership with the United Nations Economic Commission for Africa (UNECA), on financial integration as a means to foster regional trade and investment. Participants recommended the establishment of a regional fund to support SMEs and acknowledged the need—together with the Maghreb Banks Union and the Maghreb Employers Union—to lobby decision-makers to foster financial integration (UNECA, 2014). In February 2014, the third North African entrepreneurs' forum resulted in the creation of the Maghreb Initiative of Trade and Investment (IMCI) to support the UME and—more globally—the AMU, with a roadmap to foster economic integration.

Although these private initiatives have been limited by political dissensions and slow progress, they clearly indicate the rationale behind regional integration of the private sector in North Africa. Building upon that, the private sector is ready for greater openness in the region, waiting for policymakers to take the right decisions. The new economic and political context gives hope for the improvement of the business climate and competitiveness at the national level, together with positive regional effects. Most North African governments are currently elaborating strategies to diversify their economy and enhance private sector development to curb unemployment and respond to the socioeconomic demands. There should be mechanisms to make the governments more accountable with regard to the implementation of the integration process. For instance, the African Development Bank (AfDB) (2014) recommends the adoption of rule-based enforcement as well as monitoring and evaluation mechanisms. If the public and private sectors move together toward further regional integration, they will be able to build regional value chains.

Addressing the Challenge of Global Value Chains

North Africa's current integration within Global Value Chains (GVCs) is limited. From 1975 to 2008, the share of North African countries' manufactured exports in global exports only increased by a little more than 1 percent (Santi et al., 2012). North African economies still remain dependent on oil, natural resources, tourism, and remittances. Even the most diversified countries in the region export only few manufactured items (essentially, automobile spare parts, chemical products, clothing, garments, leather, and textile), which are very much labor intensive with low technological content. This kind of output often relies on imported inputs and mainly consists of outsourcing the completion of unfinished commodities abroad, essentially, to the European Union.

A key challenge for North African oil producers is to reverse their strong reliance on exports from extractive resource industries, which provides few incentives to develop forward and backward linkages with their national and regional economies or to diversify their industrial export base. All North African countries need to diversify their products and focus on more sophisticated commodities to add value to the production. The AfDB (2014) indicates that if countries have not yet reached the stage to fully benefit from global value chains, given their dependence on raw material production, linking to regional value chains is becoming a more realistic proposition. For Ben Ahmed and Othmani (2014), gas, oil, and phosphate could be for North Africa what coal and steel were for Europe's integration in the past. As a key component in fertilizers, phosphates could also allow agricultural productivity gains and ensure food security in the region.

Regional firms need to acquire and upgrade their technology and skills to compete at the regional and, ultimately, international levels, and export items with higher value addition. Value chain development is supported by regional infrastructure, financial integration, and the freer movement of persons; nonetheless, the access to different production networks remains crucial for unlocking competitive value chains. Member countries' economies need to have some degree of complementarity to integrate successfully and, according to Koffi Ehoussou (2005), there is more potential complementarity at the regional than at the bilateral level in North Africa. For example, Morocco and Tunisia experience a much more dynamic rate of private sector development coupled with significant financial needs, while Algeria and Libya exhibit a surplus of capital and represent a growing market for goods and services coming from within the region. The region could also develop an integrated energy market to fill intra-regional gaps, and needs to unlock its full potential. Investment liberalization at the regional level would also increase Foreign Direct Investments (FDI) attracted by enlarged markets and lower marginal cost of production. The potential is huge and North Africa would benefit from a greater openness to other markets, notably, given North Africa's strategic location on the world map.

The Strategic Geographical Location of North Africa: Diversifying Markets

The proximity of North Africa to the Middle East, sub-Saharan Africa, and Europe provides a strategic location for the region to diversify markets and rethink the unbalanced Euromed at a time when growth in Europe is very slow. The last forecasts by the IMF (2014a) indicate a GDP growth at 1.4 percent in the Euro area, against 4.8 percent in the MENA region and 5.8 percent in sub-Saharan Africa.

Removing Nontariff Barriers to the East

Despite regional agreements, intra-Middle East and North Africa (MENA) trade is a small fraction of North African countries' total trade. With the exception of Egypt, North African countries don't trade extensively with the Arab countries (see Appendix A8.2). Algeria and Libya have recently accelerated their exports to the MENA, but they mainly export fuels. The main obstacle to trade between North Africa and the Middle East is the nontariff measures, which are the highest in the world. The costs of complying with nontariff barriers have been estimated at 10 percent of the price of the exported commodity (Zarrouk, 2003). As described in section 2.1.1, the current divergent and complex sets of RoO also discourage regional FDI and trade (Ulgen, 2011). North African countries should work toward the elimination of nontariff barriers and the harmonization of the RoO to leverage the full potential of regional trade in the MENA region. The effective implementation of GAFTA would be a means to foster trade in the MENA, as well as to enhance its negotiating position against other powerful economic blocs such as the EU.

Looking Down the South

Sub-Saharan African countries experience a high rate of economic growth and represent a fast-growing market of over 870 million people (Malka, 2013). Demand for consumer goods in sub-Saharan Africa is rising as a result of a growing middle class, and constitutes an opportunity for North Africa's trade. The challenge for North African countries would be to diversify their export structure to deal with an increasing part of sub-Saharan Africa's prospective markets. Appendix A8.2 indicates that North African countries have increased trade with sub-Saharan Africa over the last decade. More specifically, Morocco has clearly increased its trade relationship with sub-Saharan Africa since 2009, as well as with Egypt since 2007. Burdensome procedures, tariff and nontariff barriers, cost of transportation, and corruption at the border are the most important impediments to trade between North African and sub-Saharan African countries. Tariffs vary greatly across countries in the continent. For instance, an Ethiopian exporter to Tunisia faces a mean protection rate of 50.4 percent, while a Tunisian exporter to Ethiopia faces a protection rate of 15.7 percent. In contrast, the average protection rate for Moroccan exports to Nigeria is 65.7 percent against 17.6 percent for Nigerian exports to Morocco (Mevel and Karingi, 2012).

The example of Morocco should be followed by other North African countries as a win-win strategy. For instance, Morocco has many bilateral trade agreements in Africa as well as an FTA with the West African Economic and Monetary Union (WAEMU) and the Central African Economic and Monetary Union (CEMAC). Although only 5 percent of its exports are directed toward sub-Saharan Africa, they increased by a tenfold factor between 2000 and 2013—from USD 0.12 billion to USD 1.2 billion (Appendix A8.2). Currently, agriculture represents the largest share (37 percent) of Moroccan exports to sub-Saharan Africa (Malka, 2013). However, trade potential is huge. Major comparative advantages for Morocco are its pharmaceutical sector—as Africa's second-largest producer—and its banking sector, as 3 Moroccan banks rank among the top ten banks in the continent, with a well-established presence in over 40 African countries (Malka, 2013). Morocco's cooperation with Gabon has led to a deal worth USD 2.3 billion to produce fertilizer using Morocco's phosphate and Gabon's natural gas, as well as to free-visa travel between the two countries.

Moving Forward with the European Union

With the Euro-skepticism and EU's slow demand for foreign products, the benefits of North Africa's relation with the EU have increasingly become doubtful. North African countries need to work collectively on the aspects of the Euromed that hamper North Africa's trade integration process. For instance, bilateralism tends to disaggregate the North African region, deepen their economic dependence on the EU, and create a hub-and-spoke relationship between the EU and North Africa (Nsouli, 2006). In addition, North African countries should push the EU to make more concessions on trade integration. North African countries' harmonization of standards with the EU remains minimal, even if some progress has been registered. Recently, the EU launched a new round of negotiations to set up Deep and Comprehensive Free Trade Areas (DCFTAs) with the four signatories to the Agadir Agreement (Egypt, Jordan, Morocco, and Tunisia). The goal of DCFTAs is to reduce not only tariff barriers, but also nontariff measures, by bringing North African legislations closer to the EU legislation in trade-related areas.

North African countries should take full advantage of the EU's regional support programs aimed at enhancing their trade integration prospects. For instance, the EU has been funding regional and sub-regional integration projects in the Mediterranean through the European Neighborhood and Partnership Instrument (ENPI). Although most of the ENPI funding is country-specific and has remained limited to Euro 343.3 million for the 2007–2013 period, the European Commission (2009) has also provided Euro 90 million for transnational projects such as maritime depollution programs.

Conclusion

Despite attempts to foster regional integration in North Africa, trade and economic integration have remained very low due to political reasons. The numerous North African trade agreements are poorly implemented as tariff and nontariff barriers are still significantly high. Trade is biased toward the EU and has led to increased trade deficits for North African countries. Even other emerging economies in Asia have more intense and diversified trade relations with the EU. Export structures in North Africa have remained highly concentrated in terms of products and markets. In consequence, North African countries have weak inter-industry trade potential and their low level of export diversification has contributed to poor inter-regional trade performance. Deficits in infrastructure and, more extensively, on infrastructure services are important barriers to cross-border trade. Customs modernization and administrative procedures could be further harmonized between North African countries. Conflicting rules of origin, in particular, hamper regional trade harmonization, trade volumes, and value chain development.

In a globalized context, North African countries should revive the regional trade integration process in the spirit of a win-win integration. As a first step, North African states could support private sector initiatives such as the UME to advance the institutionalization of regional trade. The private sector has been waiting for a strong political signal that would give credibility to the AMU's integration process. Regional integration has many socioeconomic benefits in many different areas, not in contradiction with the preservation of national interests. Intra-industry trade is a possible long-term strategy and the development of regional value chains would be key to successfully achieving regional trade integration and benefiting from higher value-added export.

As regional economic cooperation prospects remain limited, North African countries should look for additional opportunities with other trading partners. North African countries' trade opportunities with the Arab world and sub-Saharan Africa are multiple and increasing. Egypt and Morocco have successfully expanded their economic and political influence in the Middle East and across sub-Saharan Africa, respectively. As the post-Arab Spring era makes it easier to set new rules, North African countries should harmonize their position on such crucial issues as RoO, standards and liberalization of investment, and services to facilitate trade in the MENA region. The region should take advantage of these diversification options as a means to increase its negotiation power with the EU. In the current Euromed situation, North African countries should press the EU to endorse a regional rather than bilateral approach with them. Countries should also better examine European funding programs for projects that could *in fine* foster North African regional trade.

References

African Development Bank. (2014). *African Development Report: Regional Integration for Inclusive Growth*. Abidjan: AfDB.

Al Khouri, R. (2008). EU and US Free Trade Agreements in the Middle East and North Africa. *Carnegie Papers*, No. 8. June, 1–23.

Bchir, M. H, Ben Hammouda, H., Oulmane, N., and Sadni Jallab, M. (2006). The Cost of non-Maghreb: Achieving the Gains from Economic Integration. *Journal of Economic Integration*, 22 (3): 684–722.

Ben Ahmed, G. and Othmani, S. (2014). "North Africa Awakening: New Hopes for Faster and Inclusive Growth," in *A New Paradigm: Perspectives on the Changing Mediterranean*, edited by A. Mullins and S. Toperich. Baltimore: Center for Transatlantic Relations at the Johns Hopkins University School of Advanced International Studies.

Brunel, C. and Hufbauer, G. (2013). "Trade Agreements in the MENA Region. Contribution to Better Governance," in *Governance in the Middle East and North Africa: A Handbook*, edited by A. Kadhim. London: Routledge.

Chaponnière, J. R. and Lautier, M. (2014). Regional integration in South-East Asia: Lessons for the Southern Mediterranean countries. *Economic Brief*, Tunis: African Development Bank.

Chauffour, J. P. (2010). *Furthering Intra-Regional Integration in the Arab World*. Mimeo, Washington, DC: World Bank.

de Wulf, L., Maliszewka, M. (2009). *Economic Integration in the Euro-Mediterranean Region*. Kyrgyzstan: Center for Social and Economic Research.

European Commission (2009). *Union for the Mediterranean: Commission Increases Its Contribution to Priority Projects*. Press release IP/09/2013, July 10, Bruxelles: European Commission.

European Commission. (2014). *Directorate General for Trade*, available on http://ec.europa.eu/trade/

Havrylyshyn, O., Kunzel, P. (2000). Intra-Industry Trade of Arab Countries: An Indicator of Potential Competitiveness in B. Hoekman and J. Zarrouk (eds). *Catching Up with the Competition: Trade Opportunities and Challenges for Arab Countries*. Ann Arbor: University of Michigan Press.

International Monetary Fund. (2014a). *World Economic Outlook: Legacies, Clouds, Uncertainties*. Washington, DC: IMF.

International Monetary Fund. (2014b). *Direction of Trade Statistics*. Available at: http://www.imf.org/external/data.htm.

Kauch, K., Youngs, R. (2009). The end of the Mediterranean vision. *International Affairs*, 85 (5): 963–975.

Koffi Ehoussou, J. V. (2005). *Intégration économique régionale et commerce intra-zone: le cas de l'Afrique du Nord. Rabat*: UNECA and Abidjan: Université de Cocody.

Konsentio. (2013). Making the Case for Maghreb Business in Times of Change. Available on http://di.dk/SiteCollectionDocuments/DIBD/AE-Network/Network%20Meetings%202014/Konsentio_IMCI_Draft%20report.pdf.

Lopez-Calix, J. R., Walkenhorst, P., and Diop, N. (2010). Trade Competitiveness of the Middle East and North Africa: Policies for Export Diversification. *Working Paper*, No. 55199. Washington, DC: World Bank.

Malka, H. (2013). Morocco's African Future. *Analysis Paper*, Washington DC: Center for Strategic and International Studies.

Mevel, S. and Karingi, S. (2012). Deepening Regional Integration in Africa: a Computable General Equilibrium Assessment of the Establishment of a Continental Free Trade Area Followed by a Continental Customs Union. Paper presented at the African Economic Conference, October 30, November 2, 2012, Kigali, Rwanda.

Ncube, M., Faye, I., and Verdier-Chouchane, A. (2015). *Regional Integration and Trade in Africa*. Basingstoke: Palgrave MacMillan.

Nsouli, S. M. (2006). *The Euro-Mediterranean Partnership Ten Years On: Reassessing Readiness and Prospects*. Monaco: IMF at Crans-Montana Forum.

Oueslati, A. and Brini, R. (2013). The Arab Maghreb union: The "cost of non maghreb" and sectoral prospects. *International Journal of Economics, Finance and Management Sciences*, 1 (6): 285–291.

Santi, E., Ben Romdhane, S., and Shaw, W. (2012). *Unlocking North Africa's Potential through Regional Integration: Challenges and Opportunities.* Tunis: AfDB.

Shui, L. and Walkenhorst, P. (2010). "Regional Integration: Status, Developments, and Challenges," in *Trade Competitiveness of the Middle East and North Africa. Policies for Export Diversification*, edited by J.R. Lopez-Calix, P. Walkenhorst and N. Diop. Washington, DC: World Bank.

Ulgen, S. (2011). Time to Overhaul the European Union's Role in North Africa. *Carnegie Europe*, available at: http://carnegieeurope.eu/publications/?fa=42382.

United Nations Conference on Trade and Development. (2014). UNCTAD Stat Database. Available at: http://unctadstat.unctad.org/EN/Index.html

United Nations Economic Commission for Africa. (2013). *Regional Integration and Development of Intra-Regional Trade in North Africa: What Potential Trade?* Rabat, Morocco: UNECA.

United Nations Economic Commission for Africa. (2014). *The Industrialization for a Sustainable and Inclusive Development in North Africa.* Report on sub-regional initiatives, Twenty-ninth meeting of the intergovernmental committee of experts (ICE), Geneva.

World Bank. (2008). *Middle East and North Africa Region: 2008 Economic Developments and Prospects.* Washington, DC: World Bank.

World Bank. (2010). *Economic Integration in the Maghreb.* Washington, DC: World Bank.

World Bank. (2012). *From Political to Economic Awakening in the Arab World: The Path of Economic Integration,* Report No. 68832-MNA. Washington, DC: World Bank.

World Bank. (2014). *Export Trends and Trade Structure Indices.* Washington, DC: World Bank.

World Economic Forum. (2014). *The Global Enabling Trade Report 2014.* Geneva: WEF.

Zarrouk, J. (2003). "A Survey of Barriers to Trade and Investment in Arab Countries," in *Arab Economic Integration: Between Hope and Reality*, edited by A. Galal and B. Hoekman. Washington DC: Brookings Institution Press.

Appendix

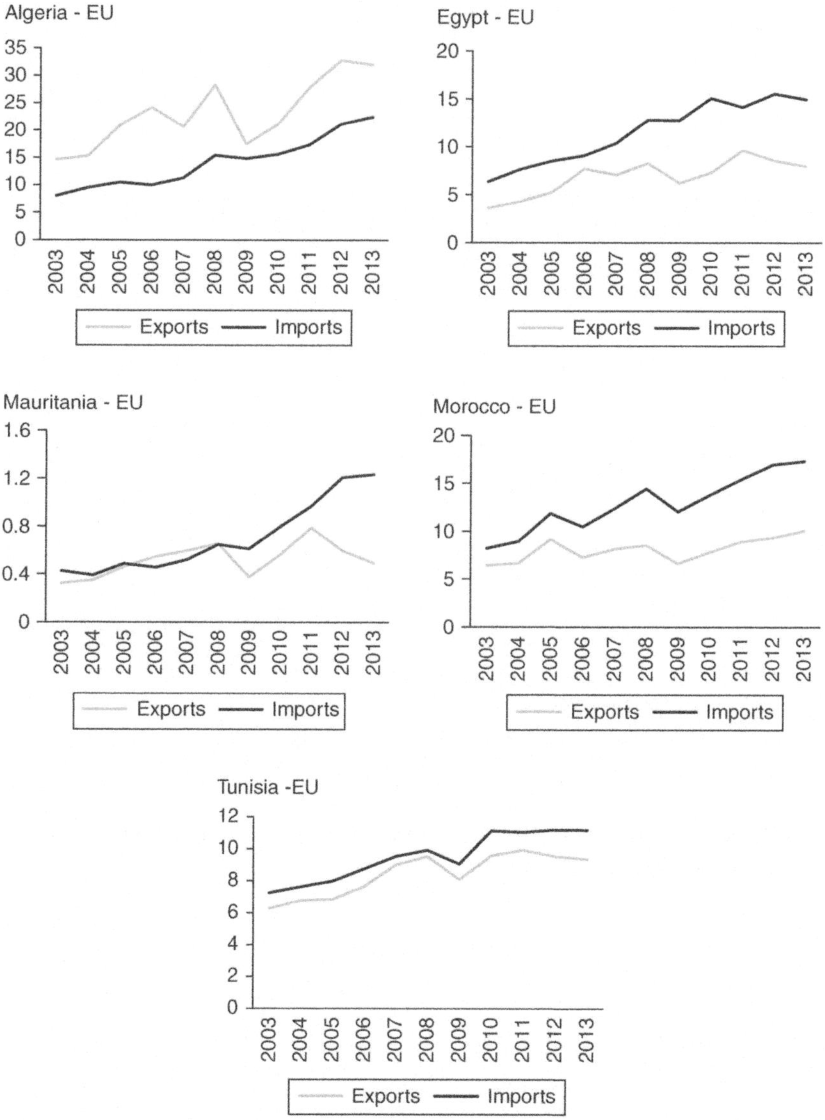

Figure A8.1 North African trade with the EU, 2003–2013 (in Euro millions).
Source: Authors, based on European Commission (2014).

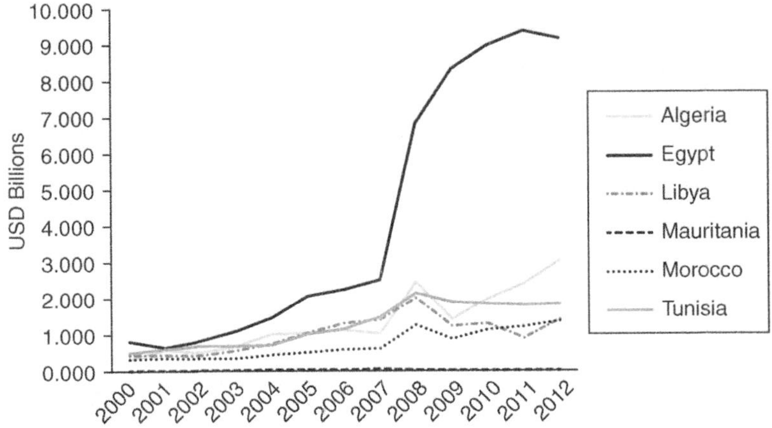

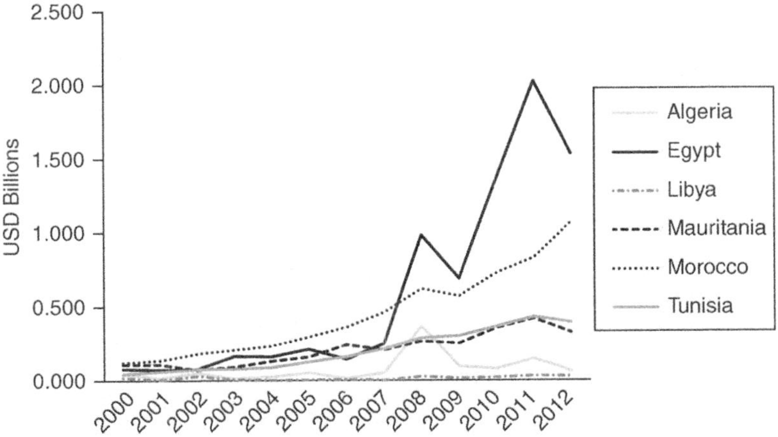

Figure A8.2 Exports to MENA, to SSA and to the EU by country, 2000–2012.
Source: Authors based on IMF (2014b).

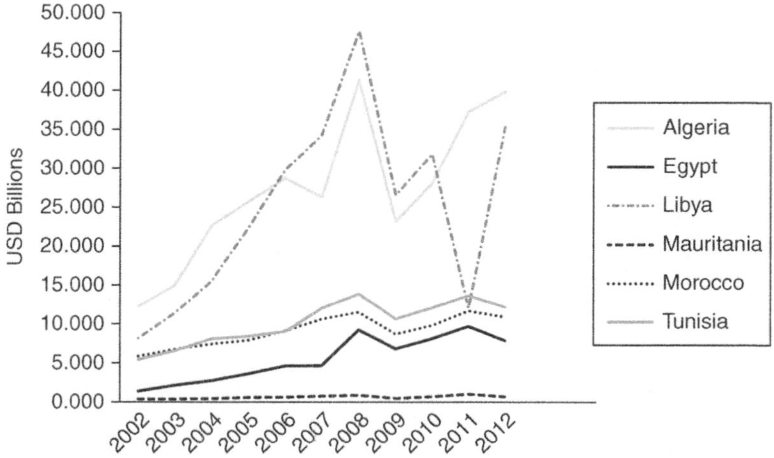

Figure A8.2 Continued.

9

FDI in the Middle Eastern and North African Countries

John C. Anyanwu, Nadège Désirée Yaméogo, and Mohamed Sami Ben Ali

Foreign direct investment (FDI), which may be flow or stock, represents the investment of foreign assets into domestic structures, equipment, and organizations. The parent multinational corporations (MNCs) may use vertical, horizontal, or conglomerate integration in carrying out the requisite FDI. Such investments may take various typologies, including resource-seeking, market-seeking, efficiency-seeking, and/or strategic (created) asset-seeking FDI.

The role of foreign direct investment (FDI) in both the national and global economies cannot be over-emphasized. Evidence has shown that FDI has contributed to the generation of more wealth and income around the world, especially since the 1980s. As a key element of the global economy, FDI is a driver for the transfer of modern technologies and technological progress, employment generation, raising of the skills of local manpower, and poverty reduction.

The key objectives of this chapter are to (a) present a brief review of the factors affecting FDI inflows to the Middle Eastern and North African countries; (b) analyze current and prospective scale, trends and other characteristics of FDI inflows to, and outflows from, the Middle East and North Africa (MENA) region; (c) examine the suite of incentives to promote FDI inflows to the region; and (d) present key policy implications for FDI policy and promotion in the region. Without doubt, an understanding of the current characteristics of FDI inflows to the MENA region is important for the design of FDI policies.

The further contents of the chapter are as follows. Section I reviews the recent empirical literature pertaining to the MENA. Section II analyzes the current scale, trends, and other characteristics of FDI inflows to, and outflows from, the MENA region. Section III examines the key incentives and policies offered by MENA countries to attract increased FDI to the region. Section IV summarizes and concludes the paper, with some policy recommendations for increased FDI inflows to the MENA region.

Brief Review of Recent Literature on the Determinants of FDI Flows to the MENA Region

Onyeiwu (2003) investigates the impacts of institutional and economic fundamentals on FDI in the MENA region during the period, 1975–1999, and concludes that trade openness increases FDI flows to the region while corruption/bureaucratic red tape reduce the inflows. Chan and Gemayel (2004) demonstrate that political instability consequent upon investment risk is an important determinant of the level of foreign direct investment for MENA countries. Méon and Sekkat (2004) arrive at similar results.

Hisarciklilar et al. (2006) analyze the locational drivers of FDI into eighteen MENA countries over the period 1980–2001. They show that firms investing in the region mainly focus on the domestic market size, and hence FDI to the region is mainly market-oriented. Elfakhani and Matar (2007), examine FDI inflows in the 19 MENA countries over an 11-year period (1990–2000), and find that the previous year's FDI, country openness, return on investment, membership of the World Trade Organization, and status of being an oil-exporting country all have significant and positive effects on FDI inflows to the region.

Shirazi, Rodrigues, and Karnik (2008), using a panel of 15 MENA countries over the period 1980–2003, show that foreign direct investment to the non-GCC countries is driven by the development of the manufacturing sector. However, results report a positive relationship between FDI inflows and the services sector.

Mohamed and Sidiropoulos (2010) examine the effects of economic and institutional variables in a sample of 12 MENA countries between 1975 and 2006. The main results stemming from this study report that FDI inflows are driven by the government size, natural resources, and the institutional variables.

Using a panel data of 19 countries in the MENA region during the period, 1995–2009, El Sayed (2011) finds that macroeconomic factors such as the size of the economy and the level of trade openness positively influence FDI inflows into the region, while inflation risk deters the inflows. Also, Rogmans (2011), using a panel data of MENA countries for the period 1987–2008, finds that in the overall results, GDP per capita (market attractiveness), trade openness, and oil prices have a positive and significant effect FDI inflows to the MENA region while overall environmental risk is insignificant. However, surprisingly, a country's endowment of oil and gas resources has a significant negative effect on FDI inflows to the MENA region. With respect to individual risk factors, the author finds that bureaucracy quality, democratic accountability, ethnic tension (strangely), law and order, and exchange rate stability have positive and significant effect on FDI inflows to the region. However, budget and current account deficits have significant negative effects on the inflows of FDI to the region.

In a recent paper, Mina (2012) revisits the policy debate on institutional reform approaches to property rights protection. The author empirically examines the debate in the context of FDI flows to eleven MENA region for the period 1991–2007. The study reports a positive relationship between the improvements in the risk of investment expropriation in non-Gulf Cooperation Council MENA countries.

In another recent paper, Burger, Ianchovichina and Rijkers (2013) analyze the investment inflows inti MENA countries from 2003 to 2012. Their study report a negative relationship with lower FDI inflows in the non-resource tradable sectors. By contrast, however, they find that FDI flows to the natural resource sectors and non-tradable activities appear to be insensitive to such shocks. Jabri et al. (2013) investigate the determinants of FDI inflows to the MENA region for the period, 1970–2010, using panel data technique. They find that the macro determinants like openness, economic growth, exchange rate, and economic instability have a long-run impact on FDI inflows to the MENA region. The results suggest that economic openness and economic growth rate increase the entry of FDI into the MENA region while economic instability and exchange rates appear to have negative effects on the inward FDI flows and can therefore deter foreign investment.

Anyanwu and Yameogo (2014) analyze the key factors affecting FDI inflows to North Africa between 1970 and 2010, using OLS and GMM estimation techniques. Their results show that trade openness, infrastructure development, and the level of education have strong positive effect on FDI inflows to the sub-region. They also find that GDP per capita, net foreign aid and being a metal exporting country are negatively and significantly related to FDI inflows to North Africa.

FDI IN MENA: CURRENT AND PROSPECTS

Trends in FDI Inflows to MENA Countries

Globally, FDI flows have risen rapidly in recent decades. For example, inward FDI flows in the world increased from US$54.1 billion in 1980 and reached US$207.7 billion in 1990. It reached the highest level at US$1401.5 billion in 2000. From 2001, a fall ensured and by 2003, FDI flows had decreased to only US$565.7 billion before reaching a new peak at US$2100 billion in 2007. Global FDI flows fell again in 2010 to US$1422 billion as a result of the economic and financial crisis (Figure 9.1 and Table 9.1). The 2011 recovery appeared short-lived as global FDI inflows fell by 18 percent in 2012, down from US$1700 billion in 2011 to only US$1300 billion. However, 2013 witnessed a 9 percent increase from US$1330 billion to US$1452 billion (UNCTAD, 2014).

Having started from a very low level and after six years of growth, FDI inflows to the MENA region decreased from a height of US$116.1 billion in 2008 to US$91.3 billion in 2009—a 21.4 percent

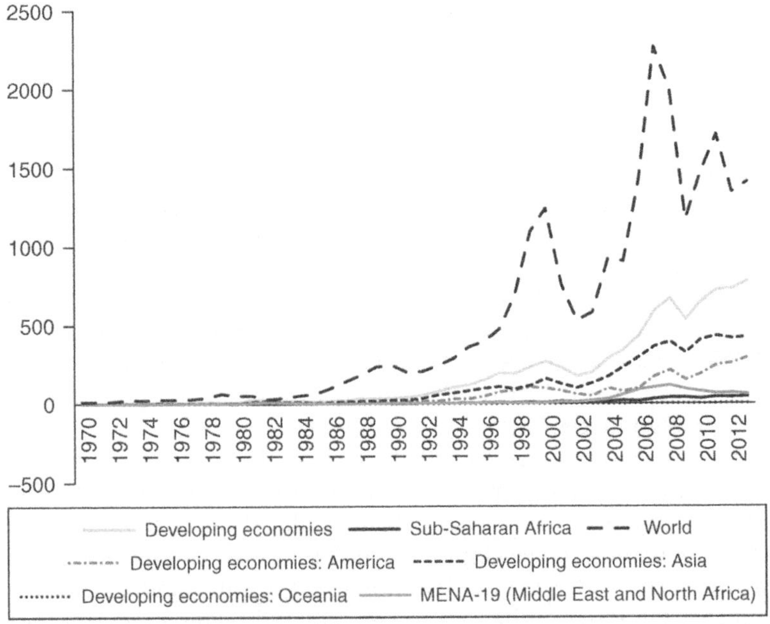

Figure 9.1 FDI inflows: Global and by selected regions (US$ billion), 1970–2013.

Source: Authors, using UNCTAD Stat online data.

Table 9.1 FDI Flows by Region, 2011–2013 (US$ billion & Percent)

Region	FDI Inflows			FDI Outflows		
	2011	2012	2013	2011	2012	2013
World	1700	1330	1452	1712	1347	1411
Developed economies	880	517	566	1216	853	857
Developing economies	725	729	778	423	440	454
Africa	48	55	57	7	12	12
Sub-Saharan Africa	42	41	45	53	89	119
Asia	431	415	426	304	302	326
Middle East and North Africa	**63**	**67**	**60**	**24**	**23**	**32**
Latin America & the Caribbean	244	256	292	111	124	115
Oceania	2	3	3	1	2	1
Transition economies	95	84	108	73	54	99
Structurally weak, vulnerable & small economies	58	58	57	12	10	9
Percentage share in world FDI flows						
Developed economies	51.8	38.8	39	71	63.3	60.8
Developing economies	42.6	54.8	53.6	24.7	32.7	32.2
Africa	2.8	4.1	3.9	0.4	0.9	0.9
Sub-Saharan Africa	2.5	3.1	3.1	0.3	0.7	0.8
Asia	**25.3**	**32.2**	**29.4**	**17.8**	**22.4**	**23.1**
Middle East and North Africa	**3.7**	**5.0**	**4.1**	**1.4**	**1.7**	**2.3**
Latin America & the Caribbean	14.3	19.2	20.1	6.5	9.2	8.1
Oceania	0.1	0.2	0.2	0.1	0.1	0.1
Transition economies	5.6	6.3	7.4	4.3	4	7
Structurally weak, vulnerable & small economies	3.4	4.4	3.9	0.7	0.7	0.7

Source: UNCTAD (2014).

fall compared to 2008 due to the economic and financial crisis. By 2013, this had fallen further to US$60 billion, representing about 11 percent decline from 2012. This represented the fourth fall since 2009 and almost a return to the 2005. As shown in Figure 9.1 and Table 9.1, the MENA region is not a major recipient of FDI inflows. It thus lags behind developing Asia and developing Americas. This is a reflection of further deterioration of the security situation in the region that adversely affected FDI inflows not only regionally, neighboring countries and those directly affected like Syria, Yemen, and Iraq. FDI inflows remained lackluster in the oil-rich Gulf Cooperation

Council (GCC) countries, in spite of enjoying strong economic growth and avoiding large-scale political unrest. Thus, FDI inflows to the MENA region had been very low due to persisting political instability and economic uncertainty; deteriorating trade, tourism, real estate, finance, and banking prospects; the recent war in Syria (especially for Jordan and Lebanon); increased sectarian violence (for example, in Iraq and Lebanon); a generally bumpy transition process; security concerns; political polarization (such as in Egypt, Yemen, and Libya); weak innovation; and a lack of technological readiness in their efforts (see, e.g., World Bank, 2013). Indeed, the aftermath of the Arab Spring had dissuaded many companies from investing in the MENA region, and hence the observed recent decline.

Other factors for the low levels of FDI inflows to the MENA region, in general, include a poor business environment, poor regulatory framework, poor institutional frameworks, and weak FDI policies and incentives. Further reasons are unfavorable comparative costs, limited market access, bureaucratic red tape, and trade protectionism. In addition, the MENA region offers the least rate of return on FDI among the major global regions, in spite of recent reductions in corporate income taxes. For example, in 2011, MENA's rate of return on FDI inflows stood at only 5.1 percent against the world average of 7.2 percent, as well as 9.3 percent in Africa, 8.8 percent in Asia, and 7.1 percent in Latin America and the Caribbean. In fact, the average performance between 2006 and 2011 show the similar outcome with the MENA region offering 5 percent, compared with 11.4 percent in Africa, 9.2 percent in Asia, and 8.7 percent in Latin America and the Caribbean.

By 1982, MENA's share of global FDI inflows reached a peak of 20 percent but, by 1990, it was a mere 0.8 percent. By 2013, MENA's share stood at 4 percent, compared to developing Asia's 29.4 percent. On average, between 1970 and 2013, MENA's share in global FDI inflows was only 3.3 percent while developing Asia received 16.5 percent (see Figure 9.2). On the whole, FDI inflows to the MENA region having started from a very low level, rose in the early 2000s, peaked in the second half of the period, but fell at the end of the decade. Indeed, as the World Bank (2013) had observed, with the Arab Spring altering the economic and political environment in the MENA region, its FDI inflows continued to decline while those of the rest of the world picked up after 2010.

As Figure 9.3 shows, FDI inflows to the MENA region represent a low percentage of its GDP (FDI rates), declining from a peak of 4.3 percent reached in 2006 to a mere 1.5 percent in 2013.

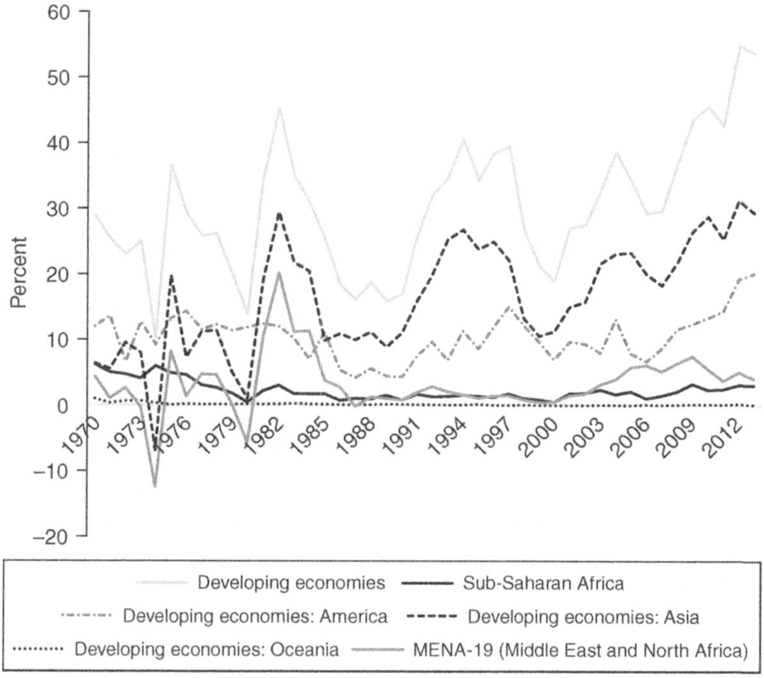

Figure 9.2 FDI inflows (Percentage of Total World), by selected regions, 1970–2013.

Source: Authors, using UNCTAD Stat online data.

FDI inflows to the MENA region vary across the two major sub-regions. As Figures 9.4 and 9.5 illustrate, the Middle East dominated North Africa by a great margin between 2000 and 2013, but with a general declining trend after 2008. The average share of the regions between 1990 and 2013 stood as follows: The Middle East (64.5%), and North Africa (35.5%). There is also a discernible reversal in the sub-regional shares between the early 1970s and the current period (Figure 9.6).

Figure 9.7 shows the relative shares of FDI inflow to the GCC bloc (Bahrain, Kuwait, Oman, Qatar, Saudi Arabia, and the United Arab Emirates) and the non-GCC ones. There is a seesaw trend, with the non-GCC countries largely dominating at an average of 67 percent while the GCC bloc had a share of 33 percent—within the Middle East, the shares are 56 percent to 45 percent.

The GCC bloc had been seen as a preferred FDI destination in the MENA region. This is because of its pro-investor environment driven

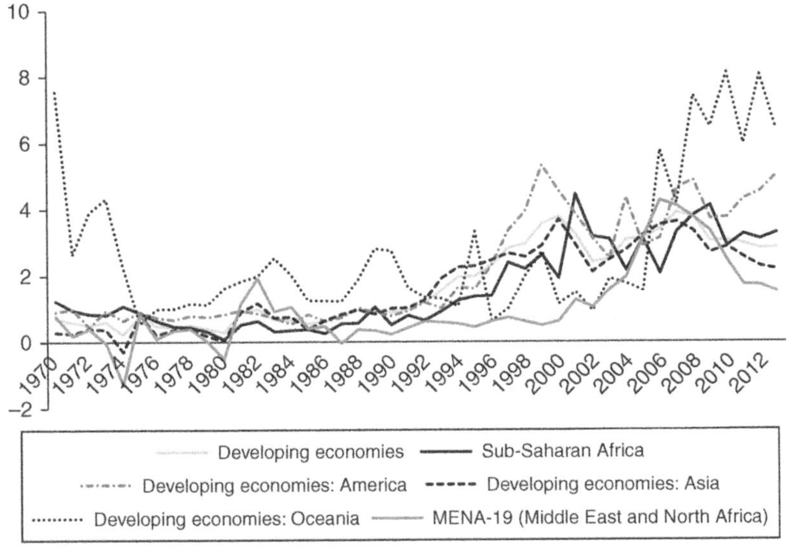

Figure 9.3 FDI inflows (Percentage of GDP), by selected regions.

Source: Authors, using UNCTAD Stat online data.

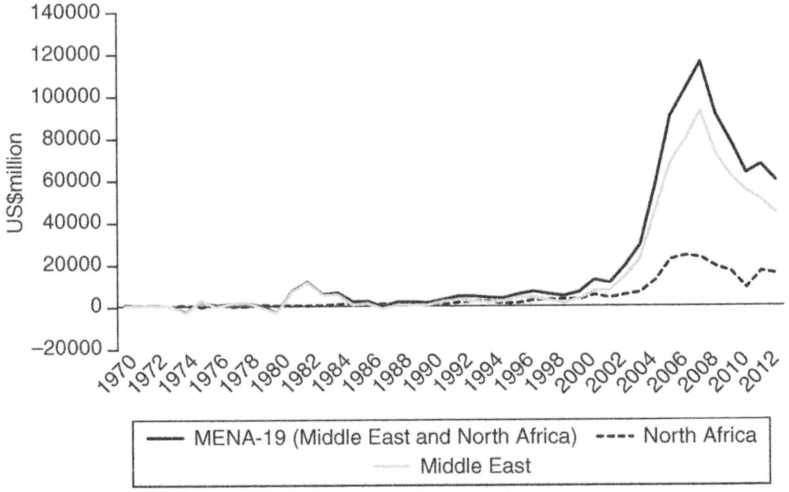

Figure 9.4 Trend in FDI inflows to The Middle East and North Africa (US$ million), 1970–2013.

Source: Authors, using UNCTAD Stat online data.

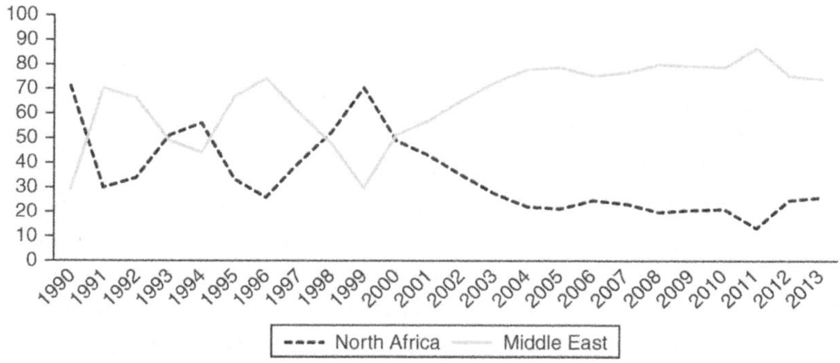

Figure 9.5 Percentage share of FDI inflows to MENA: North Africa vs The Middle East, 1990–2013.

Source: Authors, using UNCTAD Stat online data.

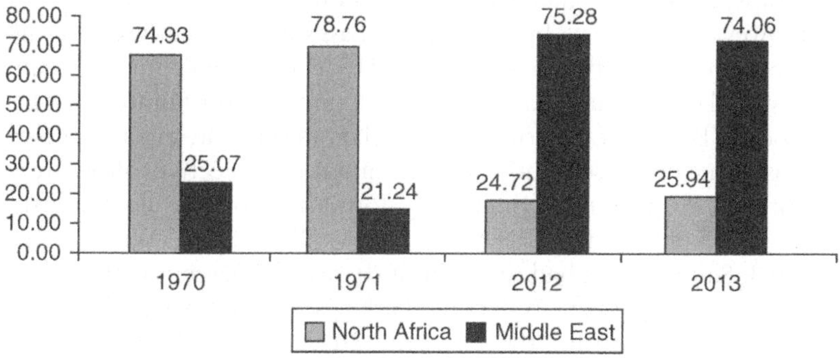

Figure 9.6 Percentage share of MENA FDI inflows, 1970/71 & 2012/13.

Source: Authors, using UNCTAD Stat online data.

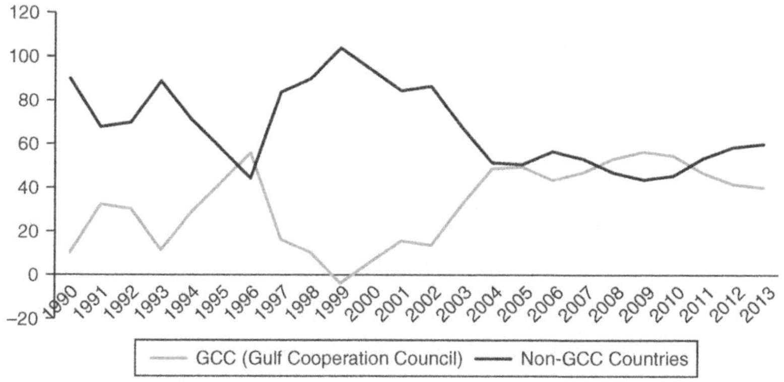

Figure 9.7 Percentage share of FDI inflows to MENA: GCC vs Non-GCC countries, 1990–2013.

Source: Authors, using UNCTAD Stat online data.

by affluent consumer markets, sophisticated banking industry, access to world-class physical infrastructure, and advanced logistics facilities. Other reasons include good quality institutions, higher scores on the World Bank's Doing Business indicators, and a source of robust growth and financing (see World Bank, 2013). However, FDI inflows to the bloc are limited because of its vast petrodollars and foreign reserves, which it has used to invest in mega development projects such as housing, electricity, petrochemicals, water, telecommunications, tourism, and leisure. In addition, the bloc has set up Sovereign Wealth Funds (SWFs), which are investing in domestic public services (hard infrastructure) and soft infrastructure (such as health and education), thus, lowering the level of FDI inflows. In addition, GCC countries are even constrained by issues relating to technological readiness, education quality, and innovation.

However, the above broad picture masks country differences and major recipients. Between 1980 and 2013, the top ten country recipients were Turkey, Saudi Arabia, Egypt, United Arab Emirates (UAE), Morocco, Tunisia, Lebanon, Iran, Jordan, and Qatar, most of which are fossil fuel producers and exporters and their collective inflows represent over 87 percent of the total inflows—the top five alone constitute over 65 percent in MENA FDI inflows (Figure 9.8). We note that in 2013, Saudi Arabia had the highest share at 23 percent with Turkey following at 16 percent, reflecting Turkey's FDI inflows declining by about 22 percent during the year from 2012.

During the past two decades, Greenfield FDI has been the dominant form of FDI inflows to the MENA region. This is because of the natural resource-rich status of many countries in the region. As

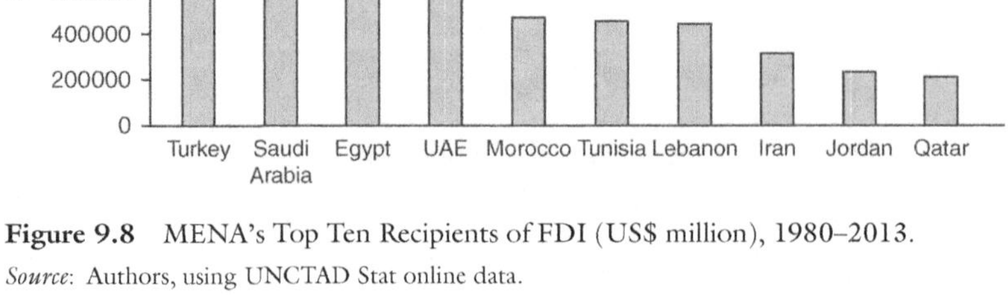

Figure 9.8 MENA's Top Ten Recipients of FDI (US$ million), 1980–2013.

Source: Authors, using UNCTAD Stat online data.

Table 9.2 shows, developed countries with strong institutions and R&D capabilities[1] had been the major sources of Greenfield investments in the MENA region. However, much fewer investments from these developed countries had gone into the region's nonoil manufacturing. The Table 9.2 also shows that over the period 2003–2012, the MENA region received the largest amount of Greenfield investments (US$ 424.7 billion) from these countries, representing 45 percent of the total Greenfield investments received by the region during this period. It also represents 61 percent of all Greenfield projects, and created 43 percent of the direct Greenfield investments-related jobs. The GCC countries (UAE, Bahrain, Kuwait, Qatar, and Saudi Arabia) were the second largest source of Greenfield investments for the MENA region. It is worth noting that most of the investments from the GCC bloc were into tradable and non-tradable services. During the period 2003–2012, Greenfield investments from within MENA totaled US$ 318 billion, representing 34 percent of the total Greenfield investment inflows the region during that period. It also represented 19 percent of all Greenfield projects, and 34 percent of the direct Greenfield investments-related jobs. The remaining 21 percent of the total investment inflows were from developing countries such as India and China, and developed economies, including Spain, Italy, and Russia.

Table 9.3 shows Greenfield FDI inflows to the MENA region by recipient and sector for the ten-year period, 2003–2012. It shows

Table 9.2 Greenfield FDI in MENA by Source, Sector, and Job Creation, 2003–2012 (US$ billion)

	Resources & Oil Manufacturing	Non-Oil Manufacturing	Commercial Services	Non-Tradables	Total Capital Investment (US$ billion)	Number of Investments	Direct Job Creation ('000)
Developed—Strong Institutions and R&D[a]	172.1 (41)	78.2 (18)	86.6 (20)	87.8 (21)	424.7 (100)	4524	580 (43)
Other Developed[b]	28 (36)	12.4 (16)	15.8 (20)	21.7 (28)	77.9 (100)	623	136 (10)
MENA[c]	23.2 (7)	29.8 (9)	125.7 (49)	139 (44)	317.7 (100)	1358	452 (34)
Other Developing Countries[d]	59.2 (51)	33 (28)	13.0 (11)	11.8 (10)	117 (100)	921	172 (13)

a. USA, France, UK, Japan, Netherlands, Germany, Switzerland, Canada.

b. Spain, Italy, Russia.

c. UAE, Bahrain, Kuwait, Qatar, Saudi Arabia.

d. India, China.

Source: Adapted from World Bank (2013). *NB*: Numbers in parenthesis are percentage shares.

Table 9.3 Greenfield FDI in MENA by Recipient and Sector, 2003–2012

	Resources & Oil Manufacturing	Non-Oil Manufacturing	Commercial Services	Non-Tradables	Total Capital Investment (US$ billion)	Number of Investments	Direct Job Creation ('000)
GCC[a]	136.6 (31)	87.1 (20)	114.9 (26)	106 (24)	444.6 (100)	4680	582 (43)
Developing Oil Exporters[b]	96.6 (39)	35.4 (14)	51.7 (21)	66 (26)	249.7 (100)	967	278 (21)
Developing Oil Importers[c]	49.7 (20)	30.9 (13)	74.4 (31)	88.2 (36)	343.2 (100)	1777	482 (36)

a. Bahrain, Kuwait, Oman, Qatar, Saudi Arabia, UAE.

b. Algeria, Iran, Iraq, Libya, Syria, Yemen.

c. Djibouti, Egypt, Lebanon, Morocco, Jordan, Tunisia, West Bank and Gaza.

Source: Adapted from World Bank (2013).*NB*: Numbers in parenthesis are percentage shares.

that the GCC countries are major FDI recipients, in addition to being the second largest Greenfield FDI investor in the MENA region. For example, these GCC countries received almost half of all Greenfield FDI inflows to the region and 63 percent of all Greenfield FDI projects during the period, 2003–2012. Two countries—Saudi Arabia and the United Arab Emirates—received large sizes (14% each) of their cumulative Greenfield FDI inflows and the number of direct Greenfield FDI-related jobs (9% and 20%, respectively). Among the developing MENA net oil importers, Egypt attracted the largest amount of Greenfield FDI (US$104 billion or 11%) while Morocco received the largest number of Greenfield FDI projects (530). While most of their investments were service activities, those of the developing net oil exporters went to the natural resource and non-tradable sectors.

Trends in FDI Outflows from MENA Countries

As observed in the previous section, while significant FDI flows into the MENA region are a relatively recent phenomenon, FDI inflows to the region are still small when compared with world flows and flows to other regions. In fact, FDI outflows from the MENA region are even lower (Figure 9.9). A significant FDI outflow from the MENA region did not occur until 2004, when it reached US$8.8 billion, rising to a peak of US$47 billion in 2008. By 2009, it had collapsed to US$20.7 billion, consequent upon the global economic and financial crisis. By 2013, it had hit US$32.1 billion, representing a rise of 42 percent from 2012. However, this was still insignificant when compared with outflows from developing Asia, which was US$326 billion in 2013, or over ten times more. It is noteworthy that the rise

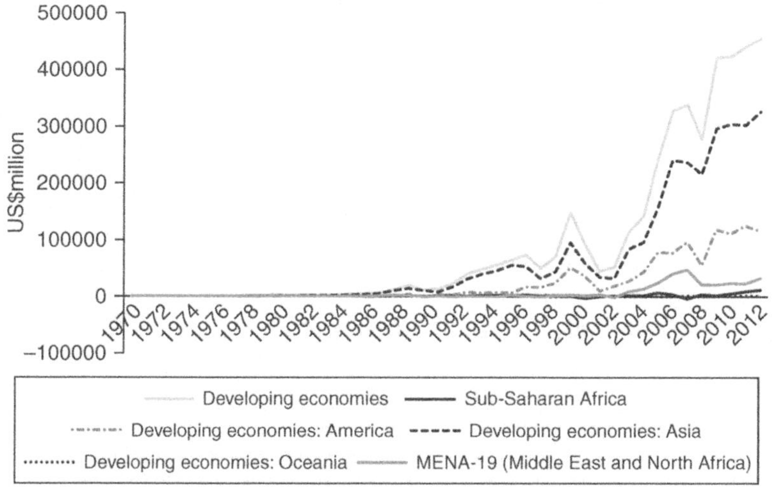

Figure 9.9 FDI outflows by selected regions (US$ million), 1970–2013.
Source: Authors, using UNCTAD Stat online data.

in the region's FDI outflows in 2013 was enhanced by increasing flows from the GCC bloc. While the GCC countries increased their investments abroad, the 336 percent increase in FDI outflows from Qatar and the 159 percent increase in outflows from Kuwait account for most of the increase between 2012 and 2013.

Average FDI originating from the MENA region stood at less than 0.4 percent of global FDI until 2003. In 2004, it rose to 0.96 percent of global outflows, peaking at almost 2.4 percent in 2008, and by 2013, it was 2.3 percent as against 23 percent from developing Asia (Figure 9.10). Indeed, between 2003 and 2013, average FDI outflows from the MENA region represented 1.7 percent of the global total.

A significant portion of FDI outflows in the MENA region is concentrated among a few countries. Between 2003 and 2013, six countries (UAE, Kuwait, Qatar, Saudi Arabia, Turkey, and Libya) accounted for 91 percent of the FDI outflows from the region. FDI outflows from UAE during the period were the largest in absolute and percentage terms while Kuwait ranked second (Figure 9.11). Between 2003 and 2013, the UAE was responsible for US$61 billion of outward FDI, representing over 26 percent of all outward FDI from the region. During the same period, Kuwait was responsible for over US$58 billion of outward FDI, representing over 25 percent of all outward FDI from

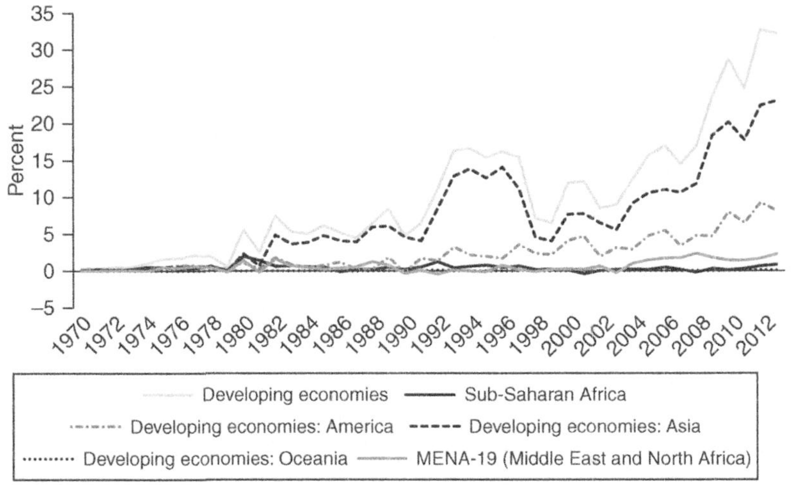

Figure 9.10 FDI outflows (Percentage of Total World), by selected regions, 1970–2013.

Source: Authors, using UNCTAD Stat online data.

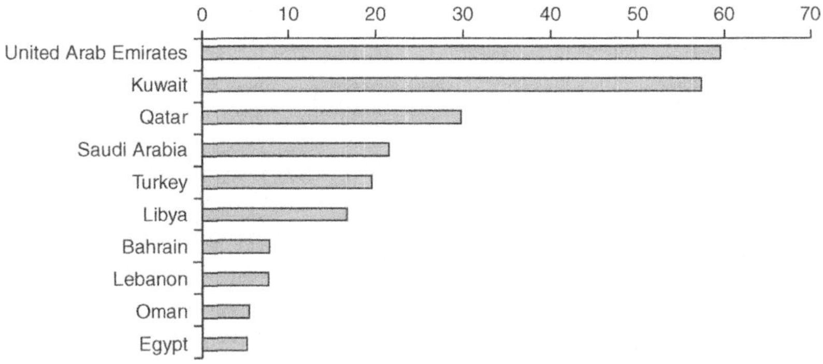

Figure 9.11 FDI outflows: Top ten MENA countries, 2003–2013 (US$ billion).

Source: Authors, using UNCTAD Stat online data.

the MENA region. However, in 2013, the six countries that accounted for 90 percent of all FDI outflows from the region were Kuwait, Qatar, Saudi Arabia, Turkey, UAE, and Oman, in that order. Five out of the six considered economies are net oil exporters, whose FDI outflows are seen as a result of the accumulation of financial resources generated by high oil prices (before the sharp price decline since late 2014) in addition to the diversification strategies followed by the Gulf countries, attempts to bolster the small domestic economies in the region, and the private sector's search for profitable investments—especially in commercial services (Ernst and Young, 2013).

We note that the United States, followed by the EU, were traditionally the main destinations of the MENA region's outward investments, but Asia is increasingly becoming a more important destination. This has been driven, partly, by the extended period of low interest rates and low yields on US and European assets (particularly sovereign debt) since the 2008–2009 economic and financial crisis, which made emerging market assets more attractive for investors globally. Essentially, MENA capital, in search of higher yield assets has turned to domestic equities and other markets, particularly in Asia. The two key Asian destinations of MENA capital had been China and India. Recent major changes in the global energy market such as the US shale revolution and the rise of those two Asian countries have contributed in shifting the MENA region's economic focus toward the Asian continent.

It has been estimated that FDI outflow from the MENA region to China increased at a fairly steady rate between 2003 and 2008 to reach a record level of US$404 million, though this only represented 0.44 percent of China's total FDI inflows. In 2009, FDI outflows from the MENA region to China declined by about 40 percent to US$241 million consequent upon the 2008–2009 economic and financial crisis that resulted in the weakening of global demand for oil and declining oil prices. In 2011, the MENA region invested in 207 projects in China, representing a 20 percent decline from the previous year. Of these, 129 projects were in wholesale and retail, 34 in manufacturing, and 25 in leasing and business services. In that year, the top-most MENA investor in China was the UAE (US$71.40 million) (55.9 percent), followed by Saudi Arabia (US$ 23.94 million) (18.7%), together accounting for 75 percent of total FDI from the MENA region to China. The GCC countries' aggregate FDI outflows to India from 2000 through 2014 totaled roughly US$ 3.2 billion, with UAE as the dominant source. For example, between 2005 and 2009, all FDI outflows from the sub-region to India came from UAE, while between 2010 and 2013, its share was about 75 percent on average. In terms of value, UAE's contribution reached a peak of US$346 million in 2012, representing about 77 percent of total MENA's contribution, with Morocco contributing the rest. The key sectors that MENA countries' outward FDI had gone to include Asian energy markets, telecommunications, and finance, among others.

Recently, intra-MENA FDI flows had become an important phenomenon. Indeed, since the terrorist attacks of 11 September 2001 in the United States, many MENA governments and investors started considering investing in their own region more actively, as it appeared at the time that there would be fewer opportunities available to them in Western economies. These shifts in focus among MENA governments and investors, together with huge government revenues among oil-producing countries as a result of the then high oil prices, had led to significant increases in intra-regional FDI into the MENA region from 2003 onward. In particular, net oil-importing countries in the MENA region such as Egypt, Jordan, Morocco, and Tunisia depend hugely on intra-regional FDI flows to fund their infrastructure investment. As noted in the previous sub-section, the GCC countries were the second largest source of Greenfield investments for the MENA region such that between 2003 and 2012, Greenfield investments from within the region amounted to US$ 318 billion or 34 percent of the total.

FDI Incentives and Policies in MENA Countries

As in many other regions, governments in the MENA region use incentives (nonmarket benefits) to stimulate FDI inflows. These incentives have often taken three broad forms: fiscal, financial, and regulatory incentives.

Recently, many MENA countries have been reforming and restructuring their fiscal (especially tax) systems to improve efficiency, spur FDI inflows, and stabilize revenue yield. One key feature of these reforms is that MENA countries have migrated from different tax investments to the general application of the same tax rate and base to all activities and hence, in the process, lowering the overall corporate statutory rate while phasing out generous tax incentives (see Figure 9.12).

In some other countries, the reduced corporate tax rates relate to general flat rates as in Lebanon (15%); flat rates applicable to different types of companies as in Syria; and in countries such as the UAE, there is currently no federal taxation but each of the individual Emirates issue low corporate tax rates, which are uniformly applied. In countries like Jordan, the corporate income tax rates for resident firms range from 14% to 30%, depending on the type of activity. Bahrain levies no taxes on income, capital gains, sales, estates, interest, dividends, royalties, or fees other than those specifically imposed on oil

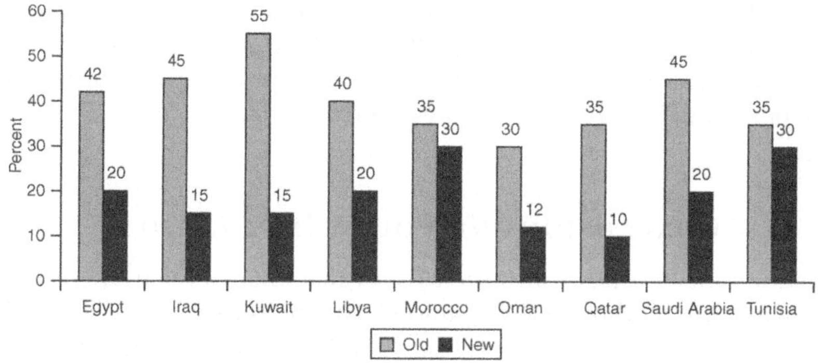

Figure 9.12 Corporate tax rate (%) reductions to attract FDI in selected MENA countries.

Sources: Sheikh (2012) and Ernst and Young (2014).

and gas firms involved in exploration, production, or oil/gas refining at 46 percent.

These are in addition to the granting of tax holidays, as in Egypt, Oman, and Syria; exemptions from indirect taxes in some specific sectors, such as in the case of or in specific economic zones like in Egypt or Jordan. There are also exemptions of reinvested profits from corporate taxation, as in Tunisia, or the exemption of foreign personnel from income taxes and social security contributions, as in Jordan. Another measure taken by MENA countries relates to the numerous tax treaties (double taxation, customs, sector-specific) signed. For example, the United Arab Emirates had more than 50 tax treaties in force by 2014.

To encourage exports and FDI inflows, almost all MENA countries have installed free trade zones (FTZs) or "free zones." These free zones offer tax and business incentives. For example, approximately 30 FTZs are located in the Emirate of Dubai (UAE) alone. These include, among others, the Dubai Airport FTZ (DAFZ), Dubai International Financial Centre (DIFC) for financial services, Dubai Internet City (DIC), Dubai Media City (DMC), Dubai Multi Commodities Center (DMCC), and Jebel Ali Free Zone (JAFZ). These FTZs offer incentives, usually include tax exemptions at the Emirate level for a guaranteed period, absence of customs duty within the FTZ and a "one-stop shop" for administrative services, and the possibility of 100% foreign ownership. While FTZs in the UAE have been adjudged successful, a number of others have had mixed success at best.

MENA countries have also created institutional structures or Investment Promotion Agencies (IPAs). These are for the promotion of FDI attraction, the majority of which were set up as "one-stop shops" to deal with all of the foreign investor needs.

Conclusion and Policy Implications

Significant FDI flows into the MENA region are a relatively recent phenomenon, though FDI inflows to the region are still small when compared with world flows and flows to other regions. This has been attributed to persistent political instability and economic uncertainty; deteriorating trade, tourism, real estate, finance, and banking prospects; the recent incidences of increased sectarian violence; a generally bumpy transition process; security concerns; political polarization; weak innovation; lack of technological readiness; poor business environment; poor regulatory framework; poor institutional frameworks; weak FDI policies and incentives; unfavorable comparative costs; limited market access; bureaucratic red tape; trade protectionism; and the least rate of return on FDI among the major global regions, in spite of recent reductions in corporate income taxes.

FDI inflows to the MENA region vary across the two major sub-regions of the Middle East and North Africa, with the former dominating by a great margin between 2000 and 2013. A significant portion of FDI outflows in the MENA region are concentrated among a few countries, dominated since 2003 by UAE, Kuwait, Qatar, Saudi Arabia, Turkey, and Libya.

Governments in the MENA region use incentives (nonmarket benefits)—fiscal, financial, and regulatory incentives—to stimulate FDI inflows. However, the evaluation of MENA countries' incentives and policies to attract FDI inflows has yielded mixed results. For example, surveys of investment drivers have shown that FDI incentives rank lower in importance than other factors. Such factors relate to the ease of doing business, political and economic stability, and market access. Practice has shown that global investors always attach far greater importance to the economic and political "fundamentals" than to incentive schemes. Thus, MENA countries need to ensure that the investment climate—including, in particular, political and economic stability and ease of doing business—is conducive, going forward, in order to attract higher FDI.

NOTE

1. United States, France, United Kingdom, Japan, Netherlands, Germany, Switzerland, and Canada.

REFERENCES

Anyanwu, J. C. and Yameogo, N. D. (2014). Foreign Direct Investment to Africa: Regional Comparison. Paper presented at the 2014 World Congress of the International Economics Association (IEA), Dead Sea, Jordan, June.

Burger, M., Ianchovichina, E., and Rijkers, B. (2013). Risky Business: Political Instability and Greenfield Foreign Direct Investment in the Arab World. *World Bank Policy Research Working Paper*, 6716, December, Washington, DC.

Chan, K. K. and Gemayel, E. R. (2004). Risk Instability and the Pattern of Foreign Direct Investment in the Middle East and North Africa Region. *IMF Working Paper*, 04/139, 1–20.

Elfakhani, S. M. and Matar, L. M. (2007). Foreign Direct investment in the Middle East and North Africa region. *Journal of Global Business Advancement*, 1 (1): 49–70.

El Sayed, L. (2011). Determinants of FDI Inflows to the MENA Region: Macroeconomic and Institutional Factors. Presented at the Finance and Economic Conference 2011, Frankfurt.

Ernst and Young (2013). FDI flows in the MENA region: Features and impacts. *IEMS Emerging Market Brief*, 13–01: 1–24.

Ernst and Young (2014). *Corporate Taxation in Middle East and North Africa 2014*. EYGM Limited: London, UK.

Hisarciklilar, M., Kayam, S. S., and Kayalica, O. (2006). Locational drivers of FDI in MENA countries: A Spatial Attempt. Munich Personal RePEc Archive (MPRA) Paper 2085, pp. 1–20.

Jabri, A., Guesmi, K., and Abid, I. 2013. Determinants of foreign direct investment in MENA region: Panel co-integration analysis. *The Journal of Applied Business Research*, 29 (4): 1103–1109.

Méon, P. and Sekkat, K. (2012). FDI waves, waves of neglect of political risk. *World Development*, 40: 2194–2205.

Mina, W. M. (2012). The institutional reforms debate and FDI flows to the MENA region: The "best" ensemble. *World Development*, 40: 1798–1809.

Mohamed, S. E. and Sidiropoulos, M. G. (2010). Another look at the determinants of foreign direct investment in MENA countries: An empirical investigation. *Journal of Economic Development*, 35 (2): 75–95.

Onyeiwu, S. (2003). Analysis of FDI Flows to Developing Countries: Is the MENA Region Different?. Paper presented at ERF 10th annual conference Marrakech Morocco, December, pp. 1–22.

Rogmans, T. J. (2011). The Determinants of Foreign Direct Investment in the Middle East and North Africa Region. PhD Thesis, Nyenrode Business Universiteit.

Sheikh, A. J. (2012). The Business Climate and the Need for Change. Paper Presented at the Better Governance and Fair Taxation, ITD MENA Regional Conference, Tunis, May 30–31, 2012.

Shirazi, A., Rodrigues, G., and Karnik, A. (2008). Determinants of Foreign Direct Investment in MENA Countries: An Empirical Analysis. University of Wollongong in Dubai—Papers, Research Online.

UNCTAD. FDI/TNC Database. Availabe at: www.unctad-org/fdistatistics.

UNCTAD. (2014). *World Investment Report 2014—Investing in the SDGs: An Action Plan*. New York and Geneva: UNCTAD.

World Bank (2013). Middle East and North Africa Economic Developments and Prospects: Investing in Turbulent Times. World Bank, Washington DC, October.

Contributors

Audrey Verdier-Chouchane is Chief Research Economist in the North Africa Regional Department of the African Development Bank. Prior to joining AfDB, Audrey taught Macroeconomics and Development Economics at the University of Nice—Sophia Antipolis, France, from where she received a PhD in Economics. She has mainly published on the analysis and measurement of poverty and inequalities in scientific journals. She recently edited a book on Regional Integration and Trade in Africa, published by Palgrave Macmillan. She has coordinated and contributed to many flagship publications within the African Development Bank, such as the *African Economic Outlook*, the *African Development Report*, and the *Africa Competitiveness Report* in collaboration with sister institutions.

Charlotte Karagueuzian has been Consultant in the Development Research Department of the African Development Bank since October 2013. She holds a PhD in Sociology from the Ecole des Hautes Etudes en Sciences Sociales, Paris, France, a Masters in Political Science from the University of Paris I Panthéon-Sorbonne, France, and a Bachelor of Arts from McGill University, Canada. Prior to that, she worked as a researcher at the Raoul-Dandurand Chair of the University of Quebec in Montreal, Canada. She also possesses teaching experience acquired in French cultural centers abroad.

Etienne Farvaque is Professor of Economics at the University of Lille (Sciences and Technologies, France) and at Skema Business School. His research interests are in Monetary Economics (and, more particularly, the Economics of Central Banking and of Monetary Policy Committees) and in Political Economics (with a focus on the Economics of Voting). He has also worked on the impact of fiscal rules. He has published several books, book chapters, and numerous articles in internationally refereed journals, in both English and French.

Eugenie W. H. Maïga is an Assistant Professor at the Université de Koudougou, Burkina Faso, where she teaches courses in Econometrics, Agricultural Policy and Finance, Microeconomics, Farm Management, and International Development. She is also currently working as a consultant for the Alliance for a Green Revolution in Africa (AGRA), in Nairobi, Kenya. She has worked as an economist at the African Center for Economic Transformation in Accra, Ghana and as a short-term consultant for the World Bank. Her research interests include agricultural economics, education and skills development, youth employment, health economics, foreign aid, and applied econometrics. Eugenie has co-authored papers published in the Journal of Public Health Dentistry, Journal of Development Effectiveness, and World Development. She holds a PhD in Applied Economics from the University of Minnesota, Twin Cities.

John C. Anyanwu is Lead Research Economist in the Development Research Department of the African Development Bank. His research interests include natural resources, international finance, governance, political economy, poverty/inequality, gender analysis, economic growth, and public finance. Prior to joining the AfDB, he was Professor of Economics, Department of Economics & Statistics, University of Benin, Nigeria; and Health Economist/Economic Adviser to Resident Representative, WHO, Lagos, Nigeria. He had also been Chief Planning Officer in the former Strategic Planning Division of the AfDB. Anyanwu holds a PhD and MSc in Economics from the University of Ibadan, Nigeria, and a Master's degree in Economic Development and Entrepreneurship from the University of Houston-Victoria, US. He had had training/executive education courses at London School of Economics and Harvard University and was a visiting scholar at Cornell University. He is Editor, *African Development Review*, a quarterly journal of the African Development Bank. Anyanwu is currently, the President of the African Finance and Economics Association (AFEA) as well as a member of NES, AEA, AFEA, NEA, IAEE, WEAI, and iHEA. He has had his papers read at more than 120 conferences/seminars/workshops worldwide. Anyanwu has authored over 100 scholarly publications in national and international journals, in addition to authoring/co-authoring more than 35 book chapters and a number of books.

Kazi Sohag is a PhD Research Fellow at Faculty of Social Science and Humanities, and Institute of Climate Change, Universiti Kebangsaan Malaysia. He has been awarded a research fund by the Malaysian education ministry's research grant. His PhD research area is environmental and energy economics. Besides that, he has worked on financial economics, political economies, and applied econometrics. He has published a number of research articles in high impact factor journals like Renewable and Sustainable Energy, Energy, Economic Modelling, Journal of Poverty, and so on. Kazi Sohag is an editorial board member of the International Journal of Applied Research in Business Administration and Economics and the International Journal of Economics. Previously, he worked as visiting lecturer at Southeast University, Bangladesh, and with several NGOs.

Lara Cockx is a researcher at the Centre for Institutions and Economic Performance (LICOS) at the University of Leuven. She holds a Masters in Advanced Studies in Economics from the University of Leuven, an Msc in Development Evaluation and Management from the Institute of Development Policy and Management at the University of Antwerp, as well as an Msc in Applied Economic Sciences from the University of Antwerp. Her research interests include, but are not limited to development issues, with a special focus on the "resource curse."

Merter Mert is an economist. He is currently working at Gazi University, Faculty of Economic and Administrative Sciences, Department of Economics, which is located in Ankara, Turkey. He specializes in economic growth, economic development, and transport economics. He received his PhD in economics from the Gazi University.

Mina Baliamoune-Lutz is Professor of Economics at the Coggin College of Business, Distinguished Professor (2012) at the University of North Florida, and Research Fellow at the Economic Research Forum (ERF). She recently served as Director of Research at the African Center for Economic Transformation (ACET) in Ghana, and as President of the African Finance and Economics Association (AFEA), and was a research fellow at the International Center for Economic Research (ICER) in Turin, Italy (2005–2012). Professor Baliamoune-Lutz's research focuses primarily on the effects of formal and informal institutions, trade, financial flows, and financial reforms on economic transformation and human wellbeing in Arab and African countries. She co-edited the book: *Women in African Development—The Challenge of Globalization and Liberalization in the 21st Century* (Africa World Press, 2005) and has published numerous journal articles and book chapters. Her empirical work on the effects of policy and institutional reforms in Africa has received significant recognition. She has been a regular contributor to research themes debated upon at the United Nations World Institute of Development Economics in Helsinki (UNU-WIDER), and has contributed to the United Nations Commission for Africa/African Development Bank/ UNDP Annual Economic Conference on Africa, and the European Report on Development. Professor Baliamoune-Lutz holds a PhD in Economics from Northeastern University.

Mohamed Sami Ben Ali is a macroeconomist. He is currently Assistant Professor of Economics at Qatar University. Previously, he was Assistant Professor of Economics and International Finance, and Head of the economics department and member of the scientific board at HEC Business School, Tunisia. Dr Ben Ali holds, since June 2013, an H.D.R Certificate (Accreditation to supervise research and PhD thesis), the highest European academic qualification for research. Previously, he received a PhD in Economics with high honors from University of Lille—France, an MPhil (DEA) in International Finance and International Trade and a BA in Business Economics. He has been teaching for the past 14 years at the graduate and undergraduate levels, in Tunisia, Qatar, and France, where he was a visiting Professor. He has published numerous articles in French and in English in internationally refereed academic journals. His research and publications focus on issues involving economic growth, capital flows, exchange regimes, workers remittances, international trade, inflation, corruption, and Islamic banking and finance. He is currently a research associate of the Economic Research Forum of the Middle East and North Africa. He is also serving as peer reviewer and guest editor for international journals. He is actively participating and chairing in numerous international conferences in the United States. Among others, he actively contributes to Pearson Education and, especially, the 2015 Acemoglu Microeconomics first international edition.

Muhammad Azmat Hayat is Assistant Professor of Economics at University of the Punjab, Lahore (Pakistan). He earned a PhD in Economics from University of Science and Technology of Lille (France). Prior to joining the University of the Punjab, he served at the State Bank of Pakistan (Central bank of Pakistan). Dr. Hayat has presented his research work in many international conferences in Europe and Russia. His teaching and research interests include applied econometrics, monetary economics, macroeconomics, and quantitative techniques. He is also serving as Assistant Managing Editor of Pakistan Economic and Social Review.

Nadège Désirée Yaméogo is Senior Research Economist in the African Development Bank's Development and Research Department. Prior to joining the ADB, she worked for Analysis Group Inc., a consulting firm in economics, finance, and strategy. She also taught econometrics, macroeconomics, international economics, and environmental economics at Laval University, Quebec (Canada) and at the Panafrican Institute for Development/West Africa/Sahel (PAID/WAS), Ouagadougou (Burkina Faso). Nadège Désirée Yaméogo holds a PhD in Economics from Laval University, with specialization in econometrics, natural resources, and environmental economics. She holds also a Masters degree in Economics from the Inter-university Graduate Programme in Economics (DEA/PTCI). She has published books and journal articles in international refereed journals.

Nahla Samargandi is currently on leave at the Department of Economics and Finance, College of Business, Arts and Social Sciences, Brunel University. She teaches at King Abdulaziz University, Faculty of Economics and Administration. Nahla is a member of Scientific Society for Saudi Students in the UK, since July 2014, member of Centre for Economic Development and Institutions (CEDI), and Brunel Macroeconomics Research Centre (BMRC), Brunel University, since October 2009. She is an applied economist whose research interests are in the areas of economic growth, financial development, natural resource, and macroeconomics policies shocks. She has published in prestigious internationally recognized journals such as World Development and Economic Modelling. In addition, she presents her work in numerous international conferences around the world.

Nathalie Francken is post-doctoral researcher at the Institute of Development Policy and Management at the University of Antwerp, Research Manager at the Centre for Institutions and Economic Performance at the University of Leuven, and Associate Researcher at the Centre for European Policy Studies in Brussels, Belgium. Previously, she has been working as Senior Economic Advisor for Irish Aid and was selected into the Young Professional Program of the African Development Bank and worked as Country Economist on Tanzania and Djibouti respectively. She defended her PhD in 2007 on "Mass Media, Government Policies, and Economic Development in Madagascar" at the University of Leuven in Belgium. She also graduated from a Masters in Development Economics and a Masters in Bio-Science Engineering. She has field experience from various developing countries and worked for the Cornell University Food and Nutrition Policy Program, TRIAS

NGO, the Government of Madagascar, UNICEF, and the World Bank while conducting her PhD research. Dr. Francken is an honorary fellow of the Belgian-American educational foundation. Her interests focus on development economics and political economy.

Senay Acikgoz is Associate Professor of Econometrics at the Faculty of Economic and Administrative Sciences, Gazi University, Turkey. She received her PhD in Econometrics from Gazi University in 2007. She has been an adjunct faculty for the academic year 2012–2013 at Rensselaer Polytechnic Institute (Troy, NY-USA) where she taught Financial Econometric Modeling. Her primary research interest lies in the area of economic growth-business cycles and time series analysis. Her additional interests include investigating relations between fertility, employment, and capital accumulation. She collaborated with Prof. Dr. Muzaffer Sarimeseli in translating three books into Turkish: *A Guide to Econometrics* by Peter Kennedy, *Fundamental Methods of Mathematical Economics* by Alpha Chiang and Kevin Wainwright and *Economic Dynamics: Phase Diagrams and Their Economic Application* by Ronald Shone. Her recent work has been to investigate the competitive balance of domestic leagues and international success in soccer related to football economics. Other works that are in progress are on IPO returns, IPO volume and economic uncertainty relations, Kaldor's technical progress function, and an alternative approach to the endogeneity of the natural rate of growth. She conducts various mathematical economics and applied econometrics courses as part of her teaching responsibilities at Gazi University. She has more than 10 articles published in various renowned international journals such as *Journal of Applied Economics*, *International Journal of Banking, Accounting and Finance*, *Panoeconomicus* and *Sage Open*.

Shrabani Saha is Senior Lecturer at the University of Lincoln, College of Social Science in the United Kingdom. She holds an MSc in economics from the University of Calcutta, India, an MEC in economics from the University of Sydney, Australia, and a PhD in Economics from Massey University, New Zealand. Her research areas include political economy, economic growth, development economics, and international trade issues. The main areas of research focus on causes and effects of corruption across nations and corruption's relations with democracy and economic freedom. She has been also engaged in research involving political instability and its effects on tourism demands and economic growth. Dr Saha has published several papers in high-ranked refereed journals in economics and tourism, such as Economic Letters, Economic Modelling and Journal of Travel Research.

Sorin M. S. Krammer is Assistant Professor of International Business and Economics in the Global Economics and Management Department at University of Groningen, The Netherlands. Prior to joining Groningen, he was a Postdoctoral Fellow and Associate with the MIT Sloan School of Business and a Visiting Scholar with Stanford Institute for Economic Policy Research. Sorin holds a PhD degree in Economics from Rensselaer Polytechnic Institute, in Troy, NY. He has previously published research at the intersection between innovation and technology and international economics and business in several peer-reviewed volumes and journals such as Research Policy, Technological Forecasting and Social Change, and the Journal of International Trade and Economic Development. Sorin has also been awarded the prestigious Haynes Prize for Most Promising Scholar (under the age of 40) by the Academy of International Business in 2014.

Index

The manufacturer's authorised representative in the EU is Springer
Nature Customer Service Centre GmbH, Europaplatz 3, 69115 Heidelberg,
Germany. If you have any concerns regarding our products, please
contact ProductSafety@springernature.com

Printed and bound by CPI Group (UK) Ltd, Croydon, CR0 4YY
13/10/2026
02232424-0013